BROTHE

Kristin Williamson is the author of *The Last Bastion*, a political history of World War Two, *Princess Kate*, a novel for young adults which was made into a telemovie, and the bestselling novels *Tanglewood* and *The Jacaranda Years*. She has an academic background in history, education and theatre, and is well known as a journalist and columnist.

Kristin Williamson lives with her husband in Sydney. They have five children.

OTHER BOOKS BY KRISTIN WILLIAMSON

The Last Bastion
Princess Kate
Tanglewood
The Jacaranda Years

BROTHERS TO US

THE STORY OF A REMARKABLE FAMILY'S FIGHT AGAINST APARTHEID

KRISTIN WILLIAMSON

WITH A FOREWORD BY JOHN PILGER

VIKING

Viking
Penguin Books Australia Ltd
487 Maroondah Highway, PO Box 257
Ringwood, Victoria 3134, Australia
Penguin Books Ltd
Harmondsworth, Middlesex, England
Viking Penguin, A Division of Penguin Books USA Inc.
375 Hudson Street, New York, New York 10014, USA
Penguin Books Canada Limited
10 Alcorn Avenue, Toronto, Ontario, Canada M4V 3B2
Penguin Books (NZ) Ltd
Cnr Rosedale and Airborne Roads, Albany, Auckland, New Zealand

First published by Penguin Books Australia Ltd 1997

3 5 7 9 10 8 6 4 2

Designed by Jo Hunt, Penguin Design Studio
Typeset in Weiss by Midland Typesetters Pty Ltd, Maryborough, Victoria
Made and printed in Australia by Australian Print Group, Maryborough, Victoria

National Library of Australia
Cataloguing-in-Publication data:

Williamson, Kristin, 1940– .
Brothers to us: the story of a remarkable family's fight against apartheid.

Bibliography.
Includes index.
ISBN 0 670 87656 9.

1. African National Congress – Biography. 2. Civil Rights workers – South Africa – Biography. 3. Anti-apartheid movements – South Africa. 4. Discrimination in sports – South Africa. 5. South Africa – Biography. I. Title.

The author and publisher would like to thank the following for permission to include material:

My Traitor's Heart by Rian Malan © 1990, published by Grove/Atlantic, Inc.

Long Walk to Freedom by Nelson Mandela, published by Little, Brown and Company, UK.

Freedom Rising by James North, copyright © 1985 by James North, reprinted with the permission of Simon & Schuster.

The Mind of South Africa by Allister Sparks, reproduced by permission of Reed Books.

CONTENTS

FOREWORD

On my first day in Johannesburg I went into a bar and wished I hadn't. A barfly wanted to tell me about his Scottish heritage and to know what I did for a living. 'A reporter, eh?' he said. 'Man, you don't buy that bullshit about the kaffir being badly off, do you?' Without waiting for an answer he shouted to the barman, 'Hey, Nick, bring out your kaffir!'

A black man of indeterminate old age emerged and the barfly crooned at him, 'Hey, boy, get me some Rothmans from the machine over there.' The old man got the cigarettes, and handed him the change, which the barfly threw on the floor. 'That's yours, boy,' he said. 'All of it! See, my friend, see how good we treat kaffirs.'

The following year I was banned from South Africa after I had been smuggled into one of the secret hearings of the Race Classification Board, where a theatre of the absurd performed in Room 33 every Thursday. Here was apartheid's horrific quackery on display, its moral and intellectual mutation made to appear normal, with forms and regulations and decision-making based on 'criteria'. Here, suited officials, models of respectability, took evidence, scribbling, nodding sagely and now and then leaning down from their magistrates' bench in order to run a comb through a human head of hair and peer at the whites of human eyes. After due consideration, 'racially borderline' people were classified or re-classified 'according to appearance and acceptance', which meant a ticket to a lifetime of privilege or humiliation. Black-skinned people, of course, need not apply.

In reporting this, I had 'defamed the good name of South Africa', said a government security official. He was a jocular man. 'You have been *naughty*, my son,' he said, 'and in time we may forgive you.' Fortunately, they never did.

That was thirty years ago. Of all the places of human upheaval I have known, none has remained in my consciousness as vividly as South Africa. I remember apartheid's evil as a presence. Mostly insidious, sometimes murderous, it corrupted everything and almost everyone. Decent whites were the equivalent of decent Germans who, under Hitler, merely went about their business. Blacks were the Jews and the hated 'pass book' their yellow star. Those who actively opposed the system embraced a danger that was spider-like in its menace. For white opponents, their secret life demanded unimaginable courage.

That makes Kristin Williamson's story of the extraordinary Watson brothers so important. Indeed, her telling of it is a landmark work, because she gives us a rare glimpse of a singular struggle against apartheid that was epic in its courage, yet intensely human in its frailty. In an age of the cynical and the clay-footed, *Brothers To Us* is a celebration of heroes, told unsentimentally and with fairness and flair. Moreover, it was the author who, apart from one other journalist in the United States, kept the Watsons' name in the international press. Not only does her work in these pages distinguish journalism as history's first draft, but her commitment to the Watsons must have helped to keep her subjects alive.

Ronnie, Valence, Gavin and Cheeky Watson embodied almost everything that white South African men liked about their breed: they were physically brave, rugby-playing and men's men. Even their Christianity fitted the mould. But their manliness and their faith embraced a universal humanity and morality that was the antithesis of the stereotype. Unlike their peers, the Watsons regarded racial equality as normal; and they hated apartheid.

Rugby is said to stand next to God in South Africa. In June 1976 – in the wake of a full-scale black uprising in Soweto – they played in the first racially mixed game of rugby ever staged in their country. Under the laws of apartheid, the event was illegal, yet 10 000 came to watch. As Cheeky was shouldered from the ground, people shouted warm greetings to him. 'I cannot explain to you,' he told Kristin, 'the love, the openness, the acceptance of these people.' Thus, in the great tradition of resisters and dissenters, the Watsons became enemies of the state.

In the following pages you will cheer and worry and be fearful and moved, from the opening scene when Ronnie, aged six, and his brother Valence are walking home from church hand in hand with Lizzie, who was black and who asks the boys to promise 'never to be like other white people who hurt the blacks', to the exhilaration and danger of that first mixed-race rugby match, and Valence's induction into the atrocious South African army, and the moment that Cheeky ran the roadblock from Koyanna Street, and Eileen and Valence's wedding ('What's this about you waiting on the Lord?' said Cheeky to his devout brother), and the stabbing of Gavin by a black man, and Ronnie's meeting with Chris Hani and the beginning of the brothers' undercover work for the banned

African National Congress, and the brothers' trial and imprisonment in Red Hell prison, and the attempted assassination of Ronnie by a British intelligence agent, and finally the dawn of a new South Africa and a kind of peace. (And throughout it all the combustion of an entire clan under one roof, including three wives and seven children!)

I cannot think of another story that so encapsulates modern South Africa. And at the end there is hope, but also a warning. As a close comrade of the late Chris Hani, Ronnie Watson's name was next on the assassin's list. Hani's loss was grievous. Had he gone on to succeed Nelson Mandela as president, he almost certainly would have set about dismantling apartheid's economic base, which Mandela has failed to do. 'We are in office, yes, but we don't yet have economic power,' Hani's widow, Limpho, told Kristin. 'The same old faces who don't want to see change are still there. The bureaucracy is still in place. There are thousands of Security police still working in the system, although they are now called something else. The bureaucrats and police try to sabotage the changes.'

And the guilty are still free. An infamous government hit squad commander, Dirk Coetsee, is not only free, but has been welcomed into the ANC. In 1981 he murdered Griffith Mxenge, the ANC's lawyer. When Mxenge's brother met Coetsee recently, wrote Kristin, 'he said with dignity that his worst suspicions were confirmed. Coetsee had become a folk hero, who went on television to confess that he's had a change of heart. In fact, he is still dangerous and untrustworthy'. The people of South Africa, Kristin Williamson found, 'do not want revenge, but justice'. Her brilliant story of the heroic Watsons is proof that only the will is needed.

JOHN PILGER

AUTHOR'S NOTE

I first heard about the Watson brothers in June 1986 from my husband, playwright and screenwriter David Williamson, who travelled from Sydney to Hollywood to meet Gavin and Cheeky Watson for the purpose of writing a television series about them. The series, commissioned by Warner Brothers, was never to eventuate, but we did not know that then and the interviews David brought back on tape were fascinating.

We listened to them and laughed at the brothers' good humour and were full of admiration for their courage. The Watsons seemed to be unaware that they were heroes. They were self-deprecating, they joked about each other but they were passionate about fighting apartheid.

They told stories of how they had driven illegally into black townships to coach rugby teams. They would sit in the middle of the ground persuading the players to support the banned African National Congress (ANC). This was one of the few places it was safe to talk politics because they could not be bugged by Security police. When the police arrived, as they often did, the Watsons would dexterously switch mid-sentence from politics to rugby tactics and leap up with the ball to demonstrate a manoeuvre.

In the mid-1970s it seemed that the four brothers had everything white South Africa had to offer – wealth, fame, good looks, female adulation and male respect. All four were successful businessmen, all were sporting champions, and in 1976 the youngest brother, Cheeky Watson, was about to become a 'Springbok', a member of the national rugby team, which in rugby-crazed South Africa is akin to becoming a god.

If they had not also been Christians who believed in racial equality and who spoke the local African language Xhosa fluently, the Watsons might have been perfect examples of what white supremacy in South Africa is all about.

Just after the Soweto riots of June 1976, a black friend invited the brothers to play a game of mixed rugby with blacks, and, because they believed such an event might ease racial tension, they accepted.

As soon as they agreed to play that match, their lives were changed forever.

No mixed game had ever been played in the history of South Africa. It was illegal under the rigid laws of apartheid. The government brought enormous pressure on the Watsons to try and prevent the game but it went ahead, watched by 10 000 wildly cheering blacks and about twenty whites. Next day, newspapers all around the world, with headlines like 'Non Race Rugby Is Born', showed pictures of the Watson brothers being carried on the shoulders of black team-mates after the match.

Internal government reaction was instant. The Watsons were banned from white rugby for life and Cheeky lost his chance of ever becoming a Springbok. Watsons' business was effectively boycotted by an angry white community, and Security began to harass them.

Three of the brothers had attempts on their lives. Gavin nearly died from a knife wound close to the heart when a black man, believed to be a police informer, attacked him. But he held no grudge. 'I blame it on the system,' he said.

The Watsons' wives and children received obscene phone calls. They were followed by Security police, their bank accounts and phones were monitored and they were constantly on the alert against car bombs.

The brothers were shocked at this sudden persecution. But now that this side of South African society had been revealed to them they became even more politicised.

They were all recruited into the ANC, which was then a banned organisation. The penalty for belonging was a minimum of seven years in prison, so even the wives were not supposed to know about their affiliation. By the early 1980s all four brothers had become deep undercover ANC operatives while continuing surface lives as whites who played black rugby as a Christian gesture.

Their Christianity was genuine. It was this, they insist, that convinced them to play non-racial rugby in the first place, and which gave them the courage to become anti-apartheid activists.

In June 1986, when I first heard about the Watsons, I was a feature writer for the *National Times*, a weekly investigative newspaper of quality that was regarded as being 'left of centre' and was distributed all over Australia. I began to phone the four brothers, Gavin, Ronnie, Valence and Cheeky, and by August I had begun to write a series of articles that would continue for nine months.

Of course I wanted to meet the Watsons, but that was impossible. Being a journalist who wrote articles that were strongly critical of the apartheid regime in South Africa, I was not permitted to enter the country, so my interviews with them were all conducted by phone. Often our conversations were interrupted because the Security police managed to trace the calls. Sometimes a sound like a storm would wipe out their voices, or else the line would go dead. I would hang up and wait, and in twenty minutes or so my phone would ring again. One of the Watsons would have found an untapped phone. Often they would change phones three or four times in the course of one short interview. (I had always found the South African accent rather repellent because of its association with white supremacy, but after talking to the Watsons the accent became attractive.)

Although the brothers worked as a close team and an injury to one was seen as an injury to all, I began to perceive that their personalities were different. Gavin, the eldest, was a successful entrepreneur who had taken charge of the family business, while the others had been pleased to let him. As a child he had been rather bossy, which irritated his brothers, but as an adult he had become responsible and good natured. He is adored by all of his nieces and nephews.

Ronnie is shrewd, forthright and can be very funny. He is the most careful and suspicious of all the brothers. Some critics have called him paranoid. He is the most politically skilled and the least interested in the family business.

Valence is gentle, diplomatic and cautious. If he had not been such a fine sportsman he might have drifted into the arts. As a child he hated conflict and physical violence, but if he lost his temper he could be ferocious. He was effortlessly successful with women, and, in his younger days, was not averse to stealing his brothers' girlfriends, for which they still tease him. He has the best academic mind and pursued university studies to postgraduate level, even in the midst of his political activities.

Cheeky is more perceptive than any of the others. He is a natural performer and comedian, the most romantic of the brothers, the most successful sportsman and the strictest Christian. He was the most helpful to Gavin in the family business; a popular person who inspired trust, even sometimes in his enemies.

As the months passed I began to feel I knew the brothers, their wives, parents and black friends quite well. The Watsons were grateful to me for writing about them because at that time, in 1986, the international press was their main source of protection. Michael Parkes of the *Los Angeles Times* and I were the two main journalists they relied upon, they told me.

Meanwhile, my husband was still determined to write a film about the Watsons. Everyone who came to dinner with us was told their story in passionate detail. As they gazed out across Sydney Harbour, our friends, the 'literati', to whom the very mention of rugby players was a turn off, were transported to a battered stadium in a black township outside Port Elizabeth in the Eastern Cape of South Africa where the first mixed match was ever played and history was made. Gradually these friends' eyes would lose their glazed expressions and they would catch a little of our enthusiasm. It wasn't so much the *sport*, we told them, but the fact that young blacks were being politicised through rugby. Rugby in South Africa was, to Afrikaans-speaking whites, a kind of religion, and the implication of playing this contact sport with blacks would fill them with horror. It would be the act of a political traitor. Therefore what the Watsons were doing was not just courageous but heroic. Would any of us be so brave?

In spite of his enthusiasm, David's hopes of a television series about the Watsons came to nothing. The series, which had been planned by Warner Brothers for the CBS network, and which would have helped the Watsons' cause a great deal, was abandoned. The main reason for this was that the script, like the brothers, was very supportive of the African National Congress. At that time in history, being pro-ANC was akin to being a terrorist. This was offensive to the American 'Standards and Practises' ruling that examined all television programs for biased or provocative material.

Another television series on the Watsons, planned by the BBC, was also abandoned when the question 'Could four brothers possibly be so heroic?' was found to be impossible to answer because the team could not get inside South Africa.

But a small German documentary team did manage to make a short film about the Watsons, which they sent to me. It was a thrill to be able to watch the brothers and their wives on film laughing and talking to black friends while they cooked meat for a 'braai' on a deserted beach where the police would not find them and order their friends to leave.

Meanwhile the brothers' continuing warfare with South African Security exposed them and their wives and children to increasing risks. Now that the Watsons had a positive international profile as a result of that first mixed rugby match, Security decided that assassination was a less attractive option than 'criminalising' them. This new thrust culminated in Security doing something so cruel, daring and unexpected that the whole family was in shock for many months. As a result, Cheeky, Ronnie and Valence were thrown into one of South Africa's toughest prisons, nicknamed 'Red Hell'.

That same day Gavin Watson phoned me in a state of shock about Security's blatant attack on the family. Although the charges were ludicrous and unsupported by evidence, the three brothers were incarcerated without trial for six months. At Christmas Gavin sent me a photo from the local press of himself with the three wives and seven children he was attempting to 'play Santa Claus' to. All were smiling bravely, but they were miserable and had almost no money for food.

A few months later, Ronnie, now targeted as the most 'political' of the brothers, was on a business trip to Botswana when he narrowly escaped being assassinated. Security had co-opted a most unexpected ally to shoot him in a hotel room. This attacker was later jailed for five years for attempted murder, but in the meantime, Ronnie was both terrified and outraged. An organisation he thought he could trust was attempting to kill him! He went into hiding in Botswana, but first he rang Valence and said, 'Get this assassination attempt into the international press or I'll have hours to live.' Valence rang me at 4 a.m. in Sydney and I managed to get the news on to the AAP wire. It was not always easy to convince editors of foreign newspapers to believe the hair-raising events that were part of the Watsons' lives. When the editors demanded, quite rightly, to know what proof I had, all I could say was, 'The Watsons don't lie'. Consequently there were several newspapers which refused to run the story, although there were enough important ones around the world to make the impact that was needed.

Meanwhile, my husband had decided that if he couldn't get Warner Brothers to make the Watsons' story into a television series, he could try to interest some other producer in making it into a feature film. Australian producer–director George

Miller had read some of the articles I had written about the brothers, and in 1989 Kennedy Miller Productions acquired the film rights to the Watsons' story from Warner Brothers. Miller brought Ronnie, Valence and Valence's wife Eileen to Sydney to tell their story to him and David, who had been hired to write the screenplay. After meeting the two brothers, Miller confided, 'I've never felt inferior to any other human being, but in the presence of the Watsons I felt I was with people who were morally superior and far more courageous and admirable than I would ever be.'

It was exciting and quite moving to meet the friends I had only ever spoken to by phone. After picking them up from the airport we drove to Kings Cross and walked through crowded streets to a restaurant, showing them a little of the local colour. Valence and Ronnie, we noticed, were very nervous. Foolishly we had not realised that mingling with crowds was a thing that their ANC training had taught them never to do. A bustling bar or street was the ideal place for an assassin to start a fight and then produce a knife or gun.

Immediately after leaving Sydney in late 1989, Valence and Ronnie, working as undercover operatives in the white community, were the first to reveal the South African Government plan to unban the ANC and free political exiles, including Nelson Mandela. While these moves gained great plaudits for the de Klerk government internationally, Ronnie and Valence learned that the real agenda for Security was to foster as much 'black on black' violence as possible, to blame it on the ANC and thus to try and gain over 50 per cent of the vote in the non-racial elections that had become inevitable.

Ronnie, Valence and Eileen returned to Sydney for another short research trip for the Kennedy Miller film in 1992. This time Valence and Eileen's three boys came too. We invited them all to share a house at the beach with us one weekend, and Valence commented that this was the first time in their lives that the boys had been able to run off unguarded down a narrow track to play on a beach without fear. During the two weeks of their stay in Sydney we watched them all begin to unwind. Their gaunt faces relaxed and their thin bodies gained weight. Nkosi, the oldest boy, who was then ten, lost the nervous tic in one eye and stopped talking compulsively about a friend who had recently been shot. We asked them if it wouldn't be better to leave South Africa for a while. They had already contributed so much to the struggle against apartheid. They were adamant, even the children, that they must go back and continue the fight. They all teased Valence, who was enjoying the food and relaxation in Sydney so much that he admitted he really wouldn't mind a few more weeks of it.

On this trip the Watsons told me that if a book was ever to be written about them, they would like me to do it. They were very pleased about the possibility of the Kennedy Miller film but, sadly, it has still not been made.

Back in South Africa the ANC was unbanned and Ronnie and Valence declared their affiliations. Both Watsons were close to Chris Hani, who was then second only to Mandela. At one stage Hani moved into Ronnie's flat, and Ronnie used his own car to transport Hani to meetings because he thought it was safer than trusting him to official cars and bodyguards. The Watsons were devastated when Hani was assassinated in 1993. When the killer was caught, Ronnie's car registration number was found in the glove box of his car. It was possible that Ronnie was to be his next target. Ronnie knew that his name had appeared on a number of hit lists. The Watsons were considered dangerous by the forces of the far right.

After the triumphant election result of May 1994, I felt that the Watsons' story should be told without delay. The Watsons, although they are reluctant heroes, agreed.

I've been very fortunate with this book because I've been able to compile a collection of testimonies from several different sources over a period of ten years. I am grateful to David Williamson for the use of the taped interviews recorded with Cheeky and Gavin Watson in Los Angeles in 1986 and to Kennedy Miller Films, who now own those tapes. I am also indebted to George Miller for allowing me access to the 2000 pages of transcripts of interviews conducted with Valence, Ronnie and Eileen Watson in Sydney in October 1989 and December 1992, and to Margaret Sixill for her research.

In May 1995, I at last travelled to South Africa to check what I had written, and add to it. You can imagine the trepidation I felt on arriving. Perhaps the story the Watsons had told was exaggerated. I had broken all the rules of journalism by relying almost completely on the Watsons themselves for their life story. What if it was untrue?

But I need not have worried. According to black friends, white associates and enemies of both colours, the Watsons, if anything, had understated the roles they had played. Both ANC and Pan African Congress (PAC) blacks admitted that the Watsons, along with people like Joe Slovo, were the *only* whites who were crucial to the struggle against apartheid. My trust in them was vindicated.

The Watsons are radicals, not liberals, but radicals who are different from the twentieth-century stereotype. The mantras they recite are not Leninist or Marxist rhetoric, but basic Christian beliefs.

For the first time, I was able to meet the whole family in their own country, to visit the farm where the brothers had grown up, to go into black townships where they had played mixed rugby, to meet activists whose lives they had saved and to interview ex-Security police who had wished them dead. I was also privileged to hear the brothers make political disclosures that they could never have made under the old regime.

I learned that although the struggle against apartheid had cost them all dearly, they were grateful to still be alive when so many of their comrades were dead.

In April 1996, South Africa's Truth and Reconciliation Commission began inquiring into crimes and human rights abuses during the apartheid era. The Watsons were asked to participate but they declined. Valence explained, 'No one was killed in our family. So many people had their whole families killed. I'd be embarrassed to take part in place of those people.' Former Security police have confessed on SABC television to being involved in the murders of many anti-apartheid activists. The former South African President F. W. de Klerk accepted the blame for apartheid crimes under minority white rule, and one of his generals, Constand Viljoen, former chief of the apartheid era defence force, acknowledged that there had been 'gross violation of human rights'. More evidence of these violations is revealed every day, as the Truth and Reconciliation Commission hearings continue.

Many different South Africans have offered their thoughts on the Watsons' contribution to the struggle against this 'gross violation of human rights' – politicians, rugby players, business people, housewives, attorneys, journalists, judges and students. Some were reluctant at first to talk to an inquisitive foreigner. There is a lot of shame about the past in South Africa.

I would like to thank my editor, Alex Watts, for her belief in this book and her constant support.

I am deeply grateful to the Watson family for being so generous, open and helpful during my time in their country. They relived events they would rather have forgotten and allowed me to trespass on the privacy they crave in the new South Africa.

And thank you to Limpho Hani, the widow of assassinated ANC leader Chris Hani, who, when I asked what the Watsons meant to black South Africans, told me that they were like 'brothers to us'.

PART ONE

I

'NAUGHTY BUT CHIVALROUS'

Ronnie Watson remembers a day in 1956 when, as a boy aged six, he and his brother Valence were walking home from church hand in hand with an old woman whom they thought of as their grandmother. The woman was black. She walked slowly because she was old, it was a hot day and her Sunday dress was too tight. When she stopped, the boys looked up at her expectantly. They waited. They were lively children, particularly Ronnie, and they were eager to get home to the farm where they could strip off their suits and go swimming in the river. But they knew better than to pull at the old woman's hands or try to hurry her in any way.

They stood quite still and stared out at the flat plains. A windmill creaked. Then there was silence. Valence, the younger boy who was four, kicked at the red earth with one polished shoe. Then Ronnie, speaking in the local dialect, Xhosa, asked, 'Did we forget the hymn book, Lizzie? I'll run back and get it, shall I?'

Valence looked back in the direction of the church. It seemed a long way to run.

'No, Ronnie. I have the hymn book.' The old woman patted

her handbag. 'I was thinking of something very important that I must ask you to do for me.'

'I'll do it! What is it?' Ronnie burst forth.

'Let me. Can I do it too?' echoed Valence, with less enthusiasm.

'Yes. Both of you can do it. You must promise me today,' said Lizzie gravely, 'that when you grow up you will never be like other white people and hurt the blacks.'

The boys stared at her, then at each other.

Ronnie promised solemnly and Valence nodded his assent, but both of them were puzzled. Why should Lizzie, whom they loved dearly, ask them not to hurt black people? Up to that moment they had barely noticed that their skins were white.[1]

The four Watson boys grew up on a farm near Alicedale, not far from Grahamstown on the east coast of South Africa. This was the Karoo country – hot, dry, red plains, purple mountains, low scrub and patches of prickly pear. Wild animals once roamed these plains – herds of elephant, springbok, wildebeest, quagga and eland. But now there were only sheep and cattle, a few wild baboons and a mass of rock rabbits, perched like weasels on every boulder.

Daniel Watson, the boys' father, was a lay preacher as well as a farmer. He was of Scottish descent, played rugby, was not afraid of a fight and taught his sons to 'Love thy neighbour as thyself'. Neighbours included the blacks. Daniel attempted to conceal his gentleness beneath a rough surface.

Their mother, Elaine Watson (known as Bobbi), was a genteel English woman. She was softly spoken, well mannered and as serene as her husband was volatile. She appeared to let him make all the decisions and would never contradict him in public, but she was, according to her sons, 'the neck that turned the head'.[2]

These very different qualities of their parents would help to turn the Watson boys into the sort of men who could not refuse a challenge and whose charm would make quite conservative people warm to them, in spite of their outrageous beliefs.

Bobbi Watson had a good head for business and she soon took over the management of the local store and butchery at Kommadagga, a tiny railway town, which was the closest settlement to the Watsons' farm. The store was the only one in town, a general dealer which sold everything from gardening hoes to groceries and working men's clothing. Half of her customers were white Afrikaner farmers and the other half black railway workers. Bobbi Watson treated each customer with equal politeness and charm and there was no racial tension within the business. She ran the store and butchery for nine years, from 1951–60. When the railway line from Port Elizabeth to Johannesburg was finished, the town shrunk back to being a farming community and the Watsons moved to Alicedale, a slightly larger town where Bobbi again managed the store and butchery. At Alicedale the ratio of blacks to whites was larger – 70 per cent. Blacks and coloureds (people of mixed blood) were obliged to live in separate parts of the town from whites. But Bobbi's stores, positioned on the border between them, continued to do well.

Bobbi Watson's business activities meant that she had to be away from the farm from six in the morning until eight at night. Consequently the boys, Gavin, Ronnie, Valence and Daniel, saw more of their 'black mothers' than they did of her.

Bobbi took care to choose African nannies who were patient, spontaneous and open so that her children did not miss her too much. One nanny who would be a loving figure in their lives for many years was Margaret.

Margaret was also the housekeeper. She took the boys into her home and brought them up alongside her own children. They sat on a cow-dung floor and ate the traditional African 'mealie meal', an oat porridge called *mphokoqo* which is served with sour milk, or stew with dumplings. They remember this food as being delicious. It would be eaten in the African style with everyone sitting around the fire and passing one spoon from the big cooking pot from person to person. In this way it took longer to eat one's meal and there was time for conversation and laughter. It created an emotionally warm atmosphere the Watson brothers remember.

But when their mother was at home she liked their dining to be formal. The family all sat up to an oak table on high-backed chairs. Table manners were insisted upon, shirts were worn, hands washed, hair brushed and mouths kept closed while eating.

If the children misbehaved in their mother's absence, Margaret would smack them. When they hurt themselves they would run to her for comfort. Because the boys spoke Xhosa with their black friends all day, Bobbi would often have difficulty understanding them and would have to ask Margaret to translate.[3]

They were brought up to feel part of the African culture, speaking Xhosa better than English and believing that blacks and whites were equal. In a society where blacks were the servants of whites, this was unusual.

Most white children in South Africa were deeply fond of

their nannies until, at the age of three or four, they learned to give orders and henceforth addressed them as 'Master' or 'Miss' and were encouraged by their parents to treat their black mothers as inferiors. The English-speaking Watsons were surrounded by a farming community of Afrikaners who treated the blacks in this way.

By contrast, the Watsons treated black people like relatives. When Margaret's children were born, Bobbi Watson acted as midwife and was given the honour of naming them. All of the children would watch the delivery. Afterwards there would be a feast and each child would be handed a bead to look after until the eating had finished. Then the beads would be given back to one of the women of the family, who would make them into a necklace for the new child. After the meal, the African men would tell stories about their heroism – what great fighters they used to be, what great horsemen. The children would listen, enthralled, until the women told the men, 'Don't lie to these children. You've never won a fight or ridden a wild horse in your life!' Then everyone would laugh, the men would defend themselves and the children would beg for one more story before going to bed.

There were also white rituals that the black people were expected to be part of. Grandfather Watson's room was at the front of the farmhouse and every Saturday he would sit in his rocking chair on the front verandah with a box on his lap. The twenty or so children who lived on the farm, both black and white, would line up along the verandah and wait to be handed their sweets.

The Watson boys swam naked in the shallow river with a mass of black children, rode donkeys together and went hunting rock rabbits with their dogs. They remember their early childhood as being idyllic. But they also remember, clearly and individually, the moment when they each became aware that their childhood of excitement and laughter had a sinister undertone that finally they could not ignore.

For Ronnie and Valence that awareness came in the summer of 1956 when Lizzie, who had once been the family housekeeper but now had retired to live on the farm and was loved as much as any grandmother, asked them not to hurt black people when they grew up.

Gavin, the oldest boy, first sensed the underlying discord in 1953 when he was five. On the farm he had a black girlfriend of the same age and when he kissed her in front of a young black man who was visiting the Watsons he was told that it was wrong.

'Why? I'm going to marry her,' Gavin declared.

'You can't.'

'Why not?'

The man turned away and gave no reply.[4]

For Daniel, known as Cheeky, the youngest Watson boy, the first intimation of bitterness in the country came in 1958 when he was four. He and his brothers and a group of black children who lived on their farm were hunting rock rabbits with his Pomeranian dog, Cheeky. (Daniel loved the dog so much that he had started calling himself Cheeky too.) The dog wandered on to their neighbour's land. Suddenly the neighbour appeared and shot it. Their father comforted young Daniel but could not bring himself to tell his sons the truth, that the dog had been killed because their neighbour was a racist who strongly disapproved of the Watson family allowing their sons to mix with the blacks.[5]

It wasn't until many years later, when the true nature of

their society was revealed to them, that these disturbing childhood memories became an explicable part of the total mosaic of their lives.

The Watson family was descended from Scottish crofters. Great-great-grandfather Watson had come as a child with the first British settlers to South Africa in 1820. His family hoped innocently to establish a farm on the Eastern Cape frontier. But they were soon to be disillusioned.

> *The diverse collection of British families who were lowered into longboats and rowed through the surf to the desolate shores of Algoa Bay on the Cape Colony's east coast between April and July, 1820 had one thing in common. They had been conned.*[6]

The new migrants had been dreadfully misled. They had been told by the colonial authorities that the coastal plains where they were to settle resembled 'a succession of parks ... particularly healthy for every description of cattle and sheep, well wooded and having very fine springs in it, it is very nearly uninhabited'.[7] In fact the plains were infertile, dry and inhabited by black tribes and Trekboers who fought constant wars over the territory and the cattle.

The Afrikaner or Boer farmers had been established in the area for over 200 years. They had large farms, were allowed black slaves and were close to the Cape Town market.

The British farmers, allotted very small farms and denied both slaves and hired labour, could not hope to compete. Interaction with the black tribes was prohibited. The purpose of settling the British so close to tribal land was to create a border which the black people would not cross. But because of economic necessity the British settlers began to trade with the Xhosa tribespeople. Metal implements, beads and trinkets were exchanged for ivory, cattle, hides and mimosa gum. Both Xhosa and British were happy with this arrangement, but the colonial authorities soon put a stop to it by building a military fort to keep the Xhosa away.

Because the farmers now occupied the land over which the Xhosa tribespeople had always roamed, they were deprived of their clay pits, which contained a red clay they had used for centuries in tribal rituals. They began attacking and killing settler families. All but a third of the families then gave up their farms and drifted towards the nearest town, Grahamstown, to try and make a living building wagons, making bricks and opening stores. Those families who remained on the land took over the abandoned farms and then had enough land to run cattle. The Watson family was one of these.

The cattle farmers fought four frontier wars against the Xhosa people between 1834 and 1878.

> *The Xhosa were a people infatuated with cattle for whom the animals held an almost mystical importance. Young men in particular needed cattle for bride price, and a daring cattle raid was also a traditional way of proving one's manhood. The settlers, in breeding larger, sleeker cattle . . . presented the tribesmen with an irresistible temptation.*[8]

While other families had their homes destroyed and their families killed in cattle raids, the Watsons managed to survive. Whether they did this by striking bargains with the Xhosa or defeating them in battle has not been recorded, but it is certain that the third- and fourth-generation Watsons had no grudge against the Xhosa and treated them with respect.

Daniel Watson went further. He allowed the Xhosa who worked on his farm to own cattle, to breed them and to share in the profits. This was an extraordinary situation in South Africa in the 1950s, and did not endear him to his conservative neighbours.

Although there was Afrikaner blood in the Watson family (great-grandfather had married a Smyman and grandfather a Schoeman), Daniel Watson was inclined to antagonise some Afrikaners for their political conservatism.

Before the Second World War Daniel had joined the other English-speaking young men in Port Elizabeth to break up a meeting of the Ossewa-Brandwag, a pro-Nazi group of Afrikaners who were openly anti-semitic. There was a fight. Chairs and tables were thrown and the meeting was disbanded. Although he was not Jewish, Daniel Watson, being an English speaker, knew what it was like to be in a minority, and therefore identified with the Jews. Also, he quite enjoyed a good stoush against the Afrikaners.

Daniel fought with a South African regiment in the Second World War and was captured by Germans three times. Later he would tell his four young sons stories about the deplorable treatment of the Jews by the Nazis and instil in them the responsibility he felt to 'protect the underdog'.

Bobbi Watson's family, at first, had reservations about their gentle and protected daughter marrying a divorcee, who was also a rugby player.

'Our mother watched every word she said,' Valence Watson recalls. 'She was a courteous person, very concerned about people's feelings. She was always ladylike. Father was very passionate. Soft but strong. He did not concern himself much about niceties. But there was never any shouting or disagreement between our parents.'[9]

'We had a lovely life together,' Bobbi Watson quietly agrees. There is a softness in her voice when she speaks of the husband who died only recently. She smiles, remembering the love they shared for almost fifty years. 'I was twenty-seven when Dan and I met, and very innocent. I was one of ten, brought up very strictly. He had been married before. A friend of mine introduced us. I wasn't impressed at all. I was far more interested in a career in nursing and planned to go overseas to study mothercraft, midwifery and theatre. Anyway, I was engaged to someone else. But soon all of that went overboard. I broke the engagement, forgot about the overseas trip and Dan and I were married. It was well worth it.'[10]

Dan Watson was working as a window dresser in Port Elizabeth when he met Bobbi, but after the marriage they moved on to their first farm near Kommadagga, about an hour and a half away. The country was harsh and dry. Farms were traditionally built in small clusters, as they had been 150 years ago, for safety from attacks by tribes of Xhosa warriors who had been driven off their land. There was bright sunlight, unmade roads and clean, crisp air.

The new young bride Bobbi Watson admitted that at farm life she was 'most inexperienced', but she loved it. It was only to help with family finances that she took on the extra responsibility of managing the local store and butchery.

'Although our mother worked long hours at the store I never think of her as being absent. She was an excellent mother,' Valence recalls.[11]

Daniel Malan had become Prime Minister on the promise of making South Africa a white man's land. He won by a narrow margin. 'Today South Africa belongs to us once more,' exulted Malan in his victory speech in May 1948.[12]

In the postwar world, segregation and white supremacy were morally objectionable. But 'As the world moved in one direction, South Africa moved in the opposite one'.[13]

Malan's election delighted the new Nationalists. It was the final triumph of the white Afrikaners, the descendants of the Dutch and German immigrants who for so long had been subjugated by South Africa's other white tribe, the English. Malan kept his promise.

Apartheid (literally 'separatehood') was the name given to a system of laws devised and enforced by the white population which prevented black South Africans from voting, living in a white area, entering a white area without a permit, marrying or making love to a white person, doing a job reserved for whites, earning what a white person earned, going to church or school or university with a white person and playing sport with whites.

There is no doubt of the influence of Nazi Germany on those who fashioned apartheid.

'Looking back, one can see two distinct strands of thought that were later to acquire a certain importance: the concept of separate nations, to save the Afrikaner "nation" from being swamped and to protect its members from black economic competition; and the more crudely racist belief in black genetic inferiority and the need to preserve the "blood purity" of the white race.'[14]

The term 'apartheid' was never mentioned on the Watsons' farm. To the four boys it would not have meant much if it had been. For the Watson brothers who had been brought up in such a way that they literally didn't see colour, the idea of 'blood purity' was quite stupid, so they ignored it.[15]

Their neighbours, the boys noticed, did not invite black people to sit at the dining table or relax on the sofa. Black and white children did not play together. They referred to the blacks as 'kaffirs' and shouted orders at them as if they were animals. The Watson boys found this odd, particularly as the neighbours professed to be Christians.

Their father Daniel preached evangelically to black congregations, and his boys shared the emotional lives of the black people on and around their farm. If there was a wedding or birth they rejoiced; if someone died they grieved as they would for a relative. The black adults who lived and worked on their farm were like mothers, fathers, aunts and uncles. Their children were like brothers and sisters. When a black grandmother grew too old to work Daniel Watson would no more think of sending her away from the farm than he would of sending his own mother.

When Gavin, the oldest boy, went to school he was shocked that his black friends were not allowed to go with him. He said it was unfair. When his new teacher asked if he could count up to ten he did so in Xhosa, as an act of defiance. English was his second language and his Afrikaans was almost non-existent. When he asked in Xhosa to go to the toilet the teacher could not understand him and he wet his pants. He was so embarrassed that he ran home, the whole five miles, and vowed to Margaret that he would never go back to a school where they didn't admit his black brothers and sisters. Margaret had to explain Gavin's trauma to his mother, Bobbi, and it took some persuading to get him back to school.

Although the young Watsons lived in perfect harmony with

black culture, there was often less than perfect harmony between the four of them. Valence remembers his older brother Gavin as being the only blot on a perfect childhood. He was bossy. The other boys, both black and white, called him 'The general'. 'All the toys used to be given to him. He'd say, "You play with those stones, you play with that brick and if you want toys you come to me." If I was annoying one of my friends, he'd give me a hiding, but if I was being bullied, he'd intervene on my behalf. He was the leader of about twenty children.'[16]

Gavin and Ronnie, the two older boys, were constantly at war over who was to dominate the children who lived on the farm, and Valence, the third and most sensitive son, found this painful. To demonstrate his superior power over the group, Gavin would force Valence to ride donkeys, which he hated because he found them difficult to control.

Cheeky (although he had named himself after his beloved dog, the nickname seemed to describe his personality quite accurately) was pampered because he was the youngest. He would tease the older boys, throw rocks at them and then run for safety behind his father. When Cheeky was three the older boys retaliated. They had been sent to fetch the cows for milking, and catching Cheeky they tied him to a calf, which he was then obliged to 'ride' around the kraal, screaming to be set free. Another time the brothers sat him in a pram and pushed it down a steep hill so that it crashed into a fence which was smashed to the ground. Cheeky, who was pleased to be 'playing' with his big brothers, neither complained about his bruises nor ran to tell his father.

When Cheeky was seven, a sister, Sharon, was born. Because of the age difference, the Watson boys did not spend much time with her, although they regarded her with great affection. When she grew up she would not take the same courageous political stand as her brothers, but Sharon would be the one in the family who collected cuttings about them and would hero worship them in the face of strong opposition from some other members of the family.

The brothers might have fought amongst themselves as children, but anyone outside the family who dared to force one of them into submission would be dealt with by all four. At primary school in Alicedale the Watsons were part of a group of ten English-speaking children in a school of 110 Afrikaners. Naturally there were fights.

Ronnie, being a good organiser, drew up the lists of which boy would fight which. Valence, who hated fighting, refused to hit back when it was his turn. After being punched hard several times until he was bleeding, he reached out and gave his opponent a bear hug. He squeezed the breath out of him until the boy began to turn blue. Ronnie claims he had to race in and stop Valence from murdering him. Ronnie had decided that, although he was only ten, he would 'take their top man'. Valence dreaded the outcome. The 'top man' was much taller and stronger than Ronnie. But once he was in the fight Ronnie 'lost all sense of what he was doing, went in for the kill and beat the living daylights out of their top guy. Even the girls were shouting "You'll kill him" and the headmaster was sent for to pull Ronnie off. It was just too horrible to watch.'[17]

The different personalities of each Watson brother were already emerging and are important in the understanding of why conflicts arose between them as adults and how they managed to support each other during their long political struggle.

Gavin, the self-appointed leader, was dominating and forthright. He said what was on his mind without considering whether feelings might be hurt. As a child he talked at the top of his voice, unaware of how annoying this was. He was inclined to trust people and not to sense danger as keenly as his younger brothers. He was dark haired and olive skinned in contrast to his brothers who were blond as children. In later life Gavin would be a successful entrepreneur, taking charge of the family business. He would consider himself head of the extended family, including the other brothers' wives and children, and they would be less pleased about this, but would humour him. He would sometimes act like a male chauvinist but in fact his wife would control him. He would be good hearted and the children would all love him. When all three brothers were in jail he would feel responsible for their families and they would be grateful.

As a child Ronnie was shrewd, perceptive and also inclined to be forthright. He was smart and funny enough not to hurt people's feelings, but to make them laugh at their own shortcomings. He had a mass of reddish-blond curls, which caused him to be nicknamed 'Ginger'. When Ronnie was really angry he found it hard to pull back. He became the most careful and suspicious of all the brothers, a perfectionist, but forgiving. As an adult he would be the most politically and interpersonally skilled of all the brothers, becoming involved in dangerous undercover work for the banned ANC. He would do anything to avoid a fight but, if pushed, would fight to win. He would take very little interest in the family business.

Valence was sensitive, gentle and diplomatic. As a child he was called 'dreamy' or 'artistic'. Sometimes he was even called 'lazy' because he did not enjoy physical work on the farm or taking risks by doing things like riding donkeys. Yet on the rugby field he was dynamic. He hated conflict and physical violence and would often give in on an argument for the sake of peace. As an adult he was tall, dark and effortlessly successful with women, which would cause some friction with his brothers. He was inclined to be anxious, self-righteous and ferocious if he lost his temper. Valence, the others agreed, had the best academic mind, could absorb complex material quickly, and at university would regularly top the class with little study. To this day he cannot bear to lie. He and Ronnie would be the most politically active of the four brothers, Valence giving direction and writing speeches for the ANC for many years before it was unbanned as well as afterwards.

Cheeky was more perceptive than any of his brothers. Perhaps because he was the youngest he learned early on to listen to people and accept guidance. As a child he was shy but people loved him. He was a natural performer who enjoyed playing tricks and embarrassing people. Later, because of his performance skills, he would be a better television interviewee than his brothers. He had light-brown hair and a winning smile. Cheeky was the only brother who was likely to become an international sportsman. He was romantic, which was probably the reason he married younger than his brothers, disregarding their advice. He would be very successful in business and would intuitively understand what people wanted – customers, sportsmen, black people in the townships and later the police who interrogated him. He would be a popular person who inspired trust.

All of the brothers are good looking. They are strongly built, open faced and from an early age had keen senses of humour. They are all gracious and have the seemingly effortless good manners of gentlemen. Some people, meeting them for the first time or interviewing them as a group, have commented that they seem to speak in the same voice. Their passions are certainly the same and they have the disconcerting knack of finishing each other's stories and sentences. Although they could never be mistaken for each other there is a distinct family likeness.

Bobbi Watson was anxious that her sons receive a good education. Gavin remembers her as 'prim and proper'. She insisted that they go to boarding school, even though she knew she would miss them terribly. 'I'd dart into Grahamstown to visit them and bring them some nice things to eat – a box of biscuits or some tins of condensed milk,' Bobbi said. 'These were to last a month, but then I'd hear that they'd called all their friends to a feast and the provisions were all gone in a day or two.'[18]

Although there was hardship on the farm, with regular droughts, no bank loans to tide the Watson family over because they would not vote for the National Party, and no bursaries for their sons because they were of English descent, not Afrikaners, Bobbi hoped that the boys would be able to go on to university. She encouraged them to think in terms of professional careers – dentistry, medicine or the law. Their father, by contrast, wanted them to do nothing more than identify with the needs of people in the community and to be good sportsmen, particularly in the field of rugby.

At primary school they were taught in English and Afrikaans. The indoctrination about the superiority of the white race began early. The blacks were born to be hewers of wood and drawers of water; they were there to serve the whites. 'We learned about the battle of Blood River, how the Afrikaners tried to negotiate with the blacks and were killed, how the blacks slaughtered the settlers' cattle, cutting their tendons and drinking the blood. They were savages, we were taught,' Gavin remembers.[19]

Afrikaans was the dominant language. As most subjects were taught in it the Watson brothers, against their wills, became fluent.

They all attended high school at Graeme College, a government boarding school at Grahamstown, about 100 kms from Port Elizabeth. Although this was an English-speaking school, the syllabus was controlled by the Afrikaner Government and reflected the growing rigidity of the apartheid system. The students were politically conservative.

In school holidays the Watson boys would come back to the farm in emotional turmoil. 'Spiritually we knew that what we were learning about the blacks being inferior was wrong. But you looked up to your teachers. You wanted to learn,' Gavin recalls. 'When you came home you couldn't really identify with your black friends as well. You didn't know why the teachers were indoctrinating you this way.'[20]

When the Watsons brought friends home from college to stay on the farm the friends would be astounded to find that the black workers were not only paid decent wages but shared in the profits. Blacks treated the young Watsons like relatives, laughing and teasing them affectionately. When the brothers played rugby with their black friends they would hug each other after a game and carry the smaller children on their shoulders. The white school friends who had been taught to avoid any physical contact with blacks instinctively wanted to push them away.

Back at school the Watson boys spoke Xhosa to the black gardeners and maids, not in the crude, cursing manner that the other boys addressed them, but as equals. Soon the Watsons found themselves being treated to extra helpings of food in the dining room.

'We always had a tremendous relationship with the blacks. I felt much closer to them than to the other kids at boarding school,' said Cheeky. 'When I was head boy I never used to tidy my room. While I was out, the black lady would do it. She wasn't paid to tidy my room. She just did it. I was lazy. I would sleep in some mornings and miss breakfast. Suddenly, breakfast was being brought into my room. I was treated like one of this lady's children. No knocking on the door. I could be standing there stark naked. She would say, "Wake up, Cheeky. Get up and eat."'[21]

Even though blacks were forbidden to attend matches, the maids and gardeners would come and cheer when the Watsons played rugby. Rugby to Afrikaners was regarded as the ultimate test of courage with an unspoken assumption that their racial superiority made it inevitable they would always be victors over the English. Thus it became a source of great conflict when Afrikaner schools played Graeme College and lost. By playing the game so well the Watsons became schoolboy heroes.

Ronnie was not above a bit of 'dirty' playing, however. 'When it looked as if we were certain to lose I'd say to my team, "Well, chaps, it looks as if we've lost the game. Let's see if we can win the war."' His father was so shocked by Ronnie's rough tactics in one match that he vowed he would never watch him play another game.[22]

Graeme College, being a government school, not a private one, was at the bottom of the ladder in the sporting competition when the Watson brothers arrived. Cheeky remembers that 'We were known as the "peasants" by the top-drawer schools like Kingswood College, St Andrews and St Aidens. Our father couldn't afford to send us to those schools. All the farm boys at Graeme College were supposed to be inferior to these highfalutin colleges but we wouldn't accept that.'[23]

Because of the leadership roles the four Watson brothers played at Graeme College, over a period of ten years the sporting abilities of the other students grew until, with Cheeky as captain of rugby, the school had an unbeaten record throughout the whole Eastern Cape and was known as the best schoolboy team in South Africa.

By now the Watson brothers had built up a strong following amongst black youngsters who lived near Graeme College. In spite of the ban on blacks attending white college matches these young Watson admirers attended every one, and whenever Cheeky Watson scored a try they would race out on to the field and grab his hands. Some parents in the crowd complained but the headmaster did not interfere.

All four brothers had a natural tendency to lead and all of them became prefects. Cheeky was also school captain.

'They were outstanding characters. Without them it would have been difficult to run the school,' said their headmaster, Steven Geldenhuys. 'I don't think many schools had four leaders like the Watsons from one family.'[24]

'They were naughty boys,' said Margaret Geldenhuys, the headmaster's wife, who was also a teacher at Graeme College. 'But there was always something very nice about them. Their manners were good. They were chivalrous.'

Mrs Geldenhuys tells the story of one female teacher rushing from her classroom in tears and being met in the corridor by Ronnie Watson. 'You tell me who made you cry, Miss Wagenaar, and I'll go and fight him,' he offered gallantly.[25]

In Cheeky's final year he was regarded more as a teacher than a pupil. One evening, noticing that a junior pupil had badly blistered heels from running, Cheeky gave him permission to wear 'flip-flops' (thongs) to the school dining room instead of the usual lace-up schoolshoes. During dinner the boy was called to the teachers' table and told that he would be given four cuts of the cane for not wearing the correct footwear. After dinner Cheeky walked across to the teachers' table and asked the teacher who had spoken to the boy, 'What right did you have to say you would give him four cuts? Have you seen his heels? I gave him permission to wear flip-flops.' The teacher said, 'Don't you talk to me like that.' At which Cheeky leant across the table, grabbed him by the shirt collar and said, 'You listen to me. Don't you ever again do what you have just done,' and threw him back into his seat, which went flying. There was consternation. The black maids screamed. The teacher leapt up and threatened to send him to the headmaster.

'Don't worry,' said Cheeky. 'I'm going.'

In the headmaster's office Cheeky said calmly, 'Sir, we have a problem.' He told the story, finishing with, 'I will be leaving within a week because I'm not prepared to tolerate that sort of thing.'

The headmaster decided it would be better if the teacher left within a week, which he did.[26]

It could be argued that such behaviour from a schoolboy

was naive, arrogant and certainly inappropriate. There would be many times in their careers when the Watson brothers would be accused of being all of these things.

During their years at Graeme College, all four were aware that there was some discontented 'muttering' about them amongst a few staff and students, but there were never any open disputes. Apparently they were too strong for anyone to argue with.

This strength of character would be really tested by what happened straight after the Soweto uprising of 1976.

2

FEELING THEIR HEARTBEAT

All his life Daniel Watson had dreamed that one day one of his four boys would be selected to play for South Africa in the Springboks rugby team.

All of the Watson boys were superb athletes who went on to play rugby at the highest levels, but from the time the youngest of them, Cheeky, was four, his father predicted that he would be the one to make the national team. When, at the age of twenty, Cheeky excelled himself as a Springbok trialist and Springbok selection seemed certain, both father and son were ecstatic.

But Cheeky was never to become a Springbok because of the extraordinary events that were to take place in South Africa, beginning in June 1976.

The riots that began on 16 June in Soweto shocked the world.

They began as a peaceful student protest against the teaching of Afrikaans, the 'language of the oppressor'. The recently formed South African Students Movement (SASM) organised a protest march of 20 000 students carrying placards to converge on Orlando Stadium in Soweto. Most of the students were in their teens. No one expected violence.

What the students objected to was not so much studying the Afrikaans language itself but the threatened introduction of Afrikaans as the language in which all subjects would be taught in a number of Soweto schools. The students argued that they were not proficient in the language and neither were their teachers. They suspected, with some justification, that being instructed in Afrikaans was intended to increase their failure rate.

They were well aware of the government's attitude. Hendrik Verwoerd, who had introduced apartheid back in 1948 and who designed the education system in the 1950s, had said in a famous speech that black students still quoted:

> *There is no place for him (the black student) in the European community above the level of certain forms of labour . . . For that reason it is of no avail for him to receive a training which has as its aim absorption in the European community . . . Until now he has been subject to a school system which drew him away from his own community and misled him by showing him the green pastures of European society in which he is not allowed to graze.*[1]

'In 1953, the year the Bantu Education Act implemented these changes, the government spent $180 on each white child in school compared to $25 on each black child.'[2]

For over twenty years black education had been declining. Many of the best black teachers had resigned rather than agree to condition their young people to accept an inferior education.

The Vorster government had ignored the students' petitions and deputations so on 16 June 1976 they called a strike.

In spite of the fact that education was an explosive

grievance, the mood of the protest marchers was cheerful. One poster read 'If we must do Afrikaans, Vorster must do Zulu'.[3] It was a totally peaceful demonstration.

As the students, some in school uniform, approached the Orlando Stadium in Soweto, the police were waiting with automatic weapons. The students slowed down. Someone started to sing a hymn and the others, rather nervously, joined in. Then the first child, a thirteen-year-old boy, fell dead. The crowd was then bombarded with tear gas, and when the students scattered, the police opened fire, killing one more student and injuring many others.

After 16 June Soweto was in a state of revolt for weeks. Street warfare broke out between police and students. Schools and government buildings were destroyed, then the students started burning anything associated with the white economy – delivery vans, trucks, shops and banks. Parents, proud of their children's courageous stand against the apartheid system they had not dared to oppose, joined in. Many of them stayed away from work and supported four general 'sympathy' strikes. Absenteeism reached as high as 80 per cent bringing Johannesburg to a standstill.

But the cost in black lives was high. The police, safe inside their armoured vehicles, went into the black townships and shot hundreds of people. It was never discovered how many. As Rian Malan, then a reporter on the *Star* newspaper, describes it:

> *When the fires finally died down several months later, there were four hundred black corpses, or five hundred or seven hundred and the police were firmly back in control. Newspapers proclaimed that the situation had returned to normal, but there was no longer any*

such thing. South Africa's psychic landscape had been transformed. Blacks saw that they had shaken the white power structure to its very foundations, and they suddenly had hope. The tide of history had turned.[4]

Solidarity protests spread to Cape Town, the townships of Cape Province and to Port Elizabeth, where the Watsons lived and had their clothing business, Dan Watson American Imports.

The Watsons had been approached by desperate black parents, customers and friends, whose children had been arrested and never seen again. They had helped to look for them and sometimes been successful in getting them out of police custody, where their bones had been broken and their half-grown bodies beaten, but usually the searches were hopeless.

It was at precisely this time, at the height of the riots in June 1976, that an astute black man named Mono Badela, supporter of the banned ANC, decided to try and recruit the Watson brothers into the struggle against apartheid. Because of his wit and gentleness they were not aware that this was what he was doing.

Mono Badela was the only black journalist working for the *Evening Post* in Port Elizabeth. He was also president of the Kwaru black rugby team. One day he wandered into one of the Watsons' smart menswear stores, noticed that there was gospel music playing and commented to Gavin, 'You Watsons are supposed to be Christians.' Ronnie remembers Badela as a bit of a joker, a teaser. 'He says to us, "Look, it seems to me that Christianity is about a white man's God; it's only for white men." And we say, "That's not true. Colour is not relevant to Christ. The politicians here are deceived. It's just a matter of showing Christian love and the differences will be overcome."'[5]

Badela is a small, engaging man with flashing eyes and a wicked wit. Ronnie Watson was very earnest and slightly indignant at being told that Christianity was about a white man's God. He blustered a little in his defence and stuck out his chest in his well-cut suit as he said that Christian love could overcome the differences – which is exactly what Mono Badela wanted.

Mono Badela's meeting with the Watsons was apparently casual, almost coincidental, but later he would admit that he had planned it carefully. He had researched the Watson brothers for some time, discovering that they were Christians, very successful in business, that all four had played for the prestigious white Crusaders rugby club, yet they spoke fluent Xhosa and could not resist a moral challenge. He also knew that Cheeky had just played a great game in the Junior Springboks against the All Blacks and was almost certain to become a Springbok. To recruit such useful young whites to the black 'struggle' would be a triumph.

After a few meetings with the Watsons in their store, Badela perceived that the time he was investing in their cultivation might have a rich pay-off. The brothers were genuinely non-racial. In many ways they thought and felt like black people.

In the political climate of early 1976 black and white playing a rugby match together was unthinkable. It had never happened in South Africa's history and it seemed that it never would as the government was totally opposed to integration of any sort.

Mono Badela knew the political impact a mixed rugby

match would have, not just in South Africa, but internationally, so he gently nudged the Watsons towards such an event. First he suggested that as Christians and rugby players the Watson brothers should go into the black township of New Brighton and unofficially help coach the Kwaru team.

Badela had judged the Watson brothers accurately. Being both idealistic and unafraid of a fight they could not resist the challenge to go into the highly volatile townships in spite of the danger. Badela did not need to ask the Watsons twice. Naively, they expected that with a little Christian love, the misunderstanding between blacks and whites could be fixed. Almost certainly they did not realise the depth of fear and hatred on both sides.

Valence recalls the first time they went into New Brighton to coach. For Valence, who was handsome, confident, used to being listened to and appreciated, it was something of a culture shock. 'The players were factory workers, people who work with their hands lifting engines all day. They'd come straight from work. They're well muscled. Nobody's overweight. Some of them greet us very nicely, you know, Hello, how are you? But one of them, named Archie, I sense is a racist. He wears a red sweat-band and is thinnish, tall; he's a bit of a hero, years younger than me, and I sense he hasn't got much respect for me.'[6]

Archie Mkele confirms that he was not impressed with Valence Watson at their first meeting. 'I regarded all white people as oppressors. All I needed was a white face and that was the enemy.'[7]

Valence continued his coaching in spite of Archie's cool reception. 'It gets dark and the only light on the field is from one car, and these guys are catching the ball like we can't catch balls under the best floodlights! There's potholes. There's rocks. I can't believe it. Cheeky and I are gingerly stepping over them, scared of breaking a leg. I can see by the end of the evening there's a sort of rapport I have with some of the players so we come again and again.'[8]

Cheeky's method of coaching was different from Valence's. 'I enjoyed shouting and egging on the players aggressively and getting tremendously involved myself,' he explained. 'Valence was more reserved. He had a quiet manner. He was never arrogant but he was used to people doing what he wanted. He was a forward first-row player and I played in the backline on the wing.'[9]

Ronnie and Gavin also began coaching in the townships. Gavin's methods, like Valence's, were quiet, but Ronnie, when explaining how to tackle or run with the ball, would do it himself.

The brothers noticed that the blacks, who were used to having no body contact at all with whites, were hesitant with them at first. 'But later they were over-aggressive, testing you to see whether your heart was in this thing,' said Cheeky. 'An occasional boot would be put in that wasn't supposed to be.'[10]

Ronnie Watson felt at this point that having demonstrated their Christian love by doing a bit of coaching, the brothers could now relax. But Mono Badela, ever so politely, invited them to watch a match in the township. Gavin and Ronnie went, as the others were busy. They were amazed at how good the black players were. Mono could see that the brothers were getting more emotionally involved, so next he asked them to play a game with the blacks.

'He put it in such a way that we could hardly refuse. So nicely he said, "You'd be shoulder to shoulder with a black man, actually scrumming with him. Would your Christian experience allow you to go that far?"'[11]

Mono Badela decided that the match should be played in Grahamstown, where the Watsons had been schoolboy heroes. Rhodes University, one of the oldest in South Africa, was in Grahamstown, so were a number of the finest private schools. Mono calculated that a small university town with a cathedral would be a safer place for the first try-out mixed game than his ultimate goal, the provincial capital, Port Elizabeth, where the media focus would be much keener.

'When the Watsons agreed to play a match in Grahamstown I wasn't surprised,' said Mono Badela. 'It was most unusual for white people to help us in rugby. We had no sponsors. The government didn't help. But the Watsons were deeply religious.'[12]

Some of the Rhodes students played alongside the Watson brothers. The game was a huge success. Black people packed the ground. Cheeky remembers one of the black maids who had worked at Graeme College screaming at him as he was shouldered above the crowd, '"Cheeky, Cheeky, do you remember me?" I said, "How can I forget you?" I cannot explain to you the love, the openness, the acceptance of these people'.[13]

Afterwards the white and black players rode into town together in cars owned and driven by the blacks. The event slipped by the national media almost unnoticed, and Mono bided his time before suggesting a much more provocative game in Port Elizabeth.

Events played into his hands. At this stage the Watsons were feeling so confident about playing mixed rugby that they suggested asking the exclusive white Crusaders club, of which they were members, whether the blacks could train on their B field. It seemed ludicrous to the politically unsophisticated Watsons that a splendid facility like the Crusaders' second-class field should be vacant while the blacks played on unlit, uneven ground covered in rocks. Mono Badela was clever enough not to resist the idea.

Before the application to play on the field was sent to the Crusaders club, all four brothers did some lobbying, asking individual Crusaders players how they would feel about having black players train on their ground. The players said they would not mind at all. To test this the Watsons brought their black team on to the B field one evening. The club hierarchy was outraged. They came down to the field and asked them to leave. Valence remembers being furious. He said, 'You even allow dogs to run on these lawns but just because the person is black you don't allow him.'[14]

One of the club members who asked the Watsons 'not to bring these people back' was the brother of the principal of the University of Cape Town, which was then the most liberal university in South Africa.

Mono Badela, without having to say a word, had revealed to the Watsons something they had not really believed until now – that even liberal whites did not want blacks on their sports grounds. 'The Watsons were shocked. I wasn't,' Badela said.[15]

The Watsons felt anger and shame at the attitude of the white club they had been proud to belong to. Now that their political consciousness was fully aroused, Mono suggested the Watsons play a second mixed match in Port Elizabeth. They accepted immediately.

The match was scheduled for 10 October 1976 and provoked a greater storm of protest than anyone had anticipated. Dr Pieter Koornhof, Minister for Sport, appealed to the players through the media – press, radio and television – to call off the game, telling them they would be breaking the law and flouting government policy. The head of the white South African Rugby Board, Dr Danie Craven, threatened to suspend the players from white rugby. The Chief Director of the Bantu Affairs Administration Board, Mr Louis Koch, said the players would be arrested if the game went ahead. Even the South African Security police telephoned the Watson brothers advising them not to participate.

Mono Badela had no fear that under pressure from the government and police the Watsons might give up the game. 'They were so sincere. That's why I asked them. Unlike other whites they were not bluffing. I knew they would stick to their guns.'[16]

When the Watsons paid no attention to their phone call, the Security police paid the four brothers a visit one evening when they were eating a meal in a Greek restaurant across the road from their clothing store in Main Street, Port Elizabeth. Three men in plain clothes with moustaches ('You always know they're Security because of their moustaches,' said Gavin) insisted that Gavin go with them to headquarters. Ronnie tried to go with him but the senior officer would not allow it.

Gavin, surrounded by five officers, was questioned for three hours about why his brothers wanted to play rugby with blacks. Eventually he became angry, shouting that it was only a game and he was not his brothers' keeper. The senior officer then pushed him roughly in the chest, so that he stumbled back against the window. The officer asked him to have a look down. Gavin, without looking down, said, 'Are you going to throw me down five storeys like you throw the blacks?'

The officer replied, 'Go back and tell your brothers that there is nothing special about them. They're not such fucking heroes that they can get away with anything. If you betray your own kind, then you'll get what's coming to you.'[17]

Gavin was furious when he got home. Ronnie, who was calm in most situations, said that Security was bluffing, just trying to intimidate them. Ronnie was reassuring at the time, but later he admitted he'd been worried.

Still, he could see the funny side of things. 'Suddenly all hell breaks loose,' Ronnie recalls. 'The funniest thing is that just before this match, Mono leaves town. He senses there will be a little controversy and he doesn't like controversy. So he's out of town. Leaves us with the players.'[18]

The brothers were amused rather than feeling betrayed by Mono Badela's hasty departure. To them he was a small 'roly-poly' man, 'very sharp politically' and a 'shrewd tactician' but 'no physical warrior'. Later they would hear that Badela had left for Durban because the police had started interrogating officials of the Kwaru club of which he was president. Also he was afraid, with good reason, of losing his job as a journalist on the conservative *Evening Post*. A year later this would happen, and Mono and his family would be severely harassed.

Cheeky Watson also had something important to lose. The convenor of the Springboks' selection panel, Ian Kirkpatrick, visited him at the Watsons' store and promised him a place in the team in early 1977 for their tour to France. 'He said, "I'm prepared to guarantee it in writing. But don't jeopardise your chances please." I said to him, "Ian, I'm going ahead with what I'm doing. I'm playing the mixed match as I promised", and off he went.'[19]

Daniel Watson, when he heard what had happened, was bitterly disappointed. Cheeky's brothers, too, knew that he was turning his back on a brilliant career. 'Doors would have opened to him all his life. Economically, as well as in sport,' Valence said.[20]

But the brothers and his father supported Cheeky's decision.

Cheeky admits it was 'painful' to give up the Springbok blazer. His selection for the team had been an exhilarating experience. 'Selectors travelled all over the country to observe prospective players. I was fresh out of the army, just nineteen and playing against the Western Transvaal. I played right wing. I was a very aggressive player, good on defence and good on attack. I had an exceptionally good game and ran rings around the chap the selectors had come to watch, and suddenly I shot to prominence. It was felt that Cheeky Watson would be the next South African wing. After one trial match I was selected for the A team in the shadow Springbok side. I felt proud, but I'd never been brought up to think of rugby as a god, so to me it was no incredible feat. It meant more to my dad. He was very proud.'[21]

Cheeky had become angry about the government's racism and the violent deaths that were still going on after the Soweto uprising. He reminded his father of the stories he had told them as children, of supporting the underdog whatever the personal cost and of 'loving thy neighbour as thyself'. There was nothing more to be said.

Cheeky's temptations were not yet over. A few days before the match he received a phone call from Pretoria. 'I was offered the position of colonel at the age of twenty, colonel in the South African Defence Force. I would never need money again, they said. I didn't have to do anything military. All I had to do was be sporting coordinator for the SADF.'[22]

Cheeky was suddenly angry. 'I was angry at a system that was trying to buy me off because I had recognised that they were racist. Buying me off. A twenty-year-old youngster.'[23]

On the day of the match tension was high. At the last minute two of the top white players, Gavin Cowley and Tommy Bedford, who had been a Springbok rugby vice captain, had pulled out of the game.

'Because of Pieter Koornhof [Minister for Sport] saying that we were communists, that we were going to be arrested and thrown into prison, these guys just disappeared. Off the scene. Gone,' Cheeky recalls.[24]

The Watsons' parents, Daniel and Bobbi, had come in from the farm and were staying with their sons in Port Elizabeth to give them support. They were extremely concerned. On the radio at lunchtime Pieter Koornhof made a last-minute attempt to prevent the match, appealing to the organisers to call it off and threatening yet again to arrest any white players who dared to enter the township. Then, as Cheeky, Valence and Ronnie waited outside their shop to leave for the game, the President of the Crusaders club arrived looking very pale. He told Ronnie, '"We've had a call from the Security police. Please don't go." He feared for us. He was pleading. He knew what it was going to mean.'[25]

Cheeky remembers feeling very nervous. 'Colin Snodgrass, from Crusaders, who is playing with us, is six foot five and enormous. He is snow white and wet with sweat. He says,

"Should we go through with this?" We said, "Boys, we've come this far. We're not turning back." And off we go, climb into the cars and go to meet the Rhodes University boys. I tell you, we are nervous wrecks because we're sure we are going to be arrested, thrown in jail.'[26]

The Watsons led the way towards the black township but when they got there they found roadblocks all around it. They got in via a back road and side streets as they had no permits. There were armoured vehicles waiting for them but they managed to avoid those too. It was the first time they realised just how the police enforced the goverment's racial sports policy. As they came within a mile of the Dan QeQe Stadium in Veeplaas they heard the chanting of 10 000 people. Pandemonium broke out as they approached. The blacks had heard the media warnings. They did not think the whites would have the courage to play.

The stadium was covered in rusted corrugated iron sheeting. It had been built for no more than 2000 but it was jam packed with five times that number. Outside, a mass of armoured vehicles were parked. Police in plain clothes were scattered everywhere amongst the crowd. The ground was dusty and uneven.

When the thirty players ran on to the field at 4 p.m. there were eight whites amongst them. The crowd cheered even louder when they recognised Cheeky Watson, the Springbok trialist and outstanding wing three-quarter for Eastern Province (equivalent to a state side) and his brother Valence, who played flank for the same team. Cheeky and Valence Watson and Colin Snodgrass from the Crusaders club were playing on the Kwaru team. The Rhodes University students Mark Rowles, Kevin Purcell, Al Weakly,

Derek Barter and Graham Bell played for Sedru.

This was the field which less than a month earlier had been seething with violence. Now the 10 000 black spectators were cheering whites, welcoming them to their teams. Each time Cheeky scored a try they seemed to erupt with joy. The commentator, addressing the crowd through a loudspeaker system, switched from Xhosa to English as a gesture of hospitality.

As a correspondent for the *Evening Post* wrote,

When Cheeky Watson went on a powerful run down the touchline the crowd roared its acclaim. When a White invitation player was brought crashing down by a Black Kwaru player half his size and only metres from the try line, they yelled their delight . . .

Towards the end of the match I heard two men talking behind me about the warnings the White players had had not to play.

'I suppose they'll all be out (of their unions) tomorrow.'

'That does not matter,' said his companion. 'They can always get a match with us.'

I asked another spectator what he thought of the idea of Blacks and Whites in the same team.

'I think it's wonderful. It should be done at every level.'[27]

Cheeky Watson scored two tries for the Kwaru team which beat Sedru 23–13.

After the match Cheeky, Valence and Colin Snodgrass were chaired off the field by the ecstatic crowd.

As the trickle of whites left the stadium blacks groped for their hands to squeeze them.

That evening the newspaper headlines declared 'Non-Race Rugby Is Born' and there were huge photographs of the teams in action, black passing to white, and the Watson brothers being carried on the shoulders of their black team-mates.

Cheeky remembers, 'We could imagine the whites watching. What do they see? "Black bastards". But we're on their shoulders and they are immediately taking us into the liberation struggle. It isn't just breaking the barriers of non-racial sport. You are on these guys' shoulders. They are lifting their fists. You suddenly feel that these guys have taken you in amongst them. You are part and parcel of them. You suddenly begin to feel their heartbeat. It is a deep, deep emotional thing.'[28]

3

FROM RAND MILLIONAIRES TO WHITE KAFFIRS

There were mixed reactions after the first game of multiracial rugby ever played in the history of South Africa.

Dr Danie Craven, President of the South African Rugby Board, was furious and warned the eight white players who had taken part that they were facing suspension from their unions. 'Craven Lashes Mixed Game' declared the headline in the *Weekend Post*. 'We have ways and means to deal with defiance like this . . .' Craven said the multiracial game was contrary to the government's new sports policy and had 'reflected badly on the country'.[1]

This seemed a contradiction because on 23 September 1976, the Minister for Sport, Dr Pieter Koornhof, had announced the government's decision to permit multiracial games at all levels. Apparently the permit did not mean quite what it said. Mixed sport could take place but only between teams of *separate* racial groups.

Dan Watson, the boys' father, defended them in the press. 'I am proud of my boys. They did the right thing . . . To them the match was sport, and politics had nothing to do with it.'

He said some people had called them 'white kaffirs' but that he would pay no attention to such remarks.

> *'My boys were nervous when they left yesterday to play. I prayed at home while they were playing. They told me afterwards that they felt completely safe in the townships. I believe that in South Africa we have got to learn to live with one another. We must love our neighbours and in this country the Africans are also our neighbours.*
>
> *'The trouble is that there is too much talking and too little doing. If we have faith and believe something is right then we must do it.'*[2]

The Watsons' younger sister Sharon, who was then a teenager and still at school, was also very proud and supportive. Although she was not particularly passionate about rugby, she began collecting newspaper cuttings about her famous brothers and pasting them in a scrapbook.

Although blacks throughout the country were euphoric about the brave stand taken by a handful of white rugby players and gave them tumultuous acclaim, only a minority of whites supported them. However, some of these were very vocal.

Dr Alan Paton, well-known author and leader of the Liberal Party in South Africa before it was outlawed in 1968, telephoned Mono Badela, the president of Kwaru, from his home in Natal to say that he was delighted to hear that the Watson brothers and other white rugby players were in the struggle for a non-racial society in South Africa. He urged them not to be deterred by any form of intimidation, and said he was 'disappointed to learn from the Press at the weekend that they were being harassed by police and others to abandon their stand'.[3]

Newspaper editor Donald Woods also supported them. In

an article in the *Rand Daily Mail* headed 'A Warning to Craven', he declared that Craven was a 'pain in the national neck' and threatened that if he dared to suspend 'the Watson brothers or any other rubgy players who took part in the Kwaru match', he would ask 'every influential editor and sports editor that I know anywhere in the world where South Africa has rugby links to oppose any suggestion of a tour here.'[4]

Donald Woods, who was at the time editor of the *East London Daily Dispatch*, later addressed a multiracial audience of 200 Kwaru fans at a dinner to present Kwaru blazers to Cheeky and Valence Watson and Colin Snodgrass. It was reported in the *Eastern Province Herald* that he said,

> *'Many of us could not believe our ears and eyes on learning that Dr Craven was speaking of punishing the Watson brothers. Dr Craven's problem is that he lives in the past although he tries to dominate the present. Springbok rugby as Dr Craven has known it is now finished and the era of ethnic teams is a closed chapter.'*[5]

These were courageous words but they made Woods an enemy of the South African Government. A few weeks later, on 1 November 1976, he received a six month jail sentence for his refusal to name witnesses in an alleged crime. An appeal court later quashed the sentence, ruling that the trial had been 'improperly conducted'.

A year later Donald Woods was banned from journalism and on 1 January 1978, he fled South Africa with his family and took refuge in Lesotho. Britain agreed to grant permission to the Woods family to settle there.

Meanwhile Cheeky and Valence Watson and Michael Ryan quit white rugby to join black clubs and play in Port Elizabeth townships without permits. They were aware that they were being watched by Security police and if they were arrested they had decided to go to jail rather than pay fines.

Cheeky told the *Sunday Times*:

> *'The pressures on us have been tremendous. We all realise we have given up our careers as white rugby players and even the chance of Springbok colours. But we are now serving a far greater cause.'*
>
> *Valence said, 'If I claim to be a Christian then let me show I am one. In politics and sport people have done nothing but talk. We felt we had to set an example.'*
>
> *Friends of Michael Ryan said he had been threatened by officials of the Port Elizabeth car company where he works . . . 'but he is still completely with us', said the Watson brothers.*[6]

The Watsons and Ryan felt they had narrowly escaped prosecution when police and officials waited for them at the Crusaders stadium where they had practised with their black team earlier that week. When they did not find the white players, who had got wind of the officials' visit and cancelled the practice at the last minute, the officials changed the locks.[7]

Despite constant harassment of this kind all four Watson brothers continued to coach and play rugby in the black townships, each brother in a separate township to spread the message of mixed rugby over a wider area.

'We taught the black players new skills,' Cheeky recalls. 'What they lacked most was exercise for the top half of the body and sprints. They'd been used to doing only long-distance runs. We changed their exercise program and made them a lot more successful in rucking and getting the ball back in the loose. At first they were surprised at us being willing to have body contact with them. Some would be aggressive. But from about the third or fourth game I played with them, I felt a tremendous act of protectiveness. My teammates would jump up and protect me. Players on the other team were not allowed to touch a hair of my body.'[8]

Frequently the Watsons were arrested for being in the townships without permits. On these occasions they would be handled roughly and interrogated for hours. In court one magistrate warned them that he was well aware they wanted to be sent to prison so they could become martyrs but he would not oblige them by sending them.

Meanwhile, their black friends lost jobs and were imprisoned without trial.

The white community turned their backs on the Watson brothers with a ferocity and suddenness that stunned them. Business fell away to almost nothing, old friends shunned them and social invitations, previously too numerous for them all to be accepted, slowed to a trickle. Their mother's brother, Uncle Frank, who was once so proud of his nephews, now refused to speak to them. 'We didn't blame him for that. He was afraid,' said Cheeky.[9]

Cheeky's new young wife was upset when a note was left on her desk at work saying *Your husband plays rugby with blacks so he can sleep with their women.*

Cheeky, in spite of being the youngest, had been the first of the brothers to marry. This had not pleased the other three. It made them question the libidinous lifestyle they had been enjoying. Before the Watson brothers became politicised they were certainly no angels.

In the early 1970s Gavin opened his own business, a men's

clothing store in Port Elizabeth. He encouraged each of his brothers to join him as equal partners in the business, which they did.

The Watson brothers at that time were regarded as 'rand millionaires'. They drove Mercedes and were handsome rugby heroes who were successful in business and popular in society. This seemed to be what white supremacy in South Africa was all about.

No one would have predicted that they would become the country's leading white activists against apartheid.

All four brothers had been sharing one large flat in Port Elizabeth. It was not unusual for one to steal another's girl. This was regarded as something of a joke. If they were all playing volleyball on the beach and a good-looking girl asked to join them, they would make her feel welcome while subtly competing with each other for her affections.

Valence recalls that 'One particular girl was doing the splits, very athletic type. Ronnie likes sporting women; I like dainty women, so I agree Ronnie can take her out, even though I can see she's angling for me. After he's taken her out and they come back to the flat and Ronnie is taking her to his room, I hang back and say, "Look, if you feel uncomfortable and want to go home tonight, I'll take you." Fifteen minutes later she comes to my room and says she can't stand Ronnie. I offer to take her home but she doesn't want to go. When Ronnie comes to wake me next morning at six there is his girl. He is extremely annoyed.'[10]

Daniel Watson was perturbed that his sons had strayed so far from the Christian path. He would encourage them to hold prayer meetings in the flat. Gavin, Ronnie and Cheeky agreed to attend but Valence would not. Gavin, quoting the Bible, said they should have nothing to do with fornication and announced that as Valence was the most guilty of this particular sin, he should be told to get out of the flat.

'But it's his flat!' their father protested. 'Anyway, the worst thing to do would be to tell him to move away. While he is here the influence that we all have on him will be very good for him.'[11]

Whenever Valence came in with a girl, his brothers would try hard not to feel jealous and pray that he would change his heathen ways.

It was Cheeky's sudden marriage and the ferment surrounding it that made Ronnie and Gavin reconsider their lifestyles. Ronnie, in particular, was beginning to feel 'Just to go to bed with a woman because it is fun or she leads you on was not what I had been brought up to do. We'd been taught to believe that the final aim was to get into Heaven, and as Christians to be an example to others.'[12]

At the age of nineteen Cheeky had fallen in love for the first time in his life. He had asked this first girlfriend to marry him. His brothers were shocked. They argued that he was too young, just two years out of school, he was inexperienced, he would fall in love hundreds of times before he should even think about marriage.

'This one is not looking at you as a wife. She is looking all around her. She is looking at *us*,' protested Ronnie, who had travelled 600 miles home from a business trip to try to dissuade his young brother from marrying her.[13]

'A lot of women are out there to have fun. She is having fun with you. Don't think she's doing it because she loves you,' warned Valence.[14]

But Cheeky was adamant that this was true love and as soon

as he returned from a rugby tour of Italy the couple would be married. In his absence the brothers conspired to prove to him that this girl was not the right one for him.

'I thought it was better to break Cheeky's heart than ruin his life,' Ronnie explained.[15]

When Cheeky arrived home his girlfriend was not at the airport to meet him. The brothers had sent their thirteen-year-old sister, Sharon, to break the news that 'Ronnie is taking your girlfriend out.' When Cheeky heard this he dropped the half dozen bottles of vintage wine he had brought back from Italy for his brothers.

There was a dreadful row between Cheeky and Ronnie. Cheeky recalls, 'I was so shocked. My first love. Suddenly she thought Ronnie had got everything. Why was she going to waste time with a little schoolboy? I was mad. I thought, "I'm going to rule the roost. I'll get her eating out of my hand." I did and she fell totally in love with me.'[16]

Cheeky announced that he and his girlfriend were getting married anyway. Valence and Ronnie refused to go to the wedding. The marriage lasted just over a year. In that time Cheeky became a father. There is little doubt that the brothers' political activism helped hasten the end of the marriage. This was a painful time for Cheeky who loved his daughter, Chantal.

From now on the Watson brothers would find that their wives and girlfriends would be harassed for their beliefs almost as severely as they were. It was a fact that would split some partnerships asunder and bind the remaining family even more closely together.

Was it just their Christianity and the attraction of a challenge that turned the Watson brothers into political activists? They each admit that as soon as they left the farm to go to school they felt at odds with their own society. Cheeky said that at boarding school he felt he had more in common with the Xhosa maids and gardeners than the other boys. Gavin, even at primary school, felt it was unfair that his black friends were not allowed to go to the same school and he could not understand why he was being taught that blacks were inferior.

But also, Ronnie, Valence and Cheeky agree that the experience of being conscripted into the South African Army in the 1970s was a very important factor in their decision to oppose the apartheid system.

Gavin was the only one who avoided doing his national service: At the time he left school it was not compulsory.

Ronnie, the first to serve his year, did so without causing any incidents. The trouble started when he returned to the army two years later to serve his compulsory three months in a camp on the border of Namibia and Angola. On one occasion he was riding through the bush inside a mine-sweeping vehicle when a group of soldiers grabbed two innocent black men who happened to be driving by and decided to use them as mine detectors. As Ronnie remembers it, 'The driver of this light aluminium Land Rover has obviously invested his whole life savings in the car. They take him and tie him to the bonnet of his Land Rover and force the other guy to drive in front of their convoy while they cover him with machine guns. They are making an example of them, saying. "We'll teach you to tell SWAPO not to lay land mines." When I get there and see this, I say, "Are you blokes mad in the head?" They threaten me with prison if I interfere but I warn them very clearly that I will speak about this when I get back to headquarters. The major then sends two guys to escort me away.'[17] Soon afterwards the black men were released.

A little later two land mines did explode in front of the convoy of trucks but none of the soldiers was hurt because they were protected by three anti-mine vehicles leading the convoy. The soldiers had all jumped out, rifles ready, to attack anyone who might try to ambush them but had found no one. Feeling disappointed at the lack of action, the unit leader decided to teach the locals a lesson by burning down every kraal (home) in the nearest village. Ronnie pleaded with him not to do this, saying that the people in the village had nothing to do with the war.

'You are going to burn a man's home, his radio, his guitar, everything that is precious and dear to his family, his bed, his crockery, pots, his animals, just burn everything in front of him. Why?' Ronnie asked. 'I said, "I am not going to do it and on no account should you chaps do it."

'The officer said, "I am instructing you to do it."

'I refused and so did the others, so he radioed the commandant, Jones Phillipson. I said, "Tell the commandant that he is a vicious person. He must come and do his own dirty work."

'The officer didn't know how to handle the situation. Was it mutiny or was it just one person's opinion? Eventually he decided not to burn the kraals.'[18]

About a week later Ronnie clashed again with his commanding officers. 'We were shooting on the range and I came out number two. I was a very good shot because I was brought up on a farm where hunting and shooting were automatic. So I was selected to go in front of an ambush. I said, "Fine. Where do you want me to go?"

'The officer said, "Watson, you are the sniper. You will be doing the shooting. Shoot at any black terrorist who comes through the bush here."

'So I take out my bullets and chuck them all on the ground and then I sit down next to a tree.

'He said, "Why are you doing that?" and I said, "Basically I am a Christian and I don't see any reason to kill people. I don't see these people as my enemies. These people have parents, children. Have they done any harm to us? No, they haven't. So why must we kill them?"

'He threatened to kill me if I didn't obey orders.

'I said, "Death is not a big thing to me. I'm going to Heaven."

'He cancelled the ambush. Everybody had to go back to camp. I had messed the thing up. When we get back he says, "I don't want any more of that fucking kaffir talk of yours. We are going to deal with you." They confiscated my rifle and bullets and told me, "From now on the army has finished with you. You will sleep in your tent and read books." They wanted me to sign a secrecy declaration promising I would not talk about the things I had seen on the border. I refused to sign it. A heck of an argument developed but I still refused. So I was refused any bedding. "You can freeze to death as far as we're concerned."'[19]

Before Ronnie received his dishonourable discharge, he was punished by being kept in solitary confinement for three weeks, ostensibly for being AWOL. After this he was brought up before the judiciary of the military command and found guilty of deserting his camp. Ronnie believed that his experiences in the army helped to radicalise him.

Valence also did his national service in the army straight

from school at the age of seventeen. He did outstandingly well in the military exams and was one of the top three young officers in South Africa in his year. His commanding officer told him that he would have a very bright future in the regular army.

After completing his year in the army, Valence, like all other young men in South Africa at that time, was obliged to do a three-month camp every two years. He was sent to the border between Zimbabwe (then Rhodesia) and South Africa, as an officer in charge of his own platoon.

During his training as an officer Valence was given 'motivation' lectures, in which he was told 'the black man is the enemy'. Every target was a black one. In all the literature handed out to young officers, 'terrorists' were black. There was frequent reference to 'the black danger'. Valence could not relate to this. He didn't believe it was so. But he could not voice his opinions. The only thing he could do was refuse to stand to attention when the National Anthem was played.

Young officers were trained to viciously attack black dummies. Valence recalls, 'You had to bayonet this dummy, screaming at the top of your voice. When they made me do it I burst out laughing. I was rolling around the ground. I remember saying to the guy in charge, "I will never kill a human being". I couldn't even *act* it. I just burst out laughing.'[20] Valence was given eight hours pack drill in the blazing sun as punishment for not obeying orders.

He was soon to meet atrocity face to face. 'My next camp was on the Namibian border with Angola. The company that had been there before us had tied a black man they suspected of being an agent to a tree and shot him. No trial. Nothing. This shocked me. A month later, when we were there, a deaf and dumb person wandered by mistake into what is called a Yattie strip, a no-man's-land area of about a kilometre between Angola and Namibia. He was a black South African in his late twenties. They brought him into our camp and tried to question him, using sign language, but he just shook his head. Later that night I heard the officers talking, planning to take him to the Angolan border. Because he was a South African they knew he would head towards home. They said, "If anybody asks what happened we'll say he was infiltrating from Angola." Then they took him out to the border and used him as target practice.'[21]

After this sinister event Valence found the army insufferable. He began politicising the soldiers in his platoon, telling them that they were not defending South Africa, just white South Africa. He told them the government was holding power over the blacks it had no right to hold, that the blacks were fighting for an ideology that was acceptable and that they were not terrorists. 'I told them, "There's no way I am part of this army. We are being used as cannon fodder. Do you see any Members of Parliament's sons up here on the border? Ask your friends if *anyone* up here on the border is the son of an MP? They're away in the US studying, while we are being *conscripted*. Clearly, chaps, if we are here to protect our population of forty million people, most of whom are black, why are only whites here? Where are the black Africans?" At first they were shocked. They said, "That's ridiculous." The white South African kid grows up in a very protected environment. They don't mix on a social level with blacks so they can be easily misinformed. Media was controlled by the State. That's why apartheid was so effective.'[22]

Eventually Valence's platoon refused to take up arms against the blacks. Valence was promptly demoted to a desk job. Later he too was given a dishonourable discharge.

By this time the Watson family was known by the government to be something of a security risk. But it did not stop the army making Cheeky, the youngest son, an officer as well.

He served his time but was kept well away from any borders. Instead he did his active service at the training camps, drilling the new recruits and teaching them military service.

Cheeky remembers his year in the army as 'an absolute waste of time'.[23] However he was efficient enough to be promoted to lieutenant and to receive a trophy for excelling as an officer. A general came down from Pretoria to try and persuade him to join the permanent South African Defence Force. He declined.

4

SECURITY STRIKES

By early 1977, a few months after the historic mixed rugby match, most whites had stopped coming to the Watsons' menswear stores in Port Elizabeth. Gavin decided to employ black assistants and to re-stock the stores with the kind of clothing that black people might wear.

He asked Archie Mkele, rugby player and accounts clerk, for some advice on how to re-stock.

'Blacks don't like white shit – Bata shoes, flared trousers, striped shirts without button-down collars. Because blacks have no power they like to buy nice clothes. Whites, because they do have power, don't care how badly they dress.'[1]

At first Archie Mkele had regarded the Watson brothers as classic liberal 'do-gooders' of whom he did not approve. Mkele was associated with the Black Consciousness Movement and was loyal to its leader, Steve Biko.

Valence remembers Archie being particularly hostile to him the first time they met on the rugby field at New Brighton township.

'First of all he arrives late. I am there with all the other players and they are saying, "Where is Archie?" I have never heard of this Archie but I sense he is the big wheel around here,' he recalls. 'As a coach I can't get any enthusiasm out of the swine. I am getting annoyed. After the practice he says to me, "Look, you are a liberal." And I say, "You are a racist. Do your homework. Find out my history." We practise again and he hears me speak Xhosa fluently and he sees the interaction I have with the blokes. By now we have two teams and we are tackling each other and being thrown around. I can sense that he is getting a bit rougher than he should, testing, is this white man for real? Archie is tackling me harder than anybody else.'[2]

In 1976 when Archie lost his clerical job, Valence offered him a job in one of the Watsons' stores and Archie accepted. 'It took some months to get used to him,' Valence admitted. 'Archie is short tempered like me.'

Jeffrey Nocanda, a cheerful and speedy little winger in the East Brighton rugby team, was also employed in the Watsons' stores. Jeffrey worked alongside Valence at Uitenhage, while Archie was kept at a safe distance and worked in the Main Street store with Gavin.

No one would have predicted that a short time later Valence and Archie would become as close as brothers and that both Jeffrey and Archie would endure torture to protect the Watsons.

One night Cheeky and his black friend Temba, who liked to call himself Cheeky's guardian angel, were driving home from rubgy training through the township of New Brighton. Cheeky had just been enthusing about the brotherly love at training between black and white when they heard sirens wailing and saw that they were being followed by three police cars. 'Welcome to the real South Africa,' said Temba.

A police sergeant ordered Cheeky out of the car and told him to get into the police car. Temba made a sign to Cheeky that he would follow. At the station Cheeky was told, in Afrikaans, that he was under arrest for entering a black township without a permit. He replied that he didn't speak Afrikaans. At this the sergeant became very angry and was about to beat him up when a senior officer appeared and told him to leave Cheeky to him. The officer told Cheeky that by refusing to speak Afrikaans he was showing contempt for the sergeant's heritage, and the officer's own.

Both officers were sweating and very aggressive.

Cheeky replied, 'I prefer English. That's my heritage.'

'Did your parents ever tell you the truth about what the English did to the Afrikaner?' asked the officer.

Cheeky said they had.

'I don't think so. Did they tell you about Lord Kitchener's concentration camps? My grandmother and four of my uncles died in those camps. The British starved 50 000 women and children to death. Did your parents tell you that?'

'No,' Cheeky replied. He had known the English took prisoners but not that they had starved them.

'What do you think the real agenda of these blacks is, Cheeky?'

'Justice.'

'Control! Total control of this nation and its resources. They didn't build this nation. We did. They want to throw us out,' the officer said furiously. 'You are playing right into their hands. If you know what's good for you, you'll keep away from the blacks.'

The officer told of atrocities committed by blacks upon each other and on whites. He showed pictures of bodies being hacked apart with knives. 'What sort of mind could do that? You are not talking about civilised men here, but savages!' he ranted. When Cheeky staggered out to the car where Temba was waiting he looked ashen.

'Did they hit you?' Temba asked anxiously.

'No, but they're so full of hate,' Cheeky said.

This was the first of many occasions when Cheeky would be taken to the police station and questioned for hours. 'The police would talk nonsense – cursing and jeering. They'd say, "Lock the rubbish up! Don't waste your time on him." And you would have to sit and listen to this because these guys are standing there with guns on their hips and they are so mad, they're sweating, even though it's winter. Eventually they charge you. You've got to go to court and the case drags on for three days. There is a lot of publicity. They find you guilty and you say you refuse to pay the fine and will go to jail. Now this is a problem for the government. This guy is just playing rugby and now he's off to jail. So the magistrate will say, "Caution and discharge".'[3]

In April 1977, the recession deepened. Over one million out of fourteen million blacks were unemployed. Following an announcement that rents in the township of Soweto were to be increased by 40 to 80 per cent to compensate for last year's riots, there were rent boycotts. Five thousand Soweto residents demonstrated.

Winnie Mandela was arrested in July for violation of a government banning order. Her offence was admitting that she'd had an unauthorised visit from friends and had talked to two neighbours. In 1975 Winnie Mandela had been banned from any involvement in politics and confined to the remote settlement of Brandfort, ninety miles from Soweto.

In August Steve Biko, acknowledged head of the Black Consciousness Movement (BCM) and advocate of peaceful opposition to apartheid, was detained under a clause of the Terrorism Act.

On 12 September, at the age of thirty, Biko became the forty-sixth black to die in custody since 1961. Officially his death was attributed to a hunger strike but an autopsy report released a month later indicated that he died from brain damage after savage beatings. Referring to Biko's death the Minister for Justice Mr Kruger said, 'I am not glad and I am not sorry about Mr Biko. It leaves me cold.'

Ten thousand mourners attended the funeral of Steve Biko in Kingwilliamstown.

His death led to renewed rioting, particularly in Queenstown, Port Elizabeth and Kingwilliamstown. The government subsequently reimposed a nationwide ban on all open-air meetings and outlawed the BCM. According to the late Biko, a medical student at Natal University, the aim of black consciousness was to channel the pent-up forces of the angry black masses to meaningful and directional opposition. It had a strong religious element, urging spiritual liberation to recover black identity. Because of certain anti-white statements, such as the South African Students Organisation (SASO) declaration that 'whites must be excluded in all matters relating to the struggle to realise our aspirations', the BCM was seen by some people as racist.

Although the Watsons had nothing to do with the BCM they were shocked by the death of Steve Biko. Some of their black friends were so angry at the way Biko had been murdered that they refused to play rugby with them because they were white.

'They tortured him. Do you know why? Because he was a better man than any white in this country,' Archie Mkele told Valence bitterly. Valence felt that Archie wanted him not only out of his team but out of his country.[4]

The government imposed a severe crackdown in which about fifty people were arrested and a score of black protest groups were banned. It also banned the country's largest newspaper for blacks, *The World*, and arrested its editor, Percy Quoboza.

It was at this time that Cheeky Watson, driving into the black township of New Brighton to play rugby, was confronted by a roadblock. Noticing that the police were not armed, Cheeky decided to burst through the roadblock at speed, which he did. 'It's five in the afternoon and there's not a dog on the street. I don't understand it. Doors are closed. Then, over the hill, just fifty yards in front, I see a crowd of about 3000 kids, wielding clubs and machetes. They'd just overturned a bus and set it alight. I don't have time to turn back. I slow right down and I'm into this mob. I don't know what to do. I wind down the window, lean out and show my face, thinking, "God, help me." The first kid looks at me and shouts, "Cheeky!" and they start chanting and hitting the car and their hands go up and my fist goes up in a black power salute. So I drive through this chanting mob, "Cheeky, Cheeky", and they are hitting the car and eventually I get to the stadium. The black players and officials just stare at me. "Where did you come from?"

'"Koyanna Street."

'"What? We would never take that risk. Are you raving mad?"

'"I drove through them."

'"What!"

'I suddenly realised why the police had let me through the roadblock.'[5]

Shortly after this incident occurred, the storeroom of the Watsons' Main Street store became a makeshift hospital for wounded radical students, who would have been taken to prison if they had dared go to hospital. The Watson brothers were aware that the penalty for harbouring 'terrorists' was ten years jail. However, they supplied money, clothing, food and cars to transport students to safety over the border to Lesotho. 'All the profits from our businesses were ploughed back into ferrying people around,' Gavin recalls. 'Every bit of money went back into the fight against the apartheid system.'[6]

Over the next ten years thousands of children would flee the country, making orphans of themselves and forming the core of the African National Congress in exile.

When the Watsons offered their Mercedes to smuggle the so-called 'terrorists' across the border, they were told by their ANC friends that they had orders from above not to let the brothers drive their own cars. Whites like the Watsons were too valuable in the struggle to be killed by the Security police. Reluctantly they handed over their keys.[7]

'Once one of our black friends smashed up two cars in one week,' says Gavin. 'The first time, coming back from Cape Town, he was chased by Security police and rolled the car. There were pamphlets all over the car but the police just left them. They looked down at him and thought he was dead so they drove off. He then came to us and said, "That car is a wreck. I need another one to transport these guys to safety."'[8]

Stores like the Watsons' were too important as ANC

meeting places to be left unguarded. It was hazardous for the ANC to hold meetings in the townships, which were riddled with black government informers. Poverty was so dire that many blacks succumbed to the temptation of government money. The Watsons' stores were relatively safe places to meet. In the event of a police raid the activists could emerge from the storeroom and pose as shoppers.

From the late 1970s onwards the leaders of the banned ANC were aware of who the Watsons were and watched them closely, sending messages and giving directions to them through ANC members.

The ANC led the anti-apartheid liberation movement. It was formed in 1912 by four black lawyers who had studied abroad and had two main objectives – to extend to the black majority the limited franchise held by non-whites in Cape Province and to oppose all forms of discrimination based on race.

By the 1950s the ANC had 100 000 members. They came from different tribal groups and believed that all Africans should be full citizens of South Africa. Being nonracial, the ANC had amongst its members radical Indians and white communists. In 1952 Albert Luthuli, Zulu chief, Christian and a follower of Gandhian non-violence, was chosen as president. In 1960 he won the Nobel Peace Prize for his peaceful leadership.

In 1955 the ANC drew up the Freedom Charter, which is still in the Congress's main manifesto. Its first premise is that 'South Africa belongs to all who live in it, black and white.'

The government, disagreeing with the Freedom Charter and fearing it was a blueprint for violent revolution, tried to crush the ANC and conducted the infamous 'treason trial', in which 156 ANC leaders were tried over a period of five years (1956–61). The charges were dismissed.

In 1960 the government outlawed the ANC. After this, certain young members of the Congress began to demand a change in the policy of non-violence to one of greater militancy and direct action. Nelson Mandela was one of these young members. He went underground and helped to found 'Umkonto we Sizwe' or 'Spear of the Nation' (known as MK).

In the 1964 Rivonia Trial Mandela and seven other ANC leaders including Walter Sisulu were convicted for their part in MK's campaign of sabotage against military installations. They remained in prison for over twenty years.

The ANC, being outlawed, was forced to establish itself in exile. Oliver Tambo, Mandela's former law partner, became leader of the ANC in exile. First the ANC established itself in Mozambique and Zambia, creating a network of bases in a number of neighbouring African countries. It was financed by independent African countries through the Organization of African Unity (OAU) and other countries.

After the Soweto unrest in 1976 ANC ranks swelled when thousands of young blacks fled South Africa to join MK and train in guerilla warfare. The ANC's guerilla campaign was limited in its effectiveness by the military force South Africa used to make nearby black states, particularly Angola, Mozambique and Namibia, agree to prevent the ANC from establishing bases there.

Despite this, support for the ANC continued to grow within South Africa and internationally. Mandela's continued imprisonment drew the attention of foreign governments, who began more and more to see the ANC as the legitimate representative of the black majority.

In 1977 Valence Watson had met a lively and attractive schoolgirl named Eileen Swanepoel and despite her parents' anxiety, he had taken her to a footballers' dance in the black township of New Brighton.

Eileen, who had never been political, was excited about going to a black township. She had a wonderful evening dancing with Valence and his friends.

Not long after this very successful first date, however, Eileen was astonished to discover that Valence had a prodigious number of female admirers, all of them older and more experienced than she was.

'His last girlfriend before me was exactly ten years older than me. I was still at school. I felt so embarrassed. Then I found that almost every woman I met had been to bed with him!'[9]

Valence said, 'I know it sounds as though I fancy myself but on the first date I told Eileen, "The last thing to do is fall in love with me".'[10]

'He *fancied* himself!' Eileen declared. 'But I decided I liked this chap. I went back to boarding school and told my friends I'd met my husband and they laughed at me. Then one asked, "Did you say your boyfriend was Valence Watson? There's a picture of him in the newspaper!" So I said, "Yes, that's him," because it was a nice picture. He used to write letters to me and they were lectures; I must exercise, I must eat properly, I must learn hard at school. That was all they were about. My friends wanted to know what was in his letters but I would only show them "Love, Valence".'[11]

Shortly after leaving school Eileen, against her parents' wishes, began dating Valence regularly. He was eight years older than she was and regarded in conservative circles as a terrorist. After a few months Eileen distressed her parents further by moving into the Watsons' family home.

In 1976 the Watsons had decided to share one house and had bought a large one in Park Drive, Port Elizabeth. It had once been a day school attached to the German Embassy. The grounds were vast and the property backed on to a large park, with rocky hills and gullies, grassland and a stream. The experience of living in this house was like being in the country.

The Watsons felt it would be ideal if they all lived together. This was partly because they were afraid of retribution from the white community and partly out of concern for their parents, who now lived alone on an isolated farm outside Alicedale. There was plenty of room for the four brothers, their parents and numerous visitors. Indeed, the whole rugby team would often come for a meal after the match and sometimes stay the night.

There was no such thing as privacy in the gracious mansion. Before one important rugby game, Cheeky decided to give his friend Temba a shaved head. His mother's bathroom was vacant so he took him in there. Bobbi, who was genteel and very polite, pushed open the door to take a shower and withdrew in alarm. All she could see was a naked black giant with a half-shaved skull spluttering into her basin.

'During the late 1970s and early 1980s our house was used as a place to stay by a lot of guys on the run. Upstairs there was a loft with a lot of beds. When you woke up in the morning there would be at least four extra people for breakfast,' Cheeky recalls. 'Often at breakfast there were African political leaders who'd be setting up meetings. The Security branch would have people sitting outside the house attempting to monitor everything.'[12]

Occasionally Security would get tired of waiting for the Watsons to do something for which they might be arrested and would try to provoke them. In June 1979 Valence was driving along Russell Road in Port Elizabeth in his Mercedes late at night when he stopped for a snack. 'Three guys came up to my car. One had what looked like a sharpened screwdriver in his hand. I reversed, and drove at them. They scattered. The next week I caught up with the ringleader . . . I gave him something to think about, like he'd have done to me. He was an ex-Railways policeman. It always goes back to the same source.'[13]

A week or so after this unnerving incident, on 23 June 1979, Valence and Eileen were married. However it was not Valence who proposed to the nineteen-year-old Eileen, but Cheeky.

'Cheeky asked me, "Do you think you and Valence will ever get married?" because at that stage they thought Valence, at twenty-seven, was the eternal bachelor,' Eileen said. 'After swearing Cheeky to secrecy I admitted that we had discussed it but that Valence was just waiting on the Lord for the right time. That very night Cheeky goes to Valence in the bathroom and I'm listening outside the door. He starts teasing Valence, saying, "What's all this I hear about just waiting on the Lord?" I was so cross with Cheeky.'[14]

Valence continued the story. 'Cheeky said to my dad, "We need a party here again. Let's have a party. It's about time Valence got married." Within days Cheeky had arranged the party, the marquee, the spit, the sheep, the whole thing. He'd phoned Eileen's mother and said, "Oh, by the way, would it be all right if Eileen and Valence were married in ten days time?"

'She replied, "That's Eileen's decision."'[15]

Eileen took up the tale. 'And Valence said, "We clean forgot about wedding rings". Gavin had got engaged and then broken it off so he had a ring and we used that. Then Cheeky said, "We haven't got a cake!" so he rushed off to the bakery and they'd made a cake for somebody getting married in a week's time, so they let us have that one.'[16]

In spite of the lack of preparation the wedding was a great success. Valence recalled, 'It was a massive non-racial party. There were 1400 people at the wedding that night and eighty were white. We refused to apply for a permit to allow the Africans to stay on in a white area after 9 p.m. We disobeyed the White-by-Night law. The party just went on. The cops didn't break it up because at this stage police were still trying to act to the outside world as if they were the good guys.

'The Afrikaner press reported our wedding, saying that the pageboy was black and the flower girl (who was Cheeky's daughter, Chantal), was white. We had an African Seventh Day Adventist choir singing. We barbecued eleven sheep and a hundred kilos of sausage, called Boerewors. As in the African tradition, the elders and senior people were seated in the marquee and the younger people sat around outside under the trees, helping themselves. It was a beautiful evening.'[17]

As part of their Christian belief the Watson brothers did not drink and the wedding was supposed to be an alcohol-free affair, so Ronnie was surprised to notice some empty champagne bottles lying at some distance from the tent. Cheeky and his rugby friend Temba were quite drunk. Ronnie said, 'Be serious. We need you for fixing things. What if anything goes wrong here?' They said, 'It's a wedding. We've got to celebrate.'[18]

In his defence Cheeky said, 'We were screening everybody just to make sure no bad elements came in. It took hours. We had to have something to keep us amused.'[19]

Soon afterwards Cheeky retired to bed in the honeymooners' room. When his father tried to get him to move, Cheeky replied that there were two beds and the couple could use the other one. 'Relax, they've got their whole lives ahead of them,' he said, and promptly fell asleep.[20]

So Valence and Eileen shared the first night of their honeymoon with Cheeky.

The next day they went off alone but before the end of a week, Eileen confessed that she was missing the family too much and asked to go home. 'I thought, "Are you crazy?",' Valence recalled. 'But it was not her family she was missing. It was the Watsons.'[21] They went home.

As it happened it was very fortunate that Eileen decided to cut short her honeymoon. The Watson family had flouted the White-by-Night law on the night of her wedding and there were soon to be violent repercussions.

A week after the wedding, on 29 June 1979, Gavin Watson was in the Commercial Road store just before closing time when two black youths who were being chased by two whites raced into the store. Gavin asked them what was happening and in an instant one of the black youths whipped out a knife and stabbed him deeply in the chest. When Gavin screamed that he'd been stabbed Archie Mkele, who was in the back of the store, came running. At that moment Valence, back unexpectedly early from his honeymoon, also entered the store.

'I saw Gavin standing there. He had a light shirt on and his hand was over his heart, and the blood was just spurting out between his fingers over his chest,' Valence said. 'His assassin then ran for the door and I caught him and knocked him down and he lay dazed. I rushed back to Gavin. Archie Mkele was in the shop. Archie had a big pair of leather brogues on and he just went berserk. He nearly stomped this guy to death. His shoes were full of blood. I shouted, "Leave him, you're killing him."'[22]

'Valence had to pull me off the guy,' Archie confirmed.[23]

Gavin was very white and sweat poured from his body. Ronnie, who had arrived shortly after the stabbing, phoned six times to get the police to send an ambulance but it took so long to come that Ronnie eventually flagged down a passing black ambulance and pleaded with the unwilling driver to take him to hospital. 'This person is dying,' Ronnie said. The black driver replied, 'I couldn't care less. I'll take my time.'[24] Apartheid was alive and well in Port Elizabeth.

By the time he arrived at hospital, Gavin's feet and hands were very swollen and Ronnie realised that he had lost a lot of blood. Ronnie noticed a row of white ambulances waiting at the hospital and asked why none of these had been sent. The hospital staff told him they had received no calls from the police for an ambulance.[25]

Suddenly two Security men in plain clothes arrived at the hospital and demanded to interview Gavin. Ronnie angrily fended them off. That night Ronnie, who did not trust them, stayed sitting up by Gavin's bed all night.

Surgeons explained to the family that Gavin was too weak

to be operated on. Twice his heart had stopped beating. They would leave the operation until midnight and hope that his condition might stabilise. Meanwhile they were still pumping blood into him. Most of the family went home to wait for news. But at 7.30 p.m. they received a phone call to say that Gavin's condition was critical. The surgeons had to take a chance and operate immediately. A theatre sister, who happened to be a close friend of the family, told the Watsons not to hold out much hope of Gavin's survival.

Twice on the operating table his heart stopped beating. The prognosis was grim. Gavin had to be given sixteen pints of blood by transfusion to replace the amount he had lost. His pulmonary artery had been ruptured. The whole family assembled at the hospital and knelt to pray. Cheeky asked that if God had to take one brother, take him, not Gavin.

But Gavin did survive. Many people thought it was a miracle.

Three days after he was pronounced to be near death, Gavin discharged himself from hospital and went home. 'We couldn't believe our eyes,' Valence recalls. 'Ronnie went off his head. He said, "Are you bloody mad?" But Gavin is impulsive. He says, "Look, chaps, we can't live in fear. We have to enjoy life. If it's God's will that I should live, then I'm not going to die just because I come out of hospital a bit early." Then, two weeks later, he asked me to come for a run with him. I said, "No way. Are you crazy?" But I went for a run and he beat me. Gavin has always been very fit.'[26]

Gavin's attacker was arrested and locked in a police cell. A few days later, rather strangely, he 'escaped' and was seen walking around in the black township of New Brighton. A woman civilian had recognised him as a criminal who had already been involved in the murder of a black youth, so she approached the CID, not the Security branch, and asked them to arrest him. She then phoned Valence Watson and said, 'Look here, Watson, the man who stabbed your brother is in the New Brighton police station. Come quick, or they'll let him go again.'[27]

Valence arrived and confronted the white policeman in charge of the station, saying, 'Don't think I am unaware of this conspiracy. We waited an hour and a half for the police to come and fetch this guy from our store. That is highly unusual. You would normally be on the scene of a black attacking a white within minutes. Next thing we hear he is running around Port Elizabeth absolutely free.' Valence recalls, 'Next they bring in two heavyweight cops from some other police station, who take me into a back room and threaten me. I tell them, "Your actions have been exposed, and that is it." After a while they let me go.'[28]

When the attacker eventually appeared in court he said he had not escaped, but that the police had let him go.

Mono Badela believed that Security had wanted the attacker to be black to embarrass the Watsons.

While the Watsons were struggling to keep themselves and their families safe, the problems of their black countrymen were not growing any less.

On 5 April 1979, despite an international appeal for clemency, the prominent black activist Solomon Mahlangu, aged twenty-three, was hanged for his part in the shooting of two whites in a department store.

The South African Government welcomed the coming to

power of Margaret Thatcher's Conservatives in Britain in May 1979. It considered the Conservatives more sympathetic to its problems than their Labor predecessors.

President Vorster resigned in June when it was revealed that he had known about the Information Ministry's secret projects and had been involved in covering them up.

In July Minister Pieter Koornhof, in charge of black affairs, eased the pass laws by enabling any black who had been working illegally in a white area for three years, or for one year for a single employer, to register as a legal worker and avoid being moved. The reforms would affect an estimated two million blacks.

This was encouraging news. But then came some that was utterly depressing.

On November 1, in a meeting with the leaders of South Africa's mixed-race community, Prime Minister Botha was unusually frank about his views on the country's racial future, saying, 'One-man, one-vote is out in this country. That is, never.'

The Prime Minister's attitude encouraged those who agreed with him to be aggressive towards those who did not.

One afternoon a carload of whites pulled up outside the Watsons' Main Street store and one hurled a brick through the large front window. They then started fighting the brothers. When the attackers appeared to be getting the worst of the encounter, a car with five whites dressed in army uniform screeched to a halt by the kerb. The driver yelled to the attackers to get in, and they drove off.

After this blatant attack on them in broad daylight the Watsons decided that they should stay away from bars and crowded places where fights could be started and they could 'accidentally' be shot or stabbed. They should check their cars, and the cars of their families, for bombs.

In January 1980, three ANC guerillas, armed with rifles, took twenty-five people hostage in a suburban bank in Pretoria, demanding the release of jailed ANC leader Nelson Mandela. The police, bungling the operation, stormed the bank, killing one hostage and three guerillas.

Underground activists said that the time had come for the Watsons to politicise the rugby players they coached in the townships and persuade them to support the ANC. The Watsons had seen the violence that the government was using against anyone who was even suspected of supporting the ANC. Yet they believed that the ANC was offering both blacks and whites the best deal they were ever going to get. Whites could keep their property, their jobs and there would be no retribution. Their friends in the ANC told the Watsons that the new South Africa would need people like them.

So Ronnie, Valence and Cheeky joined with their black friends, including Archie Mkele, in politicising the young blacks they trained in rugby. Cheeky explained how this would happen. 'After the match we didn't have change rooms to hold a meeting in so we'd find a sheltered spot on the rugby field. After we'd discussed the game, I might say, "Do you know *why* we play with you, as whites? Gentlemen, remember that we aren't here only for sport. We are all here to fight the racist system of South Africa. You've got to do it according to the M Plan (Mandela Plan). Begin by infiltrating the street committees. Work yourself up to the area committee. Use the factory floor as a platform from which to encourage activism . . ." If we had five or ten guys who didn't want to get involved with the fight against apartheid, we would isolate them from the others and work on them one by one. Most were enthusiastic but some guys said very little or were silent. Those guys were too scared to risk the repercussions or else they were informers. Very dangerous. You don't throw the informer out or punish him; you draw him closer to you, get him more involved in the team, take him on tour, elect him to office, even in a minor position. You have to know his whereabouts and try to win him over.'[29]

The Watsons would be very careful before mentioning the activities of the banned 'movement'. Their meetings were secret at first, but as they gained the confidence of players, they would become more open, explaining to them how they could take part in revolutionary activities and encouraging them to join radical trade unions.

The young men in the junior rugby teams soon began to believe they weren't just a team, but heroes. They also learned that heroes had responsibilities. They were taught that apartheid was wrong and they must fight for a democratic South Africa. The training sessions ended with fists upraised and cries of 'Viva Mandela!', 'Viva ANC!'

On Thursday nights after training, there would be a club meeting to which women were invited. Often girlfriends, mothers, wives and sisters joined in the political debate and the singing of revolutionary songs. 'There were no lights on the rugby field, so even if the police did arrive they couldn't make out who was singing,' said Valence.[30]

In March 1980, the Soweto newspaper the *Sunday Post* launched a nationwide campaign for the release of Nelson Mandela. Although it was unsuccessful, the campaign received tremendous support nationally and internationally. Fifteen million people signed the petition forms.

Mandela had been in prison for sixteen years and 1980 was the first year in which prisoners were allowed to buy newspapers, but because they were still heavily censored and appeared with large holes cut out, Mandela was deprived of the joy he might have felt at being able to read the headline FREE MANDELA!

Mandela writes in his autobiography:

> *The ANC had decided to personalize the request for our release by centreing the campaign on a single figure. There is no doubt that the millions of people who subsequently became supporters of this campaign had no idea of precisely who Nelson Mandela was. (I am told that when 'Free Mandela' posters went up in London, most young people thought my Christian name was 'Free'.)*[31]

5

DON'T GIVE THEM THE PLEASURE OF SEEING YOU CRY

Security had discovered that the Watsons' rugby coaching in the black townships was as much about politics as sport. Valence confirms that this was certainly the case. 'By now the players were well aware that non-racial rugby was about much more than just kicking the ball. It was about liberation. We never referred to the ANC; it was called "the movement". Rugby training was a place where you could discuss what was happening to your comrades in exile. For example there was "the year of youth struggle" where young people fled South Africa in thousands. You could mobilise people to resist by supporting trade unions, even though they were outlawed until 1979. We'd say, "You must strike against this company for political reasons. No scab labour. Popularise MACWUSA, the radical trade union movement. We as a rugby club support MACWUSA." The church, schools, civic organisations and rugby were all used as covers for political activism.'[1]

When Security discovered what the Watsons were up to, many officers thought they must be naive to the point of idiocy to swallow the ANC message. Now that the Watsons' wealth and fame had gone, the officers joked, it was hard not to feel sorry for them. Nevertheless, they could not resist indulging in a little crude intimidation.

One night while Gavin was training his team in the township of New Brighton, five Kaspirs (heavily armoured vehicles) drove on to the oval, surrounded the players and pointed machine guns at them. Gavin politely asked the commander what was going on. The commander told him, arrogantly, to get on with the training or leave at once. So the team continued to train with machine guns pointing at them. That evening they abandoned the political meeting that usually followed training.

Because of the danger of informers infiltrating rugby training or township meetings, ANC business was on many occasions conducted in the storeroom at the back of the Watsons' Main Street store. A printing press, which could be quickly dismantled and transported elsewhere in the boot of a car, was also hidden there. Leaflets, stating simple facts like *A white child has seventeen times more money spent on his education than a black child*, were printed and distributed to the townships. Underground organisations and individuals also had access to this printing press. Security, who had 'neutralised' every printing press in the black townships, was suspicious of the Watsons but could prove nothing.

On 17 June, coinciding with the fourth anniversary of the Soweto riots, violence broke out in the mixed-race areas around Cape Town, resulting in at least eight deaths. After this the Department of Education closed seventy-seven schools because of nationwide school boycotts in protest against unequal education.

At least fifty people died in clashes with the police during the boycott and many young students were injured.

'Some of these young kids had been shot with shotguns,' Cheeky recalls. 'They couldn't go to Livingstone (the hospital for blacks) or they'd be immediately arrested. They couldn't go to a doctor. So they came to us at the store. We'd be digging shotgun pellets out of their bodies in the back room.'[2]

During the school boycott there were riots in Port Elizabeth. Gavin remembers, 'Kids who were running away from police would come straight to us. We'd buy them food and move them from town to town, take them down to East London and when the heat was off we'd bring them back to Port Elizabeth.'[3]

In July the government attempted to replace the old Bantu Administrative Boards in the townships with new locally elected councils, but this was met with a political boycott organised by the Soweto Civic Association. In elections the total poll of eligible voters was only 5.6 per cent. Nonetheless the Botha Government pressed ahead with setting up new councils.

In the United States on 4 November 1980, the Carter administration was defeated by President Reagan. The South African Broadcasting Association declared that Reagan's victory meant 'Western Christian culture still has a chance to triumph over communism'.

On November 26, three young members of the ANC were convicted to hang for their role in a bungled terrorist attack on a rural police station in which one person was wounded. These three would become the first blacks to be executed for a terrorist action in which no one was killed.

The Watsons' family home in Port Elizabeth was still being watched day and night by Security.

Since early 1980 the family, particularly the women, had

been harassed by threatening phone calls.

Glenda, Ronnie's wife, found the strain of living with these threats too much and the couple separated. Glenda's first husband had been killed when fighting with the South African Defence Force at the border, so she had some reason to be nervous. She had three children by this husband and two children by Ronnie, a three-year-old daughter named Tandy and a one-year-old son named Samuel. When Glenda asked Ronnie to leave, young Tandy declared she was going with her father and went to pack her case. But although she was allowed to spend a lot of time with Ronnie, Tandy was not permitted to live with him.

At weekends the Watson family home was filled to overflowing with black rugby players. Every Friday after training they would come to the house to eat and would then sleep in the huge loft at the top of the house to be ready for the Saturday match. Eileen, Valence's wife, and his mother, Bobbi, would prepare food for about forty men. In the African culture men are always served by women and all the members of a family have a claim to hospitality from every other member of the family. With the Watson brothers, who had been brought up by a 'black mother', this hospitality seemed to extend to friends as well. Eileen, who was unaccustomed to the role of fulltime serving maid, became somewhat indignant.

'All those black gentlemen were used to being served by their wives, daughters and sisters. They couldn't just help themselves. Oh no. So Valence's mum and I had to prepare supper and then serve each one, not just the team but the reserves, all the officials, the old men and everyone else. I never even got to speak to Valence on those evenings because he was too busy mixing with them all. He wasn't allowed to sleep with me before a rugby match, you know. He'd sleep with the team. I slept in a little room all by myself.'

In spite of her feelings of mild outrage Eileen accepted the African tradition of females waiting on males because Valence, and indeed all of the Watson brothers, expected her to. Things might have been different if she had been older or more of a feminist – but then she would probably never have married Valence Watson.

'Then there was training,' Eileen continued. 'Every night from Monday to Thursday I used to buy six loaves of bread, slice it up and make cheese, tomato, ham and egg sandwiches. Valence's mum would make the soup. Then at 9.30 I used to drive into the township in the dark and take all this food to the rugby team so they had something to eat after training and before their meeting. It was too far for them to travel home to eat.'[4]

The brothers were aware that their house had been bugged by Security. They decided to have strong lights on outside all night in case of attackers.

Ronnie and Valence were asked by an activist to deliver a package to a special friend of his in Lesotho, a former British protectorate just over the border. The brothers did not know, but the friend was Chris Hani, head of the ANC in Lesotho, who was at that time second only to Oliver Tambo. Hani was chief of staff of MK, and one of the most popular figures in the ANC. His request to meet them personally was a great honour. The package contained many false passports, already stamped, so that ANC members could cross the border without being detected. The penalty for possession of such passports, the brothers estimated, was twenty years jail.

On their drive to Lesotho Ronnie and Valence were stopped by police and cross-examined. They explained that they were businessmen, thinking of opening a store in Lesotho. But their car was searched thoroughly, the seats ripped out and panelling unscrewed. Fortunately the false passports were not discovered.

Chris Hani had been aware for years of the Watsons' role in politicising young rugby players and in helping black people who were being harassed by the police to skip the country. He had already met some of their friends, including Archie Mkele, and had exchanged many messages with them through couriers, but now he wanted to meet them so that he could offer them new responsibilities. Unfortunately the South African police raided ANC headquarters in Lesotho just before the Watson brothers arrived and Hani had to escape out of an upstairs window. He then had to go urgently to Angola. So the Watsons did not get to meet him on that occasion. Instead they were received by his second and third in command.

Although the ANC has always stood for non-racial democracy and has attempted to avoid violence, fifty years of non-violence had brought the African people nothing but repressive legislation and fewer rights than ever, which is why, in November 1961, the ANC formed Umkhonto we Sizwe, or MK, a military organisation. It was the policy of the ANC to try and keep MK completely separate, but sometimes it was referred to as 'the military arm' of the ANC. Nelson Mandela was one of the people who helped to form MK and he played a prominent role in its affairs before he was arrested in August 1962. This is how he describes the reason the ANC formed MK:

We felt that the country was drifting towards a civil war in which blacks and whites would fight each other. We viewed the situation with alarm. Civil war would mean the destruction of what the ANC stood for; with civil war racial peace would be more difficult than ever to achieve.[5]

Mandela believed that 'sabotage offered the best hope for future race relations' but explained:

. . . the reaction of the white rulers to our first efforts were swift and brutal: sabotage was declared to be a crime punishable by death. We did not want civil war, I said, but we needed to be prepared for it . . . If war were inevitable we wanted the fight to be conducted on terms most favorable to our people . . . We decided, therefore, in our preparations for the future, to make provision for the possibility of guerilla warfare.

All whites undergo compulsory military training, but no such training was given to Africans. It was in our view essential to build up a nucleus of trained men who would be able to provide the leadership which would be required if guerilla warfare started.[6]

Valence and Ronnie Watson did not know it, but they were about to be recruited into Umkhonto we Sizwe.

A few months later they did get to meet Chris Hani.

Ronnie recalls, 'In our discussions I told him that as a Christian I had a problem with the idea of people dying in a revolution, even if they were my enemies. He replied that I should not concern myself too much with that because he was a Catholic. He said he had been a choirboy and had wanted to become a priest, but his father had asked him to go into politics. He said to me, "Let us agree to fight our common enemy. Racism." We both agreed as Christians to not being party to our enemies being killed. This region of the Eastern Cape was the only part of the country where no civilians died. We would attack no soft targets whatsoever. Once a bomb was placed in a public place by a double agent who'd infiltrated the ranks of the ANC. But still, no one was hurt.'

Later, both Valence and Cheeky would admit that although no soft targets were deliberately attacked by the ANC, occasionally people did get hurt by accident. It was inevitable in war.

Ronnie smiles when he remembers Chris Hani. 'One look at him would tell you he was a happy person. Open faced. You couldn't help but be touched by his sincerity. He was a man filled with love. He fitted the role of priest more than soldier.' Ronnie laughs with enthusiasm. 'He cared about people! Everybody who came to know Chris loved him for his warmth and compassion. He had integrity, strength. He understood fear and because of his faith he knew how to deal with it. We had enemies all around us. It was difficult. He was charged and when he got out on bail he was told by ANC leaders to leave the country. He went into exile. You couldn't buy Chris Hani. He was not driven by power, but love.'

At the time of Hani's death in 1993, Ronnie Watson's political relationship to him was the closest possible.

'In the underground structure of the ANC I reported directly to him,' he says with pride.[7]

When Chris Hani was shot in the driveway of his home by a white man, Ronnie's car registration number was found in the glove box of the assassin's car.

At their first meeting in 1980 Hani, with droll wit, had

warned Valence and Ronnie that most of those working for ANC Intelligence did not make it to thirty, their budget would cover nothing but bare expenses, they'd be asked to do impossible things and get no thanks for doing them and they'd be so deep underground that if they got themselves into trouble it would be difficult to help them.

Valence replied with a smile, 'How could we say no?'

Hani then said, more seriously, that what the Watson brothers would get in return was love and comradeship that was deep and intense, and the knowledge that the ANC path was the only path that would save South Africa from a bloody disaster.

He embraced Valence and Ronnie.

On the same trip the brothers were introduced to their commander, whose code name was Richman. Richman told them that his mother always said he would live to see the day when he'd tell a white man what to do. 'Now I've got two. My whiteboys!'

Although Richman's relationship with the Watson brothers during the days when the ANC was underground was harmonious, he was to criticise them later for being 'too individualistic' and having their own 'bright ideas, which they would try to impose on others.'[8] For a time there would be bitterness.

The Watsons were then briefed. Ronnie's task was to help destabilise the townships in the Uitenhage area, so that the white government would lose control of them and have to negotiate with the ANC.

Valence's task was to work on the trade unions, making them more pro-ANC.

Both brothers were told how to form 'cells' of five or six

people, to use code names, to beware of assassins, never to use the telephone, to assemble at a pre-arranged spot, then move to a meeting place that only one in the cell knew about.

Like all activists they were given rudimentary training and advice on how to react when threatened with physical violence. Ronnie did not realise how soon he would have to put this advice into practice.[9]

Back in Port Elizabeth Eileen, who was pregnant with her first child, became suspicious of Valence's changed behaviour. Almost every night he would suddenly rush out at 3 a.m. without telling her where he was going. He refused to speak on the phone and was constantly holding furtive meetings. One day she discovered what seemed to be a code on a paper in his jacket and demanded to know whether he was working for the banned ANC. He denied it, but Eileen did not believe him.

When she had first met Valence, he'd warned her, 'You will have to get used to the fact that there are some things about me it is better for you not to know.'[10]

She realised that he was trying to protect her from the possibility of being interrogated by Security, but it still made her uncomfortable.

Security started the first of several smear campaigns to discredit the Watsons. Pamphlets claiming that the brothers went to the townships to sleep with black women were circulated in the community. Eileen dismissed this angrily.

Shortly after Eileen and Valence were married, Gavin met a quiet and perceptive university student named Leigh Ann Shamley. She was doing a BA in social sciences, majoring in anthropology and psychology. Leigh Ann, like Eileen, would soon break the news to her politically conservative parents that she was determined to marry into the Watson family.

Eileen sympathised with the Watson brothers' beliefs about fighting apartheid. She often helped them by typing letters and pamphlets. She and Leigh Ann became close friends and a strong support to each other.

Leigh Ann's mother was secretary to the editor of the Port Elizabeth *Herald* and her stepfather was sub-editor. Both parents were approached by the Security branch and told that their daughter should not associate with the Watsons, who were 'political activists, communists and slept with black girls in the townships.' Stories about the Watsons playing rugby in the townships appeared regularly in the *Evening Post* and the *Herald*, and Leigh Ann's parents felt concerned that their daughter might also receive adverse publicity. She was followed on the university campus by Security police.

'I was an only child who came from a politically naive family,' Leigh Ann explained. 'My parents knew the Watsons were coming up against conflict because they were continuously stirring. The Watsons were controversial figures. But my mother's real concern was that I was getting involved with a man twelve years older. My stepfather got the fright of his life when the Security police started following me. He panicked and thought of the repercussions. But the more I got to know the Watson family and what they stood for, the more I started to think, and change my set of values.'[11]

Gavin admitted that he tried to politicise Leigh Ann. 'The opposition from her parents only drew us closer together,' he recalled. 'I took her away for ten days and there was pandemonium. Her parents were phoning mine to find out where this "dirty, ugly thirty-year-old, involved in non-racialism" had gone with their nineteen-year-old daughter.'[12]

Leigh Ann remembered the incident rather less dramatically. 'My mum went to see Gavin's dad and asked him, "What do you think of Gavin taking Leigh Ann away?" He said he didn't have a problem with it as long as Valence and Eileen, the married couple, went along too.

'By 1981 my mother had calmed down and accepted my relationship with Gavin. She too was becoming politically enlightened and beginning to be anti-apartheid. She'd say, "This is what the paper says", and I'd say, "*This* is what Gavin says."'[13]

In May 1982, Gavin and Leigh Ann were married.

'It was a very quiet wedding,' said Leigh Ann. 'Not as spectacular as Eileen's. About sixty people.'[14]

Since his divorce Cheeky Watson had been rather subdued. 'I went through a time of not dating anybody but being very spiritual and focused,' he said. 'My brothers kept telling me, "Why don't you take this girl out? Or that one?" One night I had a dream. My future wife was going to walk through the doors of our shop in Main Street. A few days after I had this dream, a small building next door to us became vacant and was rented by a man in the women's fashion business. The building was in a no-loading zone, the worst place for a business, but he had to make do. We had lots of parking space. One day, through our front door walked his daughter, Tracey. Now Tracey is a very outgoing type of girl, a tremendous extrovert. Anyway, she popped into the shop – '[15]

'Now I roll into the shop,' Tracey interrupts, laughing.[16] (She has put on a little weight since she was eighteen, and represented South Africa in the World Gymnastrada in Berlin.)

'I was working for my dad, doing the books, and I'd come into the Watsons' store to ask if we could use some of their parking space,' says Tracey matter-of-factly.

'I didn't at first realise she was the wife of my dream. Not at all,' says Cheeky. 'But she was lots of fun. She didn't think anything physical or sexual. She'd just get on the phone and say, "Hi". She phoned one day and I said I was playing rugby. She said, "Are you going to win?" and I said, "Definitely". We lost. When she rang to ask who had won I said, "I'll tell you over dinner." I took her out and I was so tired from playing rugby that I fell asleep over the meal.'

'And the second time he took me out, he fell asleep ten minutes after the movie had started, and snored,' Tracey adds.

In spite of this unpromising beginning, the courtship blossomed and five weeks after their first meeting Cheeky proposed to Tracey. At first she said no.

'I said, "I'm very young. Don't ask me. I will *tell* you when I'm ready."'

Six months later Tracey's parents were about to go overseas. 'But they were uncomfortable about leaving their little virgin daughter in the hands of this wolf. So I said to Cheeky, "Why don't we get married?"' Tracey laughs. 'Cheeky is very romantic. I am not.'

Becoming part of the Watson family was not as smooth a journey for Tracey as she had imagined. 'I was like my dad, very conservative and slightly nervous,' Tracey explains. 'I never wanted to live with the Watson family. I wanted my own home. I'm a very open person and the Watsons are very secretive. The brothers would go for walks together and talk politics. The wives were locked out. The brothers were obsessed with protecting themselves against the Security police, and, at that stage, I didn't know they were all ANC and I thought they were imagining things. When they took their watches off in case of bugs before going for a walk I'd say, "Do you actually think people are following you?" I'd laugh. It was so hard to believe.'

'Tracey was extremely naive,' says Cheeky. 'I think there was some resentment of her in the family because she was seen as someone coming in to break up the clan – '

' – Another woman coming in to disrupt the unity of the brothers,' Tracey adds. 'Already living in the house were Eileen and Valence, Ronnie and his wife Glenda and her children, Gavin and the Watsons' parents. Sharon, their sister, was away in London, staying with her mother's relatives. I said to Cheeky, "I don't want to live with your family." So we moved out for a while to a flat of our own.'

This only increased the resentment of the Watson family. 'I'm the one in the family who loves entertaining. I'm always in the kitchen, organising lunches and suppers,' Cheeky explains. 'So when I move out they lose the heartbeat of the home.'

Six months later Cheeky and Tracey moved back. 'We renovated an outside section of the family home and lived in that,' says Cheeky. By this time Tracey was pregnant.

'It was a converted garage. Big room, bathroom, baby's room. No toilet. I said, "This place hasn't even got a toilet!" I was so unhappy there,' says Tracey.

The family still ate together and spent almost all their time together. 'I couldn't get used to living together. It was a major problem in my life,' Tracey says frankly. 'We fought like cat and dog.'[17]

Cheeky, too, is very honest about this difficult time in his marriage. 'I thought, "She's an intruder, man. We've been a family together for a long time. We've eaten a couple of bags of salt together. She's a newcomer. She's my wife, yes, but she's not blood . . ."'[18]

Cheeky admits that at this stage their differences were so serious he considered letting Tracey go. 'We did have that discussion,' he laughs self-consciously.

'I'm a strong personality and he's a strong personality. We were newly married and I was seven years younger. It was a case of his will against mine. We both shouted a lot but we survived,' says Tracey succinctly.[19]

'We settled down,' Cheeky agrees. They smile at each other, amused by the understatement.

'Each wife has to supervise in the kitchen and I used to assist Tracey. The wives organised the cooking according to a roster. [The wives did not have to cook. The Watsons always had staff, mostly the daughters or granddaughters of African women who had worked for them on the farm.] After they married, Gavin and Leigh Ann moved out to a flat nearby but they still used to eat with us. They didn't even have a kitchen.'[20]

Although the Watson brothers expected their wives to fit in, and resented any interference with their close relationship to each other, they all acknowledge that the wives played a vital role in their political lives. 'They allowed us the freedom to do what we needed to do,' Valence explains. 'We knew that our wives were looking after the family – the kids, our parents. If you don't have the support of your wife, it makes you a very unstable activist. And with the ANC, all is stress and you *have* to have a happy family. Whenever we went to see Chris Hani he would always ask, "How's the family? How's the old man?" Because when the family unit is strong, you can actually go out and fight.'[21]

Did the women ever feel that they would like to be out there fighting too? Didn't they resent playing subordinate roles?

'They were the unsung heroes of the whole struggle,' Ronnie Watson admits. 'Take Eileen. She adapted and played a major supportive role. But never did any of the women operate as inferior citizens or junior partners. If we had to go away, they'd operate the business.'[22]

'The Watsons are vulnerable,' Valence says. 'At my father's funeral recently there were some people who seemed surprised that we should feel grief as much as anyone else. People perceive us as larger than life. They think that maybe we don't need a support system. We do.'[23]

But there was one marriage casualty. Glenda and Ronnie had moved to a flat, but Ronnie continued to spend most of his time in the Watson family home. The other wives were sympathetic with Glenda. 'Ronnie said he was a brilliant husband but he wasn't,' says Eileen. 'He'd sit with us till midnight and his mum would say, "Go home to Glenda". He'd say, "I'd better go and see my wife. I haven't seen her for two weeks." He'd have been off with his activist comrades in East London, 150 miles away. Ronnie was shocked when Glenda left him. He couldn't understand why. But Glenda had already tried living in the family home and it hadn't worked. She'd said to herself, "If you can't beat them, join them," and had moved in with her three children from a previous marriage. It was chaos. She moved out after two years and then the marriage broke up.'[24]

Ronnie has two children from his marriage to Glenda, Tandy and Samuel. He was saddened by the breakup but is realistic enough to admit that anyone who married him would have to come second to his politics.

In March 1981, the first grandson was born into the Watson family. Eileen was twenty-one when she gave birth to Nkosinathi (God be with us). 'When the black hospital staff heard his name they were delighted,' said Eileen. 'Only the parents and father of the child were allowed in to see me. The nursing sister asked, "Who is the father?" Cheeky, Ronnie, Gavin and Valence said, "We all are". She let them in.

'Nkosi was very spoilt. Valence was supposed to be his first name and Nkosi his second name, but he was always called Nkosi. Whenever we went to a petrol station or a shop where there were black people he would tell them his name and then they'd give him sweets. In white circles he learned to call himself Valence.'

'Three months after I had Nkosi I became pregnant with Daniel. When Daniel was born he didn't have a name for months because Valence wanted to call him Zwelethu, which means "our land"! I refused to call him that. In some circles Nkosi was ridiculed because of his name and I didn't want to subject the next child to the same trauma. After nine months we found a solution. Cheeky had wanted to call his first son Daniel but I asked if I could have the name and he agreed.'[25]

In May 1981, Prime Minister Botha's National Party was voted back with a massive, though weakened, majority due to the disapproval of the extreme right-wing. Botha took this disapproval as a warning to put the brakes on his reforms. Black students burned the South African flag and planted bombs to protest against celebrations to commemorate the Republic of South Africa's twentieth anniversary.

In June the Botha Government cracked down severely on

the protest movement by arresting prominent trade union leaders and student activists.

Police evicted and deported thousands of Xhosa-speaking blacks working illegally in the townships around Cape Town to their official homeland of Transkei.

In August South Africa stepped up its campaign of aggression against Angola, sending in 11 000 troops, in the biggest attack since Angolan independence.

Early in 1982 Botha's plans to allow people of mixed race and Asians a role in government caused a split in the National Party as twenty-three members, headed by Dr Treurnicht, made a vote of no confidence in Botha's racial policies. Botha won overwhelmingly and Dr Treurnicht, the right-wing leader in the Transvaal, was expelled from the party.

In April Nelson Mandela, and three other ANC leaders, Walter Sisulu, Raymond Mhlaba and Andrew Mlangeni, were transferred from Robben Island prison to more comfortable quarters in Pollsmoor Prison, Cape Town. Mandela, who had been in prison for almost twenty years, felt 'disturbed and unsettled' by the move. Although Pollsmoor was a maximum-security prison, Mandela writes that the four of them 'had been given what was in effect the prison's penthouse'. He was unhappy about the fact that the authorities had attempted to cut off the head of the ANC on the island [Robben Island] by removing its leadership', but he admitted enjoying having 'proper meat and vegetables' and a 'fairly wide range of newspapers and magazines' as well as being allowed to 'read and write during the day.'

Mandela was soon to discover the reason for this special treatment. He was shortly to be engaged in 'talks with the enemy'.[26]

As Mandela's lifestyle was in the process of improving, the Watson brothers' was deteriorating. Because every cent they earned from their business was now poured back into the ANC they were quite poor. But more importantly, they felt under siege. From being popular, successful leaders in the white community they had become the enemy. Many powerful people were against them and at times they felt close to despair.

'So many whites had such fear that when we crossed over they just drifted away from us, disappeared like mist in the morning sun,' Valence said. 'Our uncle, who was so proud of us and used to come and watch us play, didn't want to be seen supporting us any more. I knew as soon as we played that mixed match that we were now out on a limb. We had bucked the system. We realised that rugby wasn't just a sport but an integral part of the apartheid system. Suddenly we were a threat to society. We were way ahead of business, the community and the church. They had swept their consciences under the carpet and we were reminding them of the fact. We annoyed people. They didn't feel comfortable with us. It didn't shock me.'[27]

It may not have shocked the brothers to be so promptly abandoned and then persecuted for their beliefs but it certainly hurt them.

Valence expressed it this way: 'There is an orchestrated force against you that comprises the police, the politician, the business community and the army. You don't realise when you join the struggle against apartheid that it is such a powerful force. Once they would not have dared to physically attack us but after the attempt on Gavin's life, threats from the Security police, pamphlets coming out attacking us, our friends being attacked, you feel they actually want to kill you. Physical strength is not enough. You need spiritual strength. I sometimes wonder what made us take the route we did. The more powerful the opposition, the stronger we have to become. After each threat or narrow escape you get a knot in your gut. But you get used to the fear. You put it behind you quickly, and go on to the next thing. But eventually you get so tired of fighting that you are actually on the brink of becoming violent. The reason we don't is because of our Christian attitude and also because the ANC stands for nonviolence. You get to a point of no return on this journey, the journey of liberating this country and then rebuilding it, where there is no way you can turn back. You will not give up the fight and let the enemy have the pleasure of winning. An African friend said to Eileen when things were bad, "Don't cry. Don't give them the pleasure of seeing it." '[28]

6

DEEP UNDERGROUND

Gavin Watson, who had started the family clothing business and invited his brothers to join him, was concerned that pressure from the State would soon close them down. Messages were being sent from Security to the Watsons' suppliers not to supply them with goods. Then their import licence was cancelled.

Gavin had a brainwave. He had already begun to stock clothing that appealed to black males, but now to counteract the lack of smart, imported menswear he began to stock clothing suitable for black men, women and children. It was suggested by their customers that they should also sell household goods like buckets and cooking utensils, which they did.

At this time, Gavin also began to go out into white high schools and talk to the students about the need for a non-racial South Africa. He was an assured speaker and communicated with great conviction and sincerity. He spoke of a Christian vision of a South Africa where the black population had the same legal and political rights as the whites. 'You've been told in the media that if the black man is given rights he will take power and throw the white man out. It is rubbish. The black community has an enormous capacity for forgiveness and for love. We, the Watsons, have felt that forgiveness and love. We are all South Africans, black and white, and together we could make this a great country.'[1] This was a message that few of the students had ever heard. They asked many questions and were impressed by the answers Gavin gave.

But even at these highly successful meetings Security men were present, dressed in plain clothes and tape recording every word. On one occasion Gavin chased them out to their car and accused them of spying on him. They accused him of teaching terrorist rubbish. Gavin replied, 'It is you guys who are the terrorists. You're forcing apartheid on us down the barrel of a gun. We know how you deal with people. Not being man enough to do it yourselves, you pay killers to do your dirty work!'[2]

The Security men warned Gavin coldly that they would not forget him.

On 14 May 1982, the government introduced new security legislation, the Internal Security Act, which combined all previous laws on security and increased already tight restrictions on political demonstrations and on media reporting of unrest.

In July Chief Buthelezi, leader of the Zulus, won two court cases in a legal battle against the government over its decision to excise a fragment of the Zulu homeland, KwaZulu, and cede it to Swaziland. The issue was reportedly a calculated attempt by the government to retaliate against Buthelezi for his refusal to accept nominal independence for KwaZulu.

Chief Mangosuthu Buthelezi, a member of the Zulu royal family, had, as a young man, been an active member of the ANC Youth League and an opponent of apartheid, but in ANC circles he was not popular.

After becoming Chief Minister of the KwaZulu homeland he continued to speak out against the Botha regime. He demanded the consolidation and enlargement of KwaZulu and embarrassed the government by his refusal to accept independence. Buthelezi increased his position of strength by taking on the leadership of the million-strong Inkatha movement, which was originally founded in 1928 by King Solomon Ka Dinizulu as a cultural movement to preserve the Zulu heritage. Under Buthelezi's leadership, Inkatha became more political than cultural.

Despite Buthelezi's early sympathy for the ANC he was criticised by the organisation for having 'sold out' when he cooperated with the government on the homelands policy. He supported a separate government for Natal, where KwaZulu was located, in which whites and blacks would share power through a coalition. The ANC regarded this as an endorsement of Verwoerd's original plan to fragment South Africa into small black states. They thought it was opportunism on Buthelezi's part. Also Buthelezi opposed the one-man, one-vote principle advocated by the ANC and the armed struggle. He had criticised the Soweto uprising in 1976 and campaigned against international sanctions. Supporters of ANC would continue to clash with Buthelezi's Zulu gangs ('Impis') in the townships throughout the 1980s. Despite this, Mandela and Buthelezi would continue to support each other publicly. Chief Buthelezi had consistently called for Mandela's release from prison and, in 1986, Buthelezi would refuse to take part in constitutional talks proposed by Botha until Mandela was released and invited to participate.

The Watsons were sceptical about Buthelezi. Cheeky said, 'In the townships of Port Elizabeth there was a strong suspicion that Buthelezi was on the government payroll. Our feelings towards him were definitely not feelings of warmth. The township people didn't like him. He was like a burr in the saddle. Later it would be revealed that he had a certain agenda.'[3]

In August 1982, new legislation tightened the pass laws in an attempt to stop people coming from the homelands to the townships.

Prime Minister Botha outlined his plans to grant political rights to the 2.5 million coloured people and 800 000 Asians that would still ensure the 4.5 million whites dominated. The ANC saw this as an attempt to lure Indians and coloureds into the system and divide them from black Africans.

At about this time the white anti-apartheid activist Ruth First, who had served time in prison and was the wife of Joe Slovo, was killed when she opened a letter bomb.

Barbara Hogan, a white member of the ANC, received a ten-year sentence for high treason on the grounds that her membership of the ANC amounted to participation in a conspiracy to overthrow South Africa by violence. She was the first white woman to be convicted of a treason charge.

During 1981 and 1982 MK continued to launch attacks only at military targets, such as the unfinished Koeburg nuclear power plant near Cape Town, while the SADF launched direct attacks on ANC offices in Maputo, Mozambique, Maseru and Lesotho, which killed many people, including women and children.

'People we knew were killed in that raid in Lesotho,' said Valence Watson. 'They were actually shot with rifles fitted with silencers. That was a major shock. They were just sitting with friends having a couple of drinks, with the kids all around, and these Security people slipped across the border and shot them. There was one guy in the toilet and that was how he escaped. He just sat there, frozen. The attackers took a lot of ANC documents and of course our fear was that our names would be there. But apparently nothing incriminating was found.

'One time, when we arrived at Harare, the ANC office had just been bombed. And on another occasion, just as we were leaving Harare to fly to Lusaka, a third-level ANC leader climbed into his car with his girlfriend and they blew him through the top of it.'[4]

In May 1983, MK launched its first car bomb attack. The bomb exploded outside the South African airforce and military intelligence office in Pretoria, killing nineteen people and injuring about 188. This was in retaliation to the unprovoked attacks the SADF had made on the ANC, particularly in Maseru, where nineteen people were killed and over 200 injured.

The Watsons felt, with some misgivings, that this attack by the ANC was justified. Their attitude to violence had changed since they were first asked to join the ANC in 1979.

Cheeky said, 'After being under constant attack as we had been and losing many friends who were killed or had disappeared, you could almost justify MK's retaliation. It was inevitable. This type of thing had to happen at least once. Although I have a non-violent attitude I could understand it. We justified it by saying, "This is the justice of defence."'[5]

'We have always, as a family, believed that life is precious,' said Valence. 'But it was war. I feel extremely sorry for anyone injured, on either side. I can never justify why someone's child or husband should be killed. Chris Hani had told us, "On no account hit soft targets". But accidents do happen in war. When you are operating furtively and at speed there are casualties.'[6]

Unfortunately the struggle had become a military one. Exiled ANC leader Oliver Tambo said at the time of the bombing, '. . . the armed struggle was imposed upon us by the violence of the apartheid regime'.[7]

At about this time the ANC was accused of a hideous form of torture known as 'necklacing'. In order to get victims to talk, a burning tyre would be placed around their neck. The Watsons deny that this was ever part of ANC policy. They say the ANC was utterly opposed to necklacing and tried to stop it taking place in the townships.

'In fact the State would send agents into the townships to kill people by the so-called necklace method and then say the ANC did it,' Valence Watson claims. 'The problem was that the ANC had called for "ungovernability" in the townships and the State thought it could use that against us. They tried to link ungovernability with necklacing. Government agents had infiltrated our structures – our street cells – and sometimes they would use the necklace method to try and discredit the ANC. They would point out someone and say he was an informer, which he wasn't, and then necklace him. The State was able to cover up their killing in the townships by blocking off the entrances so the media couldn't get in. As well as necklacing, they'd use petrol bombs, just throw about ten of them into a house and burn the whole family. At one stage a bunch of youths came to Cheeky and said they'd had enough of it. "We cannot be killed like this and have nobody do anything about it. We're coming to town to murder the whites now." We had to persuade them it would be bad for our cause, to have blacks killing whites in retribution.'[8]

In every revolutionary movement atrocities are committed on both sides. Is it not being blinkered to believe that all necklacing was government inspired?

Valance is adamant that the South African police were behind some necklacing and the ANC was not involved. 'The ANC was always opposed to those murders. They were the outcome of complete frustration. In Uitenhage in the Eastern Cape the police were behind a certain family who terrorised people. Someone exposed them and they were necklaced. An anger built up in the people. The people in the townships were being murdered and butchered by the State and their surrogates. These people had to have some form of defence. Necklacing became one of the methods. There was nothing else they could do. The government tried to blame it on "black on black" violence. But it was the State against the people.'[9]

In August 1983, in Cape Town, the United Democratic Front (UDF) was launched. Ten thousand people of all races attended. The UDF was a powerful political movement linked to the ANC. It united over 700 local and regional anti-apartheid organisations, mainly trade unions, community, church and student organisations. Nelson Mandela was a patron.

Even though the ANC had been banned for twenty-five years it was still the most popular political organisation amongst blacks in South Africa. It also attracted international attention. Economic sanctions were being imposed on South Africa, which created pressure on the government. And in 1984 Bishop Desmond Tutu would win the Nobel Peace Prize.

In May 1984, Prime Minister Botha set off on an eight-nation tour of Western Europe aimed at reducing South Africa's international isolation.

In September Botha was sworn in as the first President under a new Constitution, which gave him potentially authoritarian powers. For the first time, Indian and coloured representatives joined the whites in Cape Town Parliament House. Outside, police fired tear gas and rubber bullets at protestors.

A month later clashes between the authorities and rioters had reached a climax and the army was brought in to quell the riots. Seven thousand police and soldiers staged a pre-dawn raid on the township of Sebonkeng and then moved on to neighbouring townships.

Trade unions, students and community groups combined to hold a massive strike as an anti-government protest. Black Labor leaders were arrested and ten blacks were killed.

By 1985 the ANC had all but achieved its objectives of making the black townships ungovernable. There were demonstrations and strikes. ANC flags were flying and placards reading *Free Nelson Mandela* and *Bring Home the Exiles* were everywhere. Many townships were in flames as the police moved in to raze whole areas.

In the Eastern Cape, the Watson brothers had been extremely active in helping to bring all this about. While Gavin and Cheeky were involved in helping to politicise sport, business and the church above ground, Ronnie and Valence worked in ANC Intelligence, which was underground.

They had been recruited by Chris Hani as people of high

calibre and were sent to Lesotho for training. 'It was not training for MK,' Valence explains. 'We were taught how to work undercover, how to keep our ears and eyes open. We might have to collect something from a dead letterbox or a desk in a government office. We would have to avoid being followed. Cells were formed and the individuals within these cells were told not to drive in cars with friends but to use public transport, so that they'd get the mood of the people, overhear their conversations and pass information back to the leadership.

'The objectives of the cells we formed were to set up alternative structures in the townships. Area committees and street committees were part of this structure. People would be elected at street and area levels and we'd make sure ANC people were centralised. The ANC was deep underground. If you said you were ANC it meant a jail sentence. UDF was above ground. So was the trade union movement COSATU and various youth and women's movements. We would make sure ANC people moved up in the hierarchies of all these movements, because we knew the Security branch and the National Intelligence Service (NIS) would be moving their informers up the hierarchies too. The Security plants would often come on strong as extreme radicals. The cell would not find it easy to collect information as to whether a person was genuine or a plant.

'Through the cells we operated on a lot of fronts. We would target particular organisations and infiltrate them. Suppose, for example, there was a quasi-government institution controlled by National Party bureaucrats. We'd introduce one of the chief bureaucrats to a few people in the ANC, then a few more, until gradually his attitude towards the ANC would change and so would the policies of the organisation with regard to the trade union movement.

'The message to us from Hani was also to work on amalgamating the unions, because if a union was divided on the factory floor, that would create divisions in above ground organisations like the church and sport. Security was pressuring the leaders of unions not to amalgamate, threatening that their homes would be petrol bombed, that they'd be attacked at night or lose their jobs. Security also harassed those members who were pro-ANC in regular meetings. So you approached these ANC sympathisers at home or church. People like Archie Mkele would preach at church, but the message would never go out from the pulpit. Before the service he'd mingle with the crowd and pass the message that way. You had to be careful.'[10]

Even though phones were tapped and mail was intercepted by the Security police, information did manage to get to the ANC in exile.

'It went by courier,' says Valence. 'Sometimes it was coded, sometimes not. Walter, an old black man, would walk through the border post wearing an overcoat. He would throw it aside as if to make it easier for the border guards to search him.'[11]

Sometimes the couriers were caught.

'One chap called Lulu, who went out on a program to Lesotho, didn't come back,' Valence recalls. 'But someone spotted him. He'd been taken to a holding cell in the Sanlam building in Port Elizabeth. Sanlam is a corporation which had close links with the National Party. The Security police had offices at the top of this building. An African playwright once wrote a play called *The Room at the Top* about the brutality that went on there. Anyway, Lulu looked a mess. I have no doubt

Security would have killed him. But we got hold of a lawyer and asked him to fight the case.

'In the meantime another ANC courier, Ndzoto, had gone on a trip, been caught and locked in a cell. On the wall he saw a drawing of Lulu's face. Beside it he drew his own face, bearded with a receding hairline. This was the way we on the outside discovered that Lulu had been arrested. Everything you do in the underground is covert because you're so scared.

'When Ndzoto returned from a trip to Lesotho he'd give us Hani's message in our shop. Comrades would come in as if they were buying clothing. Someone would say, "We'll be meeting at such and such a time at Archie's place." When we got to Archie's someone would be waiting. He'd say, "The meeting is not here. It's at Msavata's." Just in case anyone had overheard the first message.'[12]

The Watsons were instructed by Chris Hani never to carry arms because they were too valuable as facilitators to take the risk. 'But we could facilitate people who did carry arms. If an MK operative needed to get into the country he could use our cars. But we were not to drive the cars ourselves during these missions. We had to stay as far removed as possible,' Valence explains.

'MK might plant a bomb at an electric power station to cut power to certain regions but violence against innocent people was against ANC policy. The ANC was popular because it was very careful not to do anything that might create a legacy of hate in the long term. By the mid-1980s the ANC leadership realised they couldn't seize power by force and annihilate the system. A compromise settlement was needed.'

The Watson brothers were facilitators. 'Our job was to

establish cells in our area of Port Elizabeth and to popularise the ANC in all sections of South African society.

'The South African Government was also destabilising the neighbouring countries and therefore bringing added pressure on the ANC. Acts of terror were being carried out by the South African Government against Lesotho, Mozambique, Angola, Zimbabwe and Botswana.'[13]

By 1985 South Africa was facing the most violent and unrelenting uprising in its history. President P. W. Botha made what he thought was a clever offer to the people. In January, he announced that the government would free Nelson Mandela if Mandela promised not to take action which would lead to his re-arrest. That is, if he 'unconditionally rejected violence as a political instrument'.[14]

Mandela had been warned that the government was going to make this offer to him. He wrote to Botha, rejecting the conditions of his release because he felt 'Botha's offer was an attempt to drive a wedge between me and my colleagues by tempting me to accept a policy the ANC rejected.'[15]

He sent a message to the government stating that: 'while I rejected the offer because of the conditions attached to it, I nevertheless thought negotiation, not war, was the path to a solution.'[16]

On Sunday 10 February 1985 Mandela's youngest daughter, Zindzi, stood before a cheering crowd at a UDF rally in Soweto's Jabulani Stadium and read the reply Mandela was not allowed to make himself. In part it said,

> *Only free men can negotiate. Prisoners cannot enter into contracts . . . I cannot and will not give an undertaking at a time*

when I and you, the people, are not free. Your freedom and mine cannot be separated. I will return.[17]

There was wild applause. Zindzi, a handsome young woman wearing bright yellow, had spoken with passion. Huge crowds waving banners reading *Free Mandela Unconditionally* marched in the streets. The activists were in no mood to negotiate. The general feeling of the ANC executive was that if they negotiated when the enemy was still strong, they would have to make too many compromises.

The Watsons completely agreed with Mandela's decision to reject the conditions of his release. They too would not have agreed to 'unconditionally reject violence as a political instrument'. Indeed, Ronnie and Valence were acting as a recruiting agency for the ANC and they knew that many of these recruitees fled the country, then joined the military wing, MK.

Although the Watsons were not aware that Mandela had been negotiating with Coetsee, the Minister for Justice, to have talks between the ANC and the government, they would soon realise through their direct contact with ANC leaders in exile that negotiation, not force, was the path the ANC had chosen.

Soon after refusing the government's conditions for his release from Pollsmoor Prison, Mandela was separated from his three ANC companions and placed in solitary confinement but in a spacious cell. His companions were angry at being separated and wanted to protest but Mandela told them that he was now 'in a position where the government can make an approach to us. They did not care too much for this explanation as I knew they would not,' he writes.

I chose to tell no one what I was about to do. Not my colleagues upstairs nor those in Lusaka. The ANC is a collective, but the government had made collectivity in this case impossible . . . There are times when a leader must move out ahead of the flock, go off in a new direction, confident that he is leading his people the right way.[18]

It would take five hard years of negotiating and forty-seven meetings with the top men in government before Mandela would achieve what he set out to do on that day in early 1985.

On 21 March a crowd of 4000 blacks set out from Langa, a black township in the Eastern Cape, to attend a funeral near the white town of Uitenhage. The Watsons had stores in Uitenhage and were well aware of how important it was to their black friends to pay homage to the dead by attending their funeral. Funerals were now about the only legitimate place where blacks were permitted to gather together. Nevertheless, police tried to stop the crowd by opening fire and killing twenty people. This unleashed further violence in the townships, especially around Uitenhage, Cape Town and Port Elizabeth.

Each evening Ronnie and Valence went into the townships to work with black friends and sympathisers. They printed and distributed pamphlets and T-shirts with ANC slogans on them, met with area and street committees and then slipped back to their store to conduct meetings in the stockroom.

They took precautions in case of a police raid. 'There was a side door,' Valence explained. 'But if the police blocked that we could hide people in an old airconditioning duct that they didn't know about, or a deep shaft that had once been used as a lift.'[19] The brothers denied that they were members of the ANC. 'The State was fairly happy with that because very few whites were pro-ANC. It was just unheard of. In the beginning if the Security police had admitted we were ANC that would have been a positive statement for the organisation. People would have asked, "Why are the Watsons ANC? I thought it was a communist organisation full of violent thugs. If the Watsons are part of it, it can't be too bad." That was why we were never arrested as ANC supporters. The State didn't want it known that prominent whites were ANC. Later, after the State had brainwashed the white community, totally discredited us and tried to criminalise us, the community just thought we were animals. They thought the same about anyone opposed to the National Party's policies.'[20]

The State continued to circulate pamphlets to the white community, which had once revered the Watsons, saying they had only gone to play black rugby in the townships so that they could take advantage of black women. At this stage 'sex across the colour line' was still a punishable crime. The pamphlets also claimed that the Watsons were only befriending the blacks so as to increase their business. 'The blacks understood this attempt to discredit us and took it as an absolute joke,' said Valence, 'but later Security scared off our creditors by telling them we had big debts and were about to flee the country, like a lot of liberals had done.'

Security also stopped the Watsons' licence to import foreign goods. Ever since their business began they had prided themselves on stocking the highest quality imported menswear and, in spite of the fact that they now stocked cheaper goods as well, they were determined to continue the supply. 'Word came from Pretoria that the Watsons were not to get an import licence,' Valence said. 'Then, a few days later we were approached by a white businessman we had known through rugby. He offered us goods on the black market. We refused. Soon afterwards we were approached by a black businessman who made a similar offer. The offers continued over a long period of time. Security was trying to set us up. If we had accepted any of these offers they would have been successful in getting us charged as criminals, and we'd have spent five years in prison. Security believed it was safer for them if we were arrested for criminal activities rather than political activities.'[21]

Having failed to trap the Watsons into criminal activity, Security decided to threaten one of their black friends with death unless he agreed to spy on them. But the man confessed to the Watsons what he was being forced to do and asked them for advice. They decided to play along with Security and feed the spy misinformation. After four weeks, Security was suspicious. They threatened death if the information was not more accurate. At this point the Watsons arranged for their black friend to leave the country, where he joined the ranks of the ANC.

There were now hundreds of ANC cells operating deep underground all over South Africa, but the Watson cell in the Eastern Cape was one of the most effective. The Security police were aware of this and it angered them.

At about this time a German documentary film crew came to Port Elizabeth to make a film about the Watson brothers. It was called *The Whites Who Play with Blacks*. Articles were also being written about them in the *Los Angeles Times*, and the *National Times* in Australia.

Security had labelled the brothers 'terrorists', but because the international press had begun to focus on them in a positive way, they could not risk eliminating them. They could not even arrest them because they were known to be high-level ANC members. Security had been pushing the line that the ANC was a black terrorist organisation, certainly not the sort of organisation to attract intelligent whites. So it was little wonder that Security felt furious with the Watsons.

Mono Badela, the man who had originally persuaded the Watson brothers to play rugby in the townships and challenged them to join the struggle against apartheid had, all of this time, been working as a reporter on the *Evening Post* in Port Elizabeth. He was also actively involved in the street and area cells set up by the ANC.

Recently Mono had published a story about a black man named Mtimkulu, a youth leader, who was involved in student activism and had been detained by the Security branch and interrogated. Soon after the interrogation Mtimkulu went missing. It was believed that he had been abducted.

'Mtimkulu used to come into our shops a lot,' Cheeky recalls. 'A few months after he went missing he came in again and we had a problem recognising him. His hair was snow white and he was walking with the aid of two sticks.'[22]

While he was in prison Mtimkulu had been injected with rat poison over a period of several months. He collapsed and was sent to hospital. When he got out he came straight to the Watsons.

'He went into prison a man of twenty and came out like a sixty-year-old. His feet were three times the normal size. He said to us, "Chaps, they couldn't break me",' said Gavin. 'I felt like crying. To see the state he was in, and he allowed himself to get into that state to protect us as a family.'[23]

'He died a few months after he was released from prison,' Mono Badela said. 'While he was on his way to the hospital to get medicine for his condition he was abducted by police and disappeared. Later his burnt body was found. After I wrote about this in the *Evening Post* I lost my job. The paper did not like me writing stories about struggling youth leaders or organising cells either. It was a sin against the government. The Security police tried to crush me. This will all eventually come out in the Truth Commission.'[24]

Mono Badela continued, 'At two o'clock one morning in May 1985, I was woken up and taken to AZAPO headquarters, where I knew certain ANC leaders had been killed. The aim of AZAPO, the Azanian People's Organization, was to establish a democratic, anti-racist republic under black working class leadership, but government agencies encouraged them to create violence in the townships, which they did. At AZAPO headquarters I was interrogated and told that they wanted me to tell UDF, the opposition, to stop talking about AZAPO at rallies. I was hacked with a knife and spat at. Then they put me in a van, lying down, with a tyre round my neck like a pillow. They said they were going to necklace me outside Port Elizabeth. But they were divided amongst themselves about this. One said, "We didn't call him here to kill him. We want to talk to him, get him to explain about us to the UDF." My family thought I was dead when they took me out of bed. They broke the windows of my house. I was in the van with the tyre. I had given up. But they dropped me a hundred metres from my house. They said that night I must resign from the newspaper. I didn't.'[25]

In brave defiance Mono Badela refused to speak to UDF

and continued to write political stories for his newspaper. One of these was about three politically active friends of his who had suddenly gone missing. They were not violent radicals, as the police had claimed. Two of them were schoolteachers. They had been picked up by Squad 13, later known as the assassination squad, at the airport and had then completely disappeared.

Mono had written that the three anti-apartheid leaders Sipho Hashe, Qaqawuli Godolozi and Champion Galela had gone to the airport to meet a 'British consul' and had not been seen since. Many years later it would be revealed that the the PEBCO Three, as they became known, had been interrogated, savagely tortured and then murdered on the instructions of security police headquarters.[26]

On 7 June, a month after the first attack on Mono Badela, AZAPO came back to his house in the township of New Brighton.

'At 1 a.m. they came in buses and cars. Officials arrived in a Kaspir (large army vehicle). I had some boys watching my home but they were overwhelmed. They shouted to warn me,' Badela said. 'I sent my wife and children to run and hide in a neighbour's house and I thought I'd keep fighting. But there were too many of them so I ran and hid in a nearby fowl run. They were looking for me and I was flat on my stomach. The hens were clucking and I was afraid they'd find me. I saw my house burning. I stayed in the fowl run all night and in the morning I looked for my family. I phoned the Watsons and they said, "Come to us." '[27]

Mono Badela's house had been petrol bombed. He and his wife and two younger children had narrowly escaped death. His oldest daughter, aged nineteen, who was president of the

Congress of South African Students (COSAS), had just left Port Elizabeth by train for Zimbabwe, to escape a charge of possessing illegal literature.

Before he had fled to the fowl run Mono had been physically attacked so when he reached the Watsons' house he was covered in blood. Cheeky and Gavin could not help seeing the funny side of this. 'We were so happy to see the guy alive that we laughed and said, "Press (that's his nickname), you know you're not in bad condition after all. You put up quite a fight, didn't you?"' Cheeky recalls. 'He laughed and said, "I put up one hell of a fight."'[28]

'We asked him exactly what happened and there he was re-enacting it all, blocking with one hand and tackling with another,' said Gavin. 'Press is very eloquent in English and he said, "Man, when the odds are against you, Sir Lancelot doth run. I ran and ran for my life. I never knew I could jump a fence and a wall." He is very short and has a belly like a barrel.'[29]

Badela and his family were made welcome in the Watsons' home and were hidden upstairs for two days. 'We went to the shop and the Watsons told us to pick up anything we wanted. We had no clothes,' Mono said.[30]

During this time the Watsons received word that Mono's oldest daughter had been murdered on her way to Zimbabwe. 'It was terrible. We were frantic,' said Mono.[31]

Cheeky said that the word of one member of the Security police was not enough to make him believe such a thing, and he spent five hours on the phone checking the story. He and his brothers phoned every hospital, medical and railway facility along the route to Bloemfontein. Nobody had reported a murder. It had been a cruel hoax.

Soon after this Mono Badela and his family left Port Elizabeth for Johannesburg where Mono got a job on the *City Press*, a slightly more liberal newspaper, and where the family felt considerably safer. But even there they were harassed.

'In Johannesburg I was driving with my wife and my car was knocked down by a "hippo" [huge army vehicle]. My wife was hurt. It was sabotage.'

In spite of this persecution Mono Badela is a cheerful, amusing man. 'I chose rugby instead of the church,' he said. 'I think I chose right. Rugby is the centre of activism, and some of these preachers,' he winked, 'they lie.'

Badela believes that the Watsons contributed hugely to the success of 'the struggle'. 'They were heroes! They still are.'[32]

7

THE BURNING OF THE HOUSE

On 1 July 1985, President Botha declared a State of Emergency.

The State of Emergency affected the townships of Johannesburg, Port Elizabeth and thirty-four other cities and towns. The declaration, the first of its kind in twenty-five years, gave the police powers to impose curfews and to act against their political enemies without fear of any legal reprisals.

On 4 July the ANC began a boycott on the shops of white collaborators in the Port Elizabeth area. The Watsons were exempt.

In the townships vigilantes set up road blocks. They searched cars and destroyed any clothing or groceries, in fact anything at all bought at the boycotted shops. The boycott went on for months. White officials described the effect of it as 'desperately urgent'.

Although the Watsons' stores were the only ones exempt from the boycott, they had not suggested this. Black community leadership had decided that they should be exempt and had then given the Watsons the responsibility of organising the boycott in their area. They used the period of the boycott to help politicise whites in the community. 'We would say things like, "You can help lift this boycott if you react in a positive manner towards the political aspirations of the black people,"' Valence said.[1]

Meanwhile the Security forces were working to discredit the Watsons over the boycott. 'Security sent out propaganda saying we were behind it,' said Cheeky. 'They sent out pamphlets which caused tremendous resentment amongst the whites. They believed we wanted the boycott to increase our business. We had no idea how bad the backlash would be.

'The boycott committee had arrived at our shop and said, "We want you to stock the things we need – nappies, babies' bottles, dummies and inexpensive ladies' clothing." So we changed from being an exclusive menswear store. We didn't resist. It was the feeling of the leadership that this was needed. The boycott idea was to make the whites aware, to affect their pockets, so they'd be a lot more eager to get around the negotiating table. It was a fantastic tool politically.'[2]

During the first boycott, which lasted from August to November 1985, the Watsons' clothing shops in East London and Uitenhage were the only two white stores exempt from the black consumer boycott in the Eastern Cape.

'The black community had said, "the Watsons are not to be boycotted",' Gavin told the *National Times on Sunday*. He continued:

> *But the police came and stood outside our stores, sixteen at a time, and didn't allow customers in. There was tremendous political tension. The police tore up the parcels of anyone who did go in. Our wrapping paper was coloured green, black and gold (ANC colours) and that was like red rag to a bull.*[3]

Cheeky said, 'Before the police decided to stand outside and let nobody go in, they would come into our stores in groups of sixty. They jostled customers and tried to get the press to report that there was violence. Valence got a camera with no film in it and pretended to be taking photos of the police creating tension. I then phoned the police liaison officer, who was also manager of the white Eastern Province rugby side that I used to play for, but the officer said he was too busy to talk to me. The police then threatened to arrest me. I said, "On what charge?" They said, "We don't need a charge. This is a State of Emergency."

'When all their tactics to cause us to erupt into violence failed, they stood at the front door heavily armed and refused to allow customers in. There was absolutely nothing we could do.'[4]

The Watsons' wives also received unpleasant treatment from former white friends during the first boycott. Eileen, on a visit to a medical specialist, had been told that the Watson family had 'sold out the white cause and had become a threat to the white establishment'. When Eileen protested that all the family was trying to do was get black and white to work towards a democratic government, the doctor said, 'That statement is too progressive for me to understand. When I was at university I used to be a liberal, but what your family is trying to do is so forceful that the average white mind cannot comprehend it.'[5]

Eileen felt disgusted that while she was being given a gynaecological examination she could be grilled about her family's politics.

The wives had different ways of dealing with abuse from whites who had once been friends. Eileen was inclined to become upset and cry in private. She has a nervous temperament and is very energetic. Her children were the only ones old enough to be at school and she was very concerned about car bombs. 'Every morning as I got into the car to drive them to school I'd say, "Please, Lord, let this be fine."'[6] Eileen was the one who asked the most questions about what the brothers were doing.

Tracey, Cheeky's wife, is a strong personality with firm Christian principles. She had represented South Africa as a gymnast, had made recordings of her gospel singing and was not easily intimidated. Her lack of diplomacy sometimes embarrassed her husband, who did not like to offend people. But Tracey's strength came in handy when she received threatening phone calls. After one vicious threat to her children, she calmly told the caller, 'I want you to understand something. I pray for my children. I cover my children with the blood of Jesus and I want you to know that nothing is going to happen to them.'[7]

Cheeky laughed. 'It's not the way I'd have reacted.'[8]

Leigh Ann, Gavin's wife, is soft and gentle, intelligent and perceptive. She tried to hide her fears and remain calm but sometimes she too would cry in private.

None of the wives would ever show strain or emotion in public.

At this time the Watson brothers were very careful never to mention the ANC. Even to each other they would refer to it as 'the movement'. Security had bugged their house, and the wives, in particular, found this hard to bear. They deeply resented the fact that so much time, money and energy in South Africa went into spying when it might have been used for positive things like educating the community to consider a unified country with votes for all.

When Bobbi and Daniel Watson left their farm in Alicedale to come and live with their sons in the large house in Park Drive, Port Elizabeth, they brought Stompi, a domestic and sister-in-law to Margaret, who had been the boys' 'black mother', with them, and also her niece, Grace, and her daughter, Nomvula.

'Grace had no job and no way of feeding her kids so she just came to us,' Eileen recalls. 'When the inspectors came around every couple of months to see if we had anybody living with us illegally, we would quickly lock them all up in a room. The law called the Influx Control Act stated that black Africans could not move from town to town or from rural to urban areas. It was inhuman. Later we were able to buy Grace a house. When my children were small Grace looked after them while I worked for Valence. People used to say to me in horror, "Do you know that your maid smacks your children?" I said, "She is good enough to bring up my children, be mother to them while I am at work and she is not supposed to check them when they are disrespectful or cheeky?".[9]

'Most white children in South Africa are brought up by black nannies and love them dearly, but by the time the children are a few years old the relationship changes. They still love their nannies but now they say, "Fetch me this, fetch me that." The nanny treats them like a little boss. I've seen a child throw its schoolcase on the ground and then order the nanny to pick it up.'[10]

The Watsons deplored such behaviour and taught their

children to treat black people with the same respect they had for their parents.

On 6 July, in a rare interview, Nelson Mandela outlined the three principles of the ANC movement: a unified country with no artificial homelands, a black representation in central Parliament and one-man, one-vote.

Invoking the emergency powers, the authorities announced restrictions on the funerals of victims of the civil unrest. Funerals were one of the few remaining lawful forms of assembly for blacks, and this announcement caused widespread anger.

The Watsons understood this anger. They had helped to arrange the funerals of many of their friends, had been pall-bearers and had spoken at their funerals. 'Not only are funerals a time to politicise people but they are very important in the culture of black people,' Cheeky explained. 'By preventing people from attending funerals, you will really stir up their anger. The authorities restricted the times of funerals to week-days so people couldn't get off work to attend.'[11]

International trade and bank loans to South Africa were beginning to dry up. At the end of July the Chase Manhattan Bank, America's third largest bank, announced that it would stop making loans to private borrowers and would not renew existing loans. A campaign of 'disinvestment' by students, churches and charities in America withdrew deposits rather than invest in South Africa.

By the end of August Du Plessis, the Finance Minister, announced the seriousness of foreign banks withdrawing short-term finance to South Africa. Without foreign capital, he said, the country could not grow.[12]

The Australian Foreign Minister Bill Hayden announced limited sanctions against South Africa and the closure of the Australian Trade Commission in Johannesburg.

The South African Government temporarily suspended trade on the stock and currency markets when the currency plunged to an all-time low.

On 15 August 1985 in a speech in which long-awaited reforms were expected to be announced, President Botha rejected foreign and domestic calls for major concessions to apartheid and refused to compromise on terms for the release of Nelson Mandela. In a scathing reply, Bishop Desmond Tutu said that prospects for peaceful change in the country were now 'virtually nil'.

The Watsons continued to work on their cells in the black townships and rush out at all times of night to secret meetings. But occasionally they did make time to be with their families. 'Sometimes the four boys would go for a run on the beach for about ten miles,' Eileen explained. 'Tracey, Leigh Ann and I would follow in the cars, bringing sausages and chops. We'd meet up and have a braai.'[13]

It was on one of these trips that Tracey confided to her sisters-in-law that she was becoming increasingly upset by the threatening phone calls, particularly when they concerned her children. 'One caller had said he was going to necklace me and then do the same to my daughter,' Tracey recalls.[14]

The other wives agreed that their lives were becoming nightmarish. The brakes of their cars had been tampered with. They had learned never to drive alone and to constantly check the rear-vision mirror to see if they were being followed.

The wives, nevertheless, believed in the struggle. They understood why other whites were afraid of the Watson family or felt critical of them for isolating themselves from the white community.

'We were such a big family that we didn't really need anyone else,' Eileen explains. 'We did have a few white friends but some white people were a bit intimidated when they came to the house because we were all so involved with each other's interests. Some people thought we were arrogant.'[15]

Arrogance was a charge that would be levelled at the family often in the years to come. Whites, even those who thought of themselves as liberals, would be jealous of the Watsons' strength and commitment. And a few blacks, whom the Watsons regarded as corrupt, would also accuse them of being arrogant. It was to become a dangerous label.

In spite of their anxiety the Watsons' young wives, Eileen, Tracey and Leigh Ann, all believed strongly in what their husbands were doing. Was it sheer accident that made the three brothers marry women much younger than they were? Or did they hope to influence them more easily to follow their own radical politics? Whatever the reason, the wives were supportive. They were compliant but tough. They rationalised that the expectations of the Watson family were not too high – that it was not horribly suffocating living all together and coming second to the struggle. They put up with being kept ignorant of just what their husbands were doing and agreed to be part of the Watson tribe, which necessarily excluded many of their old friends who were not sympathetic. They made passionate attempts to convince other whites, mostly friends and relatives, to come to terms quickly with blacks if greater bloodshed was to be avoided. They also helped by typing documents and speeches to be delivered to white businessmen at meetings of the group called 'Concerned Citizens', formed by the Watson brothers.

'Concerned Citizens' was formed in Port Elizabeth for the purpose of explaining to white businessmen and churchgoers how South Africa could have a safe future as a non-racist country. Sometimes the brothers were invited to speak at very conservative organisations such as the Freemasons and the Hebrew Order of David.

Occasionally one of the three wives would feel like taking a more active part in the struggle.

'I sometimes wished to be part of the conversation when meetings were held at our house,' Eileen admitted. 'They were always in Xhosa and I couldn't understand what was going on. But I was doing quite a lot to help. I never did housework but I helped in the shops, drove comrades to meetings and typed pamphlets to be distributed in the townships. I trusted that Valence knew what he was doing and assisted wherever I was needed.'[16]

Tracey felt she was more useful at home, looking after her young son and daughter, than racing around being an activist. She relied a great deal on her belief in God to give her courage when things were difficult. 'Once, when I had a particularly horrible caller on the phone making threats, I said, "You listen to me. If you touch my kid, you'll not be harming me. You'll be harming God." I'd get in a preaching mode.'[17]

Leigh Ann said, 'When we were all thrown in at the deep end, I became very involved in the practical things, like getting the children to school and cooking. I'm more of a support to Gavin. I didn't always know what was going on. I didn't want to pry. I was there if he wanted to tell me. I trusted the boys enough to know that they'd make the right decision. They had our welfare at heart. I'm not a volatile person. I don't express my feelings a lot. I listen. I try to stay calm.'[18]

As Nelson Mandela had predicted, and then skilfully negotiated from his solitary confinement cell in Pollsmoor Prison, the ANC was gradually changing its position.

At a congress in Kabwe, Zambia, in June 1985, the ANC was still claiming that 'it would not seek a political settlement through negotiation and would negotiate a "transfer of power" only with a defeated white regime'.

Thabo Mbeki, then Information Officer for the ANC, spoke on ANC radio from Zambia, calling for the 'overthrow of the apartheid machine'.

Botha believed that the South African Communist Party and the ANC were 'interwoven'. After all, South Africa was fighting a war in Angola against troops whose arms were supplied by Russia. In public, Botha continued to behave as if he was uninterested in negotiation.[19]

But just a year later the ANC president, Oliver Tambo, would spell out in an interview in Lusaka the conditions under which the ANC would be prepared to negotiate:

> *if the government first released Nelson Mandela and all other political prisoners, unbanned the ANC and other political organizations, allowed exiles to return, lifted the state of emergency then in force, and scrapped key apartheid laws to demonstrate its sincerity and create an atmosphere of mutual trust.*[20]

Meanwhile Mandela wrote again and again to Kobie Coetsee, the Minister for Justice, to propose 'talks about talks'.[21] He found the minister's lack of response 'peculiar and demoralizing'.[22] But by early 1986 Mandela had found a sympathetic audience in the seven-member Eminent Persons Group, whose co-leader was Malcolm Fraser, former Prime Minister of Australia.

Mandela writes,

> *The Eminent Persons Group had come with many questions involving the issues of violence, negotiations and international sanctions. At the outset I set the ground rules for our discussions. "I am not the head of the movement," I told them. "The head of the movement is Oliver Tambo in Lusaka. You must go and see him." I favour the ANC beginning discussions with the government.*[23]

Like almost every other South African, the Watsons knew nothing of these secret messages being passed between Mandela and Tambo via the Eminent Persons. 'I would have thought there wouldn't have been much hope of negotiation at that stage,' said Cheeky. 'P. W. Botha was firmly in place. Although we hoped that someone would embark on negotiations one day, I'd have thought it was a futile process just then.'[24]

Meanwhile, in September 1985, a meeting had taken place in Lusaka, Zambia, between members of the ANC and white Johannesburg businessmen and newspaper editors. The meeting signified the first recognition by key sectors of South African society of the ANC as the most credible representative of the black majority. But Botha branded the meeting a 'betrayal'.

'I thought it was a major breakthrough,' said Cheeky. 'But I also wondered if it might be a plot to identify the weaknesses within the ANC leadership. Up until then it had suited businesses to have apartheid. Businessmen did not assist in the liberation process.'[25]

Throughout their political careers the Watsons had always been careful not to join any white-led anti-apartheid groups like the liberal opposition Progressive Federal Party (PFP). Valence said, 'We are against liberal whites because when push comes to shove, they back down. They all act as if they are anti-government because of the wrongs committed but when you ask them to do something concrete about it, they back away.'[26]

As Gavin Watson explained in an article in the *Los Angeles Times*, 'Our credibility in the black townships is very important, too important to lose on groups that are irrelevant to the process of change.'[27]

During the consumer boycotts the Watsons had worked hard to open communications between whites and blacks in Port Elizabeth. They observed that during the boycotts the illusion of the whites that their comfortable life could go on forever had been shattered. 'Many, many more whites would not only oppose apartheid but work actively to overthrow it if they were not so tightly cocooned in their artificial little worlds,' said Valence.[28]

In the same interview Ronnie boldly identified himself and his brothers with the outlawed ANC. Few whites or blacks, however radical, would have had the courage to do such a thing in October 1985 in South Africa. But Ronnie felt that there was some value in being written about in the international press and relied on it for protection.

"When the ANC is in power," he said with seeming confidence this

will be the inevitable result of the "coming revolution". The phrase, from a white South African, is startling.

"A growing number of whites, mostly at the liberal universities but some in business and the community at large, now recognize the African National Congress as the legal government of South Africa in exile ... But they can't speak out or carry ANC membership cards because it would mean 5 to 10 years in prison ... We are willing to take that chance to win others to the struggle."[29]

Some time before this Valence Watson had admitted to his wife, Eileen, that he and Ronnie were members of the ANC. He had begged her not to ask him any more questions, telling her the less she knew the better.

'I'd been very suspicious about Ronnie. He used to have bonfires and burn lots of paper,' Eileen said. 'When I asked, "What are you burning?" he'd say, "Nothing". Once I said, "Well, whatever it is, it's flying all over the street." He said, "Aaagh!" and flew after it.'

'I'd asked Valence before if he was ANC and he'd said, "What if I was?" Eventually I didn't want to know because I said, "If I get taken in, even before the torture, I'll sing like a bird."[30]

Tracey said, 'We, the wives, knew what was going on. We always knew they were ANC. We just didn't talk about it.'[31]

Security, too, had discovered that Valence and Ronnie were ANC members and that they reported directly to Chris Hani and the head of ANC Security and Intelligence, Mzuardile Piliso, which did not please them.

They had also discovered that the Watson stores had a large cash flow but because so much money went to the struggle against apartheid they were operating on a financial knife edge and were actually about 300 000 rand in debt.

The harassment from Security was now almost unbearable for the Watson family. Their phones were tapped, their cars followed, their bank accounts monitored and their homes and stores under surveillance day and night. They had to be constantly on guard against assaults, abductions and false allegations of wrongdoing. Anti-riot police had positioned themselves outside their stores on Saturdays, the busiest days, to discourage customers. Their wives continued to get obscene and threatening phone calls and their children had to be escorted to and from school and were never allowed out of sight on weekends.

In early October 1985, Eileen and Leigh Ann decided they'd had enough of keeping their young children inside all day. Eileen now had three young sons, Nkosi, Daniel and Jared. Leigh Ann had a son, Roth, aged three and a daughter, Lindsey, aged eighteen months. Their nerves were on edge. They said they all needed a weekend away. Leigh Ann's parents had a holiday house at Bushman's River Mouth on the coast. It happened to be free that weekend so Eileen cancelled Jared's first birthday party and she and Valence agreed to join Leigh Ann and Gavin for the weekend. Tracey and Cheeky were also invited but decided not to go because Tracey had a new baby daughter, Candy. They had recently moved out of the family home into a house nearby. Ronnie was away in East London, coordinating the boycott with the black leaders that weekend, so he did not go either. The Watsons' parents, Daniel and Bobbi, were staying with Bobbi's sister out of town.

The house in Park Drive had a long driveway and was situated on the edge of a large park. There was no fence between the park and the house so people could enter the grounds very easily. Recently someone had walked in from the park and tried to steal a car parked in the driveway. So it was arranged that while the family was away, Archie Mkele and Jeffrey Nokanda, who worked in the Watsons' stores and were close friends of theirs, should keep an eye on the house.

Just before midnight on Saturday 19 October 1985, the Watsons' family home exploded into flames and burnt to the ground.

Archie and Jeffrey, who had been in a car parked outside the house just before the explosion, were missing, although the car was still there.

Cheeky was phoned at about midnight by a white friend to say that the house was ablaze. 'I rush to the house and see that police have cordoned it off. There must be a thousand people all around the house. It is totally engulfed in flames. There are curtains hanging on thirty-foot-high trees.

'I see Archie and Jeff's car. The doors are hanging open and the keys are still in the ignition. I look at this and I am totally devastated. I overhear a fireman telling a policeman that there is a body inside the house and he could smell the sweet smell of flesh burning. The policeman says to me, "Look here, he doesn't know anything." I ask him, "Where are the people who were in this car?" and he says he doesn't know. Nobody knows anything. I rush around outside the house with massive flames leaping everywhere and I can't find out anything. I am highly emotional. I take it for granted that Archie and Jeff are dead.'[32]

At first it was suspected that a bomb had been the cause of the explosion, but later police discovered that the house had been doused in petrol. The house was completely gutted by the fire and only a few pieces of tottering wall were left standing.

Cheeky did not think there was a phone at the holiday house where Valence and Gavin were staying so he leaped into his car and drove there in less than an hour.

'I broke the news to Gavin and Valence. Gavin stayed behind to look after the family and calm down Eileen and Leigh Ann. Valence came back with me to Port Elizabeth. Valence was totally shocked about Archie and Jeff. I was driving at 220 kilometres an hour and he was telling me to drive faster. When he looked at the ruins of the house he couldn't believe what he saw.

'We rushed to the police and asked if any bodies had been found in the house. They said no, but there were two people found in the valley behind the house and they had been arrested and taken to the main police station in the area. We rushed there. Archie and Jeff were not there. They had been taken to Livingstone, which is the black hospital. At Livingstone we see that Archie and Jeff are critically burnt. They both have third-degree burns to 40 per cent of their bodies. The black staff recognise us. We tell them who Archie and Jeff are and they immediately rally round to help us monitor their condition.'[33]

Gavin continues the story: 'Archie and Jeff had been found by a white man and taken to Provincial Hospital, which is the nearest hospital but it's for whites. He was very upset that they were denied treatment there. He said, "They are going to die!"'[34]

Cheeky continues, 'Because this white man, out of the goodness of his heart, was making such a fuss at the white hospital the police were called. He then appealed to the police to let Archie and Jeff be treated and they said, "Don't worry about it. Leave it to us." So the guy went off and as soon as he'd gone the police took Archie and Jeff to Louis Le Grange Police Headquarters. They were interrogated for three hours without any treatment. Police were shouting and screaming at them, "Who attacked you? Did you see any whites? What did they look like?" In other words, they were just trying to find out if Archie and Jeff knew what they already knew and might give evidence against them.'[35]

Archie and Jeff were too weak to speak for a few days after their ordeal but eventually they told the Watsons that on the night of the fire they had been attacked by men in balaclavas, dragged out of their car and left semi-conscious inside the petrol-soaked house. After the explosion they had managed to crawl outside and get away into the bush at the back of the house.

Meanwhile newspaper headlines declared *Horror in Watson Inferno*, *Watson Home Gutted in Fire Blast* and *'No bomb' in gutted home*. The explosion was heard ten kilometres away.

The residents of Park Drive had watched in disbelief as flames four storeys high leaped out of what had been the Watsons' stately mansion. In a newspaper report one neighbour said, 'I thought it was a plane crash! I looked out my window and the entire house was on fire. The roof and every room were burning.' Another neighbour was 'shot out of her bed by the force of the blast'.[36]

Gavin, Eileen, Leigh Ann and the children returned, in shock, from their weekend away and gathered at Gavin's flat nearby. Ronnie came back from East London to join them. Everything they owned had been lost – antique furniture, clothing, keepsakes and sporting trophies. The family home, where they had expected to live their whole lives, had gone. Here the sons had been married, there had been great parties in the gardens; here the whole rugby team would spend the night before a match, activists on the run would hide out in the loft. It had been a welcoming house and one from which the Watsons would gain the reputation from some Africans in the community of being 'like the Kennedys' and 'living in a house like Dallas'.

Eileen Watson and her mother-in-law, Bobbi, spent hours picking through the rubble looking for any remnant of their lives in the family home – a charred photograph, a blackened toy, a melted bracelet. But there was nothing.

'When Mono Badela's house was burnt down, and he was the first person really close to us it had happened to, I asked Valence and Ronnie if they thought Security would do that to us,' Eileen recalls. 'But they said no. So when our house burnt down I thought that the ANC had stashed arms underneath. I was annoyed. I thought, "How could they do that to us? They don't care two hoots about us or our kids." But later I found that it wasn't the case. It was just that everyone was talking about nothing but bombs, bombs, bombs.'[37]

The brothers were in no doubt that the destruction of their home and all their family possessions was part of an intense campaign being carried out against them because of their active resistance to government policies. In an interview in the *Evening Post* Ronnie said that recently

> *... the campaign had intensified since the brothers had initiated meetings with others of the Port Elizabeth business community.*
>
> *Ronnie said the purpose of the discussions was to emphasise the urgent need for negotiation between race groups as the means to*

solving South Africa's current political crisis. Ronnie reiterated the brothers' belief in a 'one-man, one-vote' policy and said the release of Nelson Mandela was of paramount importance.

Asked if they could link the campaign they talked of to the explosion which demolished his family's home, Gavin said, 'There is only speculation at this stage, we cannot say anything – but just look at the newspaper articles which have been published recently.'[38]

Gavin was referring in particular to an article in the *Los Angeles Times*, the introduction to which read, 'The four Watson brothers can see the revolution coming in South Africa, and they are determined to be on the winning side – the side of the blacks.'[39]

This was provocative stuff. But Gavin agreed with Ronnie about the wisdom of getting themselves into the international press as a means of protection.

Archie and Jeffrey, meanwhile, were under police 'protection' in Livingstone Hospital and the Watson brothers were not permitted to visit them. But being well known and respected by the hospital staff, they soon developed a network within the hospital. 'It started when one of the sisters came to Ronnie and said that two plainclothes policemen had been in to see Archie and Jeff and been overheard saying, "Why are these two still alive? They're supposed to be dead",' said Cheeky.[40]

'At that time political detainees were treated as prisoners at Livingstone Hospital,' Gavin recalls. 'So we confronted the hospital authorities and asked them whether they were working independently or as part of the police system. Then a real confrontation started. Eventually the black sisters and doctors confronted the police and said they would work independently, not under their orders.'[41]

Cheeky recalls indignantly, 'The security police would be sitting right there in the burns ward, smoking a cigarette. In a place like that you need total hygiene – a sterile environment, masks and gloves to prevent infection getting into the burnt skin, and there is this guard, who is supposed to be protecting Archie and Jeff, smoking.'[42]

'Ronnie eventually got access to Archie and Jeff through his attorney. He got rid of that security guard quite legally, via the doctors who stood up against the superintendent who wanted to allow police authority in the hospital,' said Gavin. 'Captain Prinsloo, the investigating police officer on the case, didn't like it at all.'[43]

'The police had to let us in to visit. But then they tried another tactic to get Archie and Jeff to make incriminating statements about us. They disguised themselves as a TV crew from International News Media. Now Archie and Jeff know that we are always completely open with the international media and now these News Media people have come to interview them, they will be open too,' said Cheeky. 'But the sister recognises Captain Prinsloo and immediately gets on the phone to Ronnie and says you have to get down here. When Ronnie arrives there is a confrontation. Prinsloo hits Ronnie on the chest and says, "Ronnie, you people are treading on dangerous ground once more, and we are going to teach you a lesson."

'Ronnie tells him that if he was truthfully investigating the burning of the house they would all cooperate, but his moves are sinister. "If Ronnie is bucking the system," he says, "then Prinsloo's moves are worse". He tells Prinsloo to leave Archie and Jeff alone and get out. The doctors arrive and stand beside Ronnie, saying, "Move out. You are not allowed in here."'[44]

Meanwhile Valence Watson was so depressed about the dreadful state his close friends Archie and Jeff were in, and the fact that he could do nothing to retaliate, that he was put under sedation for two days. He blamed himself for his friends' serious injuries, because it was he who had asked them to keep an eye on the house.

Ronnie and Valence, Eileen and the three children all moved into Gavin Watson's three-bedroom flat. Their parents moved in with friends. Fortunately the Watsons' younger sister, Sharon, was away working in Cape Town when the house was burnt.

The police denied the Watsons access to their own house, destroyed though it was, for four days because they said they were carrying out an investigation. At the end of this time they declared that the situation was 'suspicious'. The insurance company refused to pay any money on the house because of this.

The Watsons' house was destroyed and creditors were lining up for their money. Their shops were receiving bomb threats and their customers were being harassed by police who tried to stop them from buying anything. The local media would not defend them because of the State of Emergency.

In Gavin's overcrowded flat the Watson family knelt and prayed.

8

CRIMINALISING THE WATSONS

For several days after the explosion of their house the Watson family was in a state of shock.

In spite of being tremendously frightened, a lot of their black friends came to offer sympathy. If whites who stood up against apartheid could have their house destroyed by Security then what would happen to blacks? The Watsons' house had been a refuge to them. Now there was nowhere.

Recently four black leaders had been murdered and three others had disappeared. The Watsons' activist friends felt despondent.

The black community did not dare to visit Archie Mkele and Jeff Nocanda in hospital but they sent messages through the preacher and a choir of six who pushed past the police guard to sing hymns for them and pass on their condolences.

In the early stages it was not at all certain that Archie and Jeff would live. Their second day in hospital was the most critical. On this day Security police persuaded a doctor to get Archie and Jeff to sign a form saying that they could be moved to Tygerburg Hospital in Cape Town. The doctor was not a regular at the hospital so he was not aware of Archie and Jeff's close connection with the Watsons. The excuse given by Security for this eight-hour drive, which almost certainly would have killed the critically ill men, was that there were better facilities in Cape Town.

A regular doctor came quickly to the Watsons' Main Street store to warn them of what was about to take place. Archie and Jeff were still delirious and did not know what they had signed. Ronnie rushed to the hospital and found them in the back of an ambulance all ready for the journey.

He asked them both, 'Do you know who I am?'

'Ginger,' they said. (Ginger was his nickname.)

'Do you want to go to Tygerburg?'

'No!' they chorused.[1]

They had already been interrogated for three hours while lying in the back of the ambulance with the doors wide open to the winter wind.

The plan to take them to Tygerburg was cancelled and Ronnie hired two security guards to sit outside Archie and Jeff's room and not allow anyone in who was not on the list he gave them.

Ronnie continued regularly visiting the hospital during the six months that Archie and Jeff were there, at the end of which time the nursing staff were awarded a cup for helping the two men to make such a miraculous recovery.

Meanwhile Valence Watson was still in a state of depression as a result of his close friends' brush with death. Archie, in particular, was like a brother to him. When they first met at rugby training he and Valence had been enemies, perhaps because their personalities were so similar. They were both very certain of themselves and used to commanding respect. They would each remain calm until they were pushed too far and then would become very angry. It was Valence who'd had to pull Archie off Gavin's attacker to stop him being killed. They had shared a great deal in recruiting people for the ANC. Archie had transported many people in hiding using Valence's car. He had met his future wife, Carol, while working in the Watsons' store. Archie and Valence trusted and understood each other completely.

Cheeky explains, 'We were so concerned about the welfare of Archie and Jeff, running around trying to get them the best treatment we possibly could, and we were also organising furniture from friends for the flat and getting another flat for everyone to move into, that we hardly noticed Valence was in such a poor state. He was sedated for days and he'd ask the stupidest questions, like, "What's business like? Has the Uitenhage shop been opened?" We'd say, "Do us a favour. Just go upstairs. Lie down. Don't worry." '[2]

The brothers decided that it would be too distressing for Valence to see Archie and Jeff for at least a month and deliberately kept him away. Archie, too, knew that Valence would be traumatised and did not want him to visit.

'The sight of them was gruesome. We painted such a bad picture of them to prepare Valence for the worst that when he did see them he was relieved they looked so good,' said Cheeky.[3]

While they waited until a second flat became available in the same apartment block, almost all of the Watsons lived in Gavin's three-bedroomed flat. Eileen recalls it was hopelessly crowded.

'Myself, Valence and the three kids were in one room, Gavin, Leigh Ann and their children in another room, the Watsons' parents in another room and Ronnie in the lounge. One evening two African friends who were on the run came by and they slept in the lounge too. I couldn't handle it. There were so many people, and the phone rang all night with obscene and cranky calls. I remember one Afrikaner woman calling several times, telling us, "We missed you the first time but we'll get you next time. We'll get your children and slit their throats from ear to ear." I couldn't face people. Gavin's wife, Leigh Ann, was very sweet to me. She took the kids to school and so on. You must realise I had no clothes. We'd been away for the weekend so we only had shorts and vests. Jared was only a year old and still into nappies and bottles. And when at last another flat became vacant and we walked into it, there was nothing. No curtains, no beds, no furniture.

'Valence's mum and I spent a lot of time going back and forth to the burnt house, just to see if we could find anything in the rubble. I'd kept albums for each child and videos, the first lock of hair, the first footprint, the first words, that type of thing. Because there'd been a blast at the house things were scattered. I thought maybe we'd pick something up but we didn't.

'Valence was in a hell of a state and so was I. I was very upset with him. I would burst out crying. It was the shock of losing the house. He was so upset about Jeff and Archie and he was annoyed because we were going through the rubble, trying to find certain things that were sentimental to us. He told us we were crazy and the walls would fall on us. But we persisted.

'If the kids went downstairs and just put one foot outside the door there'd be total panic because we thought someone was waiting to grab them. We told the teachers that if anyone else came to collect them from school they must not let them go, because of the threats we were having. That went on for a long time.'[4]

The police investigation of the house had dragged on for months. Meanwhile no insurance had been paid to the Watsons, who had spent 20 000 rand on hiring an attorney and 45 000 rand to relocate the families. They had very little clothing and almost no cash.

At this very low point in their lives, Gavin Watson and his friend Brian Bird, a white minister of religion, were called in by the National Intelligence Service (NIS) and interrogated by two colonels about the organisation the Watsons had started called Concerned Citizens. Security was afraid that Concerned Citizens was already changing the ideas of conservative white businessmen about apartheid. During the interrogation Colonel Chris Koleski said to Gavin, not unpleasantly, 'You know, Gavin, why don't you as a family start marching to the beat of the drum, and work in the system? Then you won't find yourself with all these problems. If you do not work with us, we'll eradicate you.'

Gavin recalls that Brian Bird got such a fright at hearing this that he didn't speak for fifteen minutes.[5]

The colonel then repeated to Gavin that if he and his brothers would not cooperate with the NIS that they would 'isolate them, destroy them and eradicate them as a family'.

Gavin said, 'After Brian Bird heard this he became completely involved with Concerned Citizens and started standing up against the government.'[6]

Shortly after this the NIS sent a Security police agent to two retailers who had attended Concerned Citizens meetings. He told them that the Watsons were giving out armaments in the black townships. As a result the two retailers no longer attended meetings and avoided the Watsons. When Gavin confronted them to ask why, they were very angry with him. After he had convinced them that the story was nonsense, they took him to the black agent, who confessed he had been bribed by NIS.

Security tried other tactics to disrupt the Watsons' ANC work. They reported trouble had broken out in a remote black township so that the leaders rushed there and missed important meetings of their organisation back in Port Elizabeth.

'They caused us to have to cancel meetings of Concerned Citizens so that we'd look as if we were disorganised. But the meetings became increasingly larger and more successful. We had 250 at some meetings, made up of retailers, lawyers and accountants, all of them against apartheid. At one of our meetings the National Party sent people to try and break it up by interjecting. One of them stood up and said, "P. W. Botha's heart is in the right place. Let's try and work with the government, get in the system. Let's not be a bunch of radicals and communists doing our own thing." So Brian Bird got up and told him, "We're not setting up another rebel group. We are looking for a solution for this city and the country. We have come here to discuss that, not the National Party."

'At another meeting there were four men carrying guns, probably hoping some violence would erupt. I stood up and said to the one I recognised, "David, we appreciate you coming here this evening but we know you work for the Security branch and are paid by them. If you're here to break up the meeting we'd ask that you leave." Then everybody got up and slow clapped them and said, "Out, out, out," until they left.'[7]

It is easy to imagine the charming manner in which Gavin Watson would have humiliated the Security man. The Watson brothers are always scrupulously polite, immaculately dressed and gentlemanly, even when they are furious.

Sometimes the Watsons' black friends would get discouraged by the level of abuse they suffered from angry whites and would ask them if they thought the struggle for non-racial policies was worth it. Gavin recalls, 'They'd say to me, "Gavin, you guys have gone through so much. Your house has been burned, your wives and children are threatened. Why waste your time?" But we felt it was God's will that we should get involved with the white community as well, to mobilise them, to get them to feel what the blacks were feeling. The whites are the ones who created the apartheid system. They've got to feel the pain that comes with it.'[8]

The Watsons were seen as very important political figures in the Eastern Cape region. Naturally they had enemies. A few years later, they would discover just how much they had been hated by certain people in Security and how determined Security had been to eradicate them.

On Christmas Day 1985, just outside the town of Durban, fifty-three people died as a result of a clash between 2000 Zulus and 3000 members of the Pondo tribe. Newspaper reports declared that the reason for the fighting was unclear. But the Watson brothers were quite clear about it.

'Duncan Village was a small African community on the edge of East London, about 250 kilometres from Port Elizabeth,' Valence said. 'Most of the blacks had been moved to Ndantsane, a township fifteen kilometres away. But those remaining in Duncan Village didn't want to move. They were more political people. So the Security police sent in the hoods. The comrades operating in the underground in Duncan Village were identified by Security, who then targeted these leaders. Security had their operatives within the village. It was not "black on black" violence. The State was doing it, so they could then say, "Look there. They can't govern themselves. We should do it."'[9]

The massacre occurred in Duncan Village during a peaceful rally against apartheid. The Watsons had helped to prepare for the mass funeral of those killed in the demonstration by manufacturing T-shirts and printing leaflets.

'We lost 15 000 rand on those T-shirts because the police confiscated most of them,' Cheeky said. 'The company we hired to make them had to disclose what was printed on them. They had *Stop Killing Innocent People* on the back. That was approved by Security. But later we had stencilled on the front of the T-shirts *SADF*, so they now read *SADF Stop Killing Innocent People*. We sent the first lot of T-shirts by panel van to Duncan Village and these got through. But the second lot were sent by air. One of the comrades working at the airport saw Security open a box. He told us, "Your T-shirts are gone."'[10]

'A massive funeral, attended by 60 000 people, was held in Duncan Village for the twenty-nine who had been killed,' said Valence. 'I was there. Steve Tshwete gave a rousing speech, the last one before he skipped the country. He said, "We will burn Oxford Street [main street of East London] to the ground and on the ashes we'll build a new South Africa." [In the new South Africa, Steve Tshwete is currently the Minister for Sport.]

'After the funeral the police withdrew from the township,'

Valence continued. 'But first they "bought" a very powerful group in the township by giving them cars and money. There is a very high rate of unemployment in Duncan Village. In spite of the tremendous unity in the village after the massacre, this group, which was involved in government and community structures, was able to buy off people all around them. They brought in criminals, got them drunk or gave them hash to smoke, then sent them to attack the political activists. Two close friends of ours were given a hundred lashes each by this reactionary group set up by South African Security. The guys were hospitalised for two weeks. That was the divide and rule policy of the government.'[11]

The Watsons, in their collective, had tried to politicise the reactionary group and failed. 'I tried to explain to them that by belonging to this group they were doing the struggle great harm,' Gavin said. 'But after three or four hours I and several other political guys decided we were making no headway. Knowing that the government was so completely behind them, the reactionaries were feeling very confident. Their homes were completely secure. They pretended to be on our side, to be in fact ANC, but their real purpose was to nullify anything progressive we tried to do. They were cunning. For example, they gave a hundred lashes to one guy who had a great following in the township because he was going out with a girl from the black consciousness-raising movement. This was a ploy by the government to cause a division, to blame their violent behaviour on the ANC. This was part of their plan to make people believe there was "black on black" violence. The ANC would never agree to give a guy a hundred lashes for going out with someone who didn't entirely agree with their ideology!'[12]

On 7 March 1986, South Africa rescinded its State of Emergency and released the last 327 of 8000 people detained since the previous July.

But the government failed to meet a 31 March deadline for changes in the apartheid system, so on 7 April a second wave of boycotts commenced. The first boycotts had lasted three months and had crippled white businesses.

This time the Watsons' stores were not exempt.

There were several reasons for this. The first was that there had been a rumour their stores would be bombed by disgruntled whites. There had been a severe backlash from the whites against the Watsons for being exempt from the first boycott, and after consultation with the black underground movement, they decided to take the bomb threat seriously.

The black leaders had told the Watsons, 'We don't want to put you guys' necks on the line. We can't afford to lose you now.'[13]

The second reason for including them in the boycott was that the Watsons were embarrassed by the rumours that they were only supporting the black imposed boycott because they were benefiting from it financially.

The third reason was that they had been told by black comrades that some white storekeepers had copied the bags used by the Watsons, which were in ANC colours, and their goods were being bought and carried into the townships, fooling the comrades who were on guard against any white goods other than the Watsons'.

There was also a fourth reason that the Watsons did not know about at the time. This was disturbing because it proved that the Watsons had enemies within the black community.

Maxwell Mamase, now the Minister for Housing and Local

Government in the Eastern Cape, explained, 'The Watsons had spent all their money financing the revolution, but there were a few individuals on the boycott committee who said they were making money out of the black community, and who thought that they should be boycotted too. At the time there was a strong anti-white feeling across the spectrum. To us, who had played rugby with the Watsons, they were not whites. They were part of us. But a few key people were opposed to them.'[14]

The Watsons themselves were not aware until many years later that they'd had enemies on the boycott committee who wished they would fail.

They did fail. Soon after being included in the second boycott, the Watsons became bankrupt.

At about the same time as the Watsons' business failed, Tracey got a phone call to say that the house she and Cheeky lived in would be bombed next. Cheeky immediately phoned the officer investigating the bombing of the Park Drive house and asked for protection. The officer said he did not believe it was necessary. Cheeky told him to call Pastor Fraser, who had been running their East London shop and had been getting phone calls threatening to blow up all their stores if the Watsons did not stop what they were doing. The officer did so and Pastor Fraser confirmed what Cheeky had told him. A liaison officer from the police then phoned Cheeky and said that he would receive protection for one night only. After that time protection would be his problem, not that of the police.[15]

Soon after this the Watsons' father, Daniel, had a stroke. He had always encouraged his sons to take the difficult,

Christian path and had instilled in them since childhood the need for equality for the blacks, but he was shocked by the punishment his sons were receiving from the white community.

Anyone who supported the Watsons was also targeted. An old school friend of theirs who lived in Port Elizabeth was taken in by the NIS and offered 600 000 rand to infiltrate the family and find out how involved they were in the political struggle. Just before he was asked to spy, his children had been threatened. This friend was never involved with the Watsons politically but he knew what they were doing, believed in it and went to church with them. He refused Security's offer.[16]

With the onset of the second boycott several powerful whites, who had previously been unsympathetic to the anti-apartheid struggle, came to Gavin Watson and asked him to approach black leaders to ask them what they could do to prevent the boycott. 'City councillors, businessmen, even the deputy mayor came. I told them there was nothing they could do. If the mayor couldn't even open up the beach to the blacks, how could he help any other structure of the community? We called a meeting of Concerned Citizens and asked for the resignation of all city councillors and Eastern Cape Province representatives in Parliament. The whites were beginning to realise you can't run a town council without the involvement of the black community.'[17]

'We contributed ideas to help the second boycott,' Valence said. 'We knew that the leaders in the black townships would be willing to speak to the white leaders, but the ANC, being a banned organisation, could not communicate directly. The ANC's call was to make the country ungovernable. Internally we had organisations such as UDF, COSATU, women's organisations and sporting bodies agitating for change and calling for the release of political prisoners and the return of the exiles. Elements of the national democratic struggle started to be propagated through the boycott.

'Slabbert of the PFP and other PFP members had meetings with us, and members of the National Party met with Ronnie to discuss how new structures could be formulated. But the National Party and the PFP refused to become involved with the idea. We had been asked by ANC leaders Chris Hani, Mzuardile Piliso and others to speak to whites right across the political spectrum, but at this time, early in 1986, white South Africa was not prepared to change.'[18]

In April 1986, Bishop Desmond Tutu was elected as the first black Anglican Archbishop of Cape Town and became the titular head of the Anglican Church in South Africa.

'When we first played non-racial rugby in 1976 the church as an institution did not support us. It was part of the racist establishment,' Valence said. 'But this was starting to change. The appointment of Tutu would mean that the Anglican Church, which was very powerful, would help to speed up the liberation struggle.'[19]

Also in April the government announced that it would abolish laws restricting the movement of blacks, which effectively allowed them to take up work or residence anywhere in the country, except white areas. The hated 'pass laws' were abolished. But segregation of hospitals, schools and residential areas was to remain.

'The abolishment of the pass laws made very little difference to the lives of average people,' Valence said. 'The motivation of the government was nothing more than window dressing. Political pressure from outside the country was becoming more powerful. The more the international community attacked South Africa the more they had to make *some* change. It wasn't a change from the heart.'[20]

On 1 May the biggest strike ever in South Africa was waged with 1.5 million blacks staying away from work. Many students boycotted school in support of the strike. In Johannesburg and Port Elizabeth the stoppage was almost total.

As Nelson Mandela wrote, 'Oliver Tambo and the ANC had called for the people of South Africa to render the country ungovernable and the people were obliging.'[21]

On 24 June 1986, the British Minister of State, Lynda Chalker, met with ANC President Oliver Tambo. This was a major turnaround in British Government policy. Prime Minister Thatcher had up till then dismissed ANC members as 'men of violence' with whom she would not deal.

On 4 August, at a meeting of Commonwealth Heads of Government in London, Margaret Thatcher finally bowed to pressure and agreed to the imposition of limited economic sanctions against South Africa. Her refusal to back stiffer sanctions was a source of bitterness amongst the other nations.

The Watsons were feeling bitter about problems of their own. A short time after the explosion, armed police had surrounded their burnt-out house and refused to allow them anywhere near it. 'We said, "This is our property. We have a right to be here." But they put their hands on their guns and said, "If you walk over this line you could find yourselves with problems."' Gavin said. 'You always get one policeman with a loose mouth, and a few days later we found out they were searching for armaments. There was a whisper campaign that we'd blown up our house to get the insurance. Was that likely? We had lost all our personal belongings for the last thirty-six years.'[22]

Some months later Archie and Jeffrey, still badly scarred and barely able to walk, left Livingstone Hospital with their wives and a crowd of black well-wishers. Shortly after leaving hospital they went back to work at the Watsons' stores. A few weeks later Jeffrey Nocanda was arrested. Two months later, on 30 July, while he was at work, Archie Mkele was also arrested. Valence Watson, who was with him at the time, tried to prevent it.

'Six police, carrying handguns, entered the store and one said they were arresting Archie. I said, "What for?" and they said, "We don't have to tell you." I said, "Of course you have to tell me. Do you have a warrant for the arrest?" He said he didn't. He said, "We have the power to do as we please in the State of Emergency. We're answerable to nobody." I asked if Archie could phone his wife, if I could phone his attorney. They allowed nothing.' said Valence. 'They frogmarched Archie to the front door and I'm standing there helplessly. There's *nothing* I can do.'[23]

Later his attorney, Leon Schubart, told Valence and Archie's wife Carol that under the State of Emergency regulations there was nothing he could do to stop the arrest. Although each arrest was only supposed to hold the prisoner for six months, there was nothing to stop Security from re-arresting the prisoner immediately he was released. Carol was very distressed.

Valence was angry and asked Schubart what they could do. Schubart advised him to keep bombarding Security with letters and queries. He was sympathetic and implied that he thought the laws of South Africa were unfair.[24]

insurance totalling R572 992 could be used to pay the

State alleges that Mr Mkele and Mr Nocanda were d to set the house on fire in such a way that they would in the process – giving rise to the attempted murder charge.[31]

e photograph in the *Evening Post* showed Gavin and the four female partners, including Glenda, ex-wife, leaving the court after the bail hearing.

and Bobbi were also present at the hearing. 'I only :e,' Bobbi said. 'I couldn't take it. My boys shackled. cent children. I went home and prayed.'[32]

ives made certain that they always dressed well for t hearings and never showed emotion. 'It was trau- etting dressed up nicely for the TV crews and smiling ameras before we went inside. It was almost as if it eal,' said Tracey. 'I couldn't bear the sight of the hand- was as if I'd been shot, a physical impact. It was a hollow feeling.'[33]

said, 'I cried only when I got home. Once Glenda arm around me near the court and I pushed her away anyone thought I might be crying.'[34]

da, who had separated from Ronnie, continued to the court hearings to support him. Her sisters-in-law ateful.

Watsons' attorney Leon Schubart argued that as the ad offered no evidence at all of the charges of murder, nd fraud, there could be no question that bail should ted.

Prosecutor, Henning Van der Walt, said that the State d bail because the Watsons were known political

Meanwhile Archie and Jeff were being interrogated and tortured. Their horrific experiences would not become public knowledge for many months.

The whole Watson family, except for Cheeky and Tracey, was now living in two flats, one above the other. Ronnie, Gavin, Leigh Ann and their children were downstairs and Daniel and Bobbi, Valence, Eileen and their children were upstairs. On Tuesday 12 August at 5 a.m., when everyone was asleep, there was a thunderous banging on the door and six heavily armed police burst in, surging into every bedroom. Another dozen or so stood guard outside.

Valence, thinking it must be activists, had gone to the door wearing nothing but a towel. When the police burst in he asked if they would mind leaving the bedroom while he and his wife dressed. Eileen, who was wearing only a T-shirt, had heard loud Afrikaans being spoken and saw that the passage was full of police. She asked Valence what was going on and he told her, 'I'm under arrest.' Police streamed into the bedroom. Valence quietly told Eileen not to say anything. 'He went to the toilet and they went with him,' she recalls in disbelief.[25]

Bobbi, in her dressing-gown and bare feet, ran downstairs to warn the others and was jeered at by the police.

The police handcuffed Ronnie and Valence, but left Gavin behind. They were marched outside to a van, where some sixty police were waiting. The arrest was a huge operation. Gavin kept demanding to know why they were being taken and where. Valence, trying to be cheerful, told Eileen not to tell the children. 'We'll be out on bail before they realise we're gone,' he said. Their father, Daniel, still weak from his stroke

Meanwhile Archie and Jeff were being interrogated and tortured. Their horrific experiences would not become public knowledge for many months.

The whole Watson family, except for Cheeky and Tracey, was now living in two flats, one above the other. Ronnie, Gavin, Leigh Ann and their children were downstairs and Daniel and Bobbi, Valence, Eileen and their children were upstairs. On Tuesday 12 August at 5 a.m., when everyone was asleep, there was a thunderous banging on the door and six heavily armed police burst in, surging into every bedroom. Another dozen or so stood guard outside.

Valence, thinking it must be activists, had gone to the door wearing nothing but a towel. When the police burst in he asked if they would mind leaving the bedroom while he and his wife dressed. Eileen, who was wearing only a T-shirt, had heard loud Afrikaans being spoken and saw that the passage was full of police. She asked Valence what was going on and he told her, 'I'm under arrest.' Police streamed into the bedroom. Valence quietly told Eileen not to say anything. 'He went to the toilet and they went with him,' she recalls in disbelief.[25]

Bobbi, in her dressing-gown and bare feet, ran downstairs to warn the others and was jeered at by the police.

The police handcuffed Ronnie and Valence, but left Gavin behind. They were marched outside to a van, where some sixty police were waiting. The arrest was a huge operation. Gavin kept demanding to know why they were being taken and where. Valence, trying to be cheerful, told Eileen not to tell the children. 'We'll be out on bail before they realise we're gone,' he said. Their father, Daniel, still weak from his stroke and arterial sclerosis, hobbled in on a stick and stared at the scene in disbelief. The women sat together in shock and felt grateful that none of the children had woken.

Later Bobbi said, 'The police had been all over the flats. I was simply amazed. I thought I'd quickly phone Cheeky and let him know. Tracey answered and said, "Cheeky has been taken too." I just put the receiver down. When you look back, you wonder how we endured it.' She spoke very quietly, a gracious, dignified woman who was obviously deeply hurt by the events. 'Daniel had a turn after the boys were arrested,' she added.[26]

'I thought Bobbi would have a turn herself,' said Eileen. 'Her three sons were taken. Her husband had just had a stroke. I phoned our family doctor. He was wonderful. He came at seven that morning to see her. When we opened the door a newspaper reporter was waiting. Gavin chased him away.'[27]

Tracey, too, had received a rude shock when the police burst into the room where she was in bed, asleep. 'They just stormed in, shining torches on her and her kids who were in bed with her,' said Eileen indignantly. 'It was a show of power.'[28]

Tracey recalls, 'It was pitch black and there was a thump on the door. Cheeky got up and saw that there were cops surrounding the house and all over the garden. They put handcuffs on him and then his mother rang. He asked me, "How are the family taking it?" I said, "Very well. Valence and Ronnie have been arrested too." '[29]

The family had not been told where the police were taking Ronnie, Valence and Cheeky. They had to find that out for themselves.

'We phoned from police station to police station,' Eileen

recalls, 'and each one said they knew nothing. Eventually we went to Louis Le Grange Police Station and found that Cheeky was there. But they would not tell us where the others were. We had to push and push for information. They sent us all over the place. They had separated the brothers as part of the harassment.

'Our lawyer said there was no evidence against them and they would get out on bail, so we felt quite confident. Meanwhile, the nights were frightening. Valence's mum and I somehow felt the police might come back and arrest us. Just a few days earlier, a black woman friend of ours, named Zoe, who'd been arrested, had told us what they did to her. They had stripped her and opened her legs and used electric rods to shock her and worse. Terrible things! I was petrified. A lot of women who'd been taken into detention had had this happen to them. We didn't sleep for five nights. We kept waiting for 5 o'clock.'[30]

Ronnie, Valence and Cheeky Watson and their two black employees, Archie Mkele and Jeff Nocanda, were charged with arson and fraud. The trumped-up charge was clearly an attempt by the authorities to victimise the brothers for their anti-apartheid stance. They all vehemently denied the charges.

The next day, in Port Elizabeth Magistrates' Court, they were ready to defend themselves. But when they got to court the three brothers found to their astonishment they were also being accused of attempted murder.

On 13 August the *Evening Post* reported:

It is alleged that a conspiracy was entered into between the accused to get Mr Archie Mkele and Mr Jeffrey Nocanda to destroy the house so insurance totalling R572 992 could be used to pay the debts.

The State alleges that Mr Mkele and Mr Nocanda were instructed to set the house on fire in such a way that they would be killed in the process – giving rise to the attempted murder charge.[31]

A large photograph in the *Evening Post* showed Gavin Watson and the four female partners, including Glenda, Ronnie's ex-wife, leaving the court after the bail hearing.

Daniel and Bobbi were also present at the hearing. 'I only went once,' Bobbi said. 'I couldn't take it. My boys shackled. My innocent children. I went home and prayed.'[32]

The wives made certain that they always dressed well for the court hearings and never showed emotion. 'It was traumatic, getting dressed up nicely for the TV crews and smiling at the cameras before we went inside. It was almost as if it wasn't real,' said Tracey. 'I couldn't bear the sight of the handcuffs. It was as if I'd been shot, a physical impact. It was a horrible hollow feeling.'[33]

Eileen said, 'I cried only when I got home. Once Glenda put her arm around me near the court and I pushed her away in case anyone thought I might be crying.'[34]

Glenda, who had separated from Ronnie, continued to attend the court hearings to support him. Her sisters-in-law were grateful.

The Watsons' attorney Leon Schubart argued that as the State had offered no evidence at all of the charges of murder, arson and fraud, there could be no question that bail should be granted.

The Prosecutor, Henning Van der Walt, said that the State opposed bail because the Watsons were known political activists who had made many pro-ANC and anti-government statements in the local and international press. 'He argued that we had connections with the ANC and that we would skip bail if released,' Valence said. 'Part of their case against us was that we might kill the witnesses. There were 163 of them!'[35]

Schubart argued that the charges being brought against the Watsons were criminal charges, not political ones.[36]

Van der Walt replied that it was the State's opinion that if the Watsons were released on bail they would be helped by political sympathisers to flee the country. Ronnie was accused of going to Harare in Zimbabwe to seek possible asylum there. This Ronnie denied emphatically. Valence supported him, telling the court that 'because of the brothers' financial situation he had visited Harare to explore a new business venture.' (In fact the brothers had been involved in such a venture; they were selling a pharmaceutical product called 'Sof 'n Curl', which was supposed to improve the texture of African hair.)[37]

That day the *Evening Post* reported:

> *[Ronnie had] no intention of leaving P.E. and the East Cape where he has lived all his life and, if bail was granted, he would accede to his passport being confiscated.*
>
> *He had no intention of not attending the trial, or interfering with State witnesses.*
>
> *Under cross-examination from the State, he said he was opposed to apartheid, but denied he or his family were liberals and politically controversial figures in the East Cape.*
>
> *He repeatedly replied 'Rubbish' to a suggestion by Mr Van der Walt of political asylum being sought in Zimbabwe.*[38]

Valence recalls, 'Ronnie emphasised that he was an activist against apartheid and not a liberal because, as we Watsons were aware, most South African liberals gave liberal politics a bad name.'[39]

It was some time since a court case in Port Elizabeth had caused such a stir. But the small crowd that attended the first hearing, mainly the Watsons' wives, friends and a few journalists, was greatly outnumbered by police in riot and camouflage gear, carrying batons and quirts, which are plastic whips nearly two metres long.

Reporter Debbie Booysen wrote in the *Weekend Post*:

The atmosphere was tense as the men were led, handcuffed to each other, into a small courtroom – usually used for traffic cases – at the back of the New Law Courts.

For men who until recently were running trendy clothing outlets, the three looked rather dishevelled after their early arrest and a day spent in separate police cells.

Everyone seemed more relaxed on Thursday – the three men looking encouraged by the presence in court of their fourth brother, Gavin, and their wives who had brought along fresh clothing.

It was evident that the food and paper cups of coffee were also very welcome . . .

The attractive, fashionably dressed wives sat close to each other all along, seeming to draw comfort from the thought that they were all in the same unhappy position . . .

The relatives had established good rapport with the court officials, exchanging laughs with them and being allowed to speak to their husbands at the dock during adjournments and to stay with them during the tea-break.

Yet everyone was aware of the seriousness of the case and the general atmosphere was subdued.[40]

Beside this article a large photograph appeared of three of the wives certainly looking 'attractive and fashionably dressed'. Glenda has her head bowed, Eileen, perhaps to escape scrutiny, is looking away from the camera but Tracey is beaming triumphantly straight into the lens.

When the case continued on Thursday, Ronnie was accused of not cooperating with the police and physically barring the investigating officer from seeing the two men who were badly burnt in the fire at the family home.

According to the *Evening Post*:

Mr Watson said the men were still in a critical condition when the investigating officer, Captain Prinsloo, went to see them at hospital.

'My main concern was that the men live and I just told the police not to see them until they had stabilised.'

Afterwards he had apologised to Captain Prinsloo for things said under emotional stress and said he was prepared to co-operate.

Mr Van der Walt also quoted from a report by an independent forensic expert who the family employed to investigate the cause of the blaze and who had expressed reservations about the 'failure of the family to co-operate'.

Mr Watson replied that they had terminated the expert's services after he had remarked 'I see there was an explosion. There must be some dead kaffirs around.'

Mr Watson denied he had been hiding in a cupboard when the police arrived to arrest him on Tuesday morning.

He said he had been standing outside the cupboard tying his shoelaces.[41]

There was a good deal of humour in court. Ronnie, according to Valence, was so relaxed that the courtroom occasionally roared with laughter. 'The magistrate asked him, "When the police came to arrest you, what happened?" and Ronnie gave his version of events, finishing with, "And then I looked up into the very good-looking face of Warrant Officer Fourie". He insulted the guy in such a nice way that the court laughed and laughed.'[42]

Ronnie continues, 'The magistrate said to me, "Look, calm down. This is not a comedy. Don't turn my court into a theatre." '[43]

Throughout the proceedings Cheeky was dignified and quiet. Valence was sometimes aggressive. Once Leon Schubart warned him to be careful. Valence said, 'I was annoyed because every time Leon stood up to say "This is a criminal trial, not a political trial" he was overruled.'[44]

Valence was questioned about a letter written by Gavin to their father shortly after the provisional liquidation of their businesses the year before. In the letter Gavin had said they had 'reached the end of the road' in their businesses in Port Elizabeth, Uitenhage and East London and could not repay their father the R30 000 he had lent them.

According to the *Evening Post*, 'It was further stated that the family home in Park Drive was mortgaged to try and save the business and that creditors, to whom the brothers owed 700 000 rand, had already instituted proceedings against them.'[45]

On 19 August, to their great shock and dismay, the three Watson brothers were refused bail.

The reasons given by the magistrate, T. K. Morgenthal, were that the court believed the evidence of the investigating officer, Captain Prinsloo, and the officer involved in the men's arrest, Warrant Officer Fourie, who were 'straightforward and even fair to the accused'.

He said, 'The same cannot be said about, especially, Mr Valence Watson and his brother, Ronnie.'[46]

The magistrate said he believed that the brothers were seeking political asylum in Zimbabwe, that Ronnie had seriously interfered with Captain Prinsloo's questioning of the two burnt men and that he had hidden in a cupboard to avoid being arrested.

The case was postponed until 29 August and the three brothers were taken to North End Prison, known as 'Rooi Hel' (Red Hell).

9

INSIDE RED HELL

At the time the brothers were admitted to 'Rooi Hel' Prison there were thirty white prisoners and almost 3000 blacks. The Watsons realised they were being taken there so that in the eyes of the white community of Port Elizabeth they would be criminalised.

When they arrived at the prison, which is a stark, dull-red stone building, which could, if it had windows, have a fine view of the sea, the brothers were taken through some huge wooden doors and marched down a long corridor as gate after gate closed behind them. Their fingerprints were taken and they were told to undress so they could be checked for distinctive body markings. After this they were told that as 'awaiting trial' prisoners they could put their own clothes back on.

The lower floor of the prison was primitive and squalid and because summer was approaching, it was also fiercely hot. The sergeant recognised Ronnie and told him, not unpleasantly, that he had once played rugby against him.

What happened next was as much of a shock to the Watsons as it was to their four white warders.

In order to get to the top floor where white prisoners were held, the Watsons were marched up past three levels of black prison cells. Suddenly a black prisoner recognised them and shouted out, 'Viva, Viva ANC! Viva Cheeky! Viva Comrades!'

His cellmates jumped up from their beds on the floor and raced to the bars. Black power fists sprouted from other cells and voices shouted, 'Cheeky! Cheeky! Viva Watsons!'

The whole floor suddenly came alive. The shouting became thunderous. 'Viva Mandela! Viva Umkhonto we Sizwe! Long Live the Spirit of No Compromise!' as thousands of prisoners on all levels joined in. The Watsons raised their fists and shouted 'Viva! Viva!' in reply as they were marched past. The faces of the warders were white with anger but they could do nothing but prod their prisoners to go faster.

Then the black prisoners began to sing an ANC liberation song, 'Si'khokele, Si'khokele Tambo' ('Lead us, Lead us, Tambo'). As they sang they stamped their feet in rhythm, a sound that seemed to rock the prison to its foundations. They sang other protest songs and danced the Toyi Toyi. The warders on either side of the Watsons looked frightened as the noise swelled to an enormous echoing frenzy.

The Watson brothers looked at each other, stunned and deeply moved.

On the top floor the prison commandant awaited the new white prisoners. The tumult below had not pleased him. With a stony face he introduced them to the sergeant in charge of the white floor who told them that prison was a place of punishment so they needn't expect an easy time.

'There was a sense of absolute antagonism towards us,' Valence said. 'They said the bare minimum to us.'[1]

As they were pushed into a crowded cell one prisoner told them that there were three murderers amongst their cellmates.

They had tried to hang a man in this cell the week before, the prisoner continued, but the guards had cut him down just in time. He warned the brothers not to all go to sleep at the same time.

It was late and most of the other prisoners were asleep. The Watsons had to share one thin, dirty mattress on the floor near the lavatory bowl.

Valence recalls that later that night another prisoner, a boy of twenty, woke up and asked, 'Who did you say you guys were?' One of the prisoners said, 'This is Cheeky Watson', and he said in amazement, 'Are you Cheeky Watson?' His face just beamed and he said, 'I can say I was in prison with Cheeky Watson!' This was the biggest thing in his life. He'd spent all his life in orphanages, reformatories and prisons. Nothing else.

'Another of the guys had made himself a sandwich. It was a bit dirty, but he came up and offered it to us as something to eat. After that most of the other prisoners were very warm to us.

'Very quickly these guys realised that we were in prison on trumped-up charges,' Valence said. 'They'd been fed a diet of stories that the Watsons were ANC terrorists and had sold out the white race, but as they mixed with us and ate with us they realised that we had not sold out any cause but were trying to make a positive difference, and their attitude towards us changed.'[2]

After a few days the warders noticed that the three Watsons were getting on extremely well with their criminal cellmates. The usual fighting had stopped. There was laughter and joking and some of the prisoners were even joining the Watsons in singing hymns and praying! But there were still a number of prisoners in the cell who were suspicious and hostile towards the brothers.

One warder took Ronnie aside and asked him to do the authorities a favour.

'He said, "Look, one of the guys in this cell has been trying to commit suicide. We don't want that on our records. Why don't you guys look after him? Put him in your prayer meetings. Sing songs with him." So we did. Soon the guy was laughing and joking and there was no more fighting.'[3]

'Eventually we got the worst offenders playing volleyball with us,' Valence said. 'On our team was the mass murderer who killed his wife and kids, and the guy who had wanted to die.

'Later we organised a hunger strike to protest about the food, which was mostly porridge full of weevils, and when we pulled it off we also demanded a twenty-first birthday cake for the guy who had wanted to die. He got it too!'[4]

The Watsons were also on a hunger strike over the lack of exercise they were allowed. Except for half an hour a day, when the thirty prisoners were allowed into a small courtyard, they were confined to the crowded cell. 'In that courtyard you couldn't run. You could only do a couple of pushups or pullups on the bars,' said Valence. 'But after the hunger strike they gave us volleyball.'[5]

The brothers were allowed visitors for half an hour twice a week. Eileen described the cubicles in which visitors had to sit as 'like phone booths, but with very thick glass between you and the prisoner, so you had to shout to be heard. If there was anything I wanted to tell Valence that I didn't want anyone else to hear, I'd write it very small on a tiny piece of paper and then eat the paper so it wasn't discovered by the guards. The things I wrote were political news or details that were worrying us about the forthcoming court case. It was frustrating not being able to tell Valence much about what was happening to me and the kids but I didn't want to upset him.'[6]

Three days after the brothers were taken to prison Eileen had gone out and found a job through a friend. She was working as a personal assistant to the marketing manager of a pharmaceutical company. 'I had to pay the rent and keep a car. Otherwise we had no transport,' she explained.[7]

Tracey had moved in with her parents to save on rent, had given up her car and taken a part-time waitressing job.

Leigh Ann also took a part-time job as a waitress and started doing an MBA by correspondence at Stellenbosch University.

Bobbi, who was then sixty-five, went back to nursing. 'She used to leave for work at five in the morning and not be home until seven in the evening,' Eileen said.[8]

'It was necessary. We had no income whatsoever,' said Bobbi quietly. 'I worked for four or five years after the boys went to prison.'[9]

'She has letters and cards asking her to come back to that job to this day,' Tracey said proudly.[10]

Bobbi Watson was so traumatised by her sons' imprisonment and the court cases which stretched over many long months that her hair fell out. 'I was completely bald,' she confessed shyly. 'I had to wear a wig. The hair took eight years to grow back.'[11]

In her job Eileen discovered that she was the subject of malicious gossip. 'The people at work were very right wing. They avoided the issue of my husband being in jail, but they would continually start talking about "kaffirs" in front of me.

One day a woman turned to me and laughed. She said, "Your husband must think very little of you and your children. He obviously doesn't love you if he's brought this upon you." I would often get into arguments with this woman, which was upsetting to me. After a while I decided to just keep quiet.'[12]

At school the Watson children had unpleasant experiences. 'I remember taking the kids to school just after the boys went to prison and people just staring and staying away from me. One child said to Daniel, who was four, "Your father burnt his house down."' Eileen said. 'But then, gradually, people you would least expect to support us came forward. A pensioner sent us 100 rand. And a student asked if he could help us. An elderly lady stopped me in the street and said, "I want you to know something. You've nothing to be ashamed of." Then one friend took me out for supper, another, Nitza Levin, phoned me every third day and gave me furniture for the flat and presents for the children at Christmas. But my parents were still very scared for me.'[13]

Tracey said, 'Very few people were kind to us. No one phoned me. My parents went overseas. It didn't worry me being on my own. But none of Cheeky's black friends came to visit me. They were too scared as our movements were scrutinised by the police all the time.'[14]

Gavin and Leon Schubart met frequently to discuss the court case. Schubart is about the same age as the Watsons, intelligent, pleasant and unassuming. At first Schubart did not think the Watson brothers trusted him. 'Gavin was fairly paranoid and Ronnie was very intense. I got on best with Cheeky and Valence,' he told me. 'The Watson brothers were well known from sport. They were interesting, strong personalities. Those who knew them at school said that they were real thugs, so a lot of people wouldn't have liked them.

'They are a close-knit family who stick together really well. They kept very much to themselves. They don't socialise, don't drink; they are very insular. They socialised with the blacks. So the white community generally was not sympathetic to them and initially believed they did burn their house down. The newspapers were probably inaccurate. During the State of Emergency the press was vetted and gave the wrong impression of the Watsons.

'I believe that the police did criminalise the Watsons. I had the feeling that this trial was set up to convict them.'[15]

On one occasion Leon Schubart and Gavin met to discuss what to do about Archie Mkele. Schubart told Gavin that he was afraid his office may be bugged, so it was safer to walk in the park. Schubart said that both Mkele and Nocanda were being called as State witnesses to testify against the three Watson brothers. The State was claiming that the brothers had ordered them to burn the house and that Mkele and Nocanda would testify to this, he said.

Gavin could not believe that this would happen, even if the two men had been tortured. He said, 'They're like brothers to us,' but Schubart advised him to expect the worst.[16]

Schubart did not believe the imprisoned brothers would get a hearing until December or January. Because they were bankrupt their case was being paid for mainly from funds donated from outside South Africa. They had a few supporters, who had read about them in articles published in the United States and Australia.

The Watsons' only media support inside South Africa came from Jayne La Monte who wrote for the *Eastern Province Herald* and their old friend Mono Badela, now a journalist with *City Press* in Johannesburg. But even Badela found it difficult to publish positive articles about the Watsons.

Sometimes he had to rely on foreign newspapers to publish his comments. When Badela was asked by the Australian newspaper the *Times on Sunday* whether he thought the Watsons' lives were in danger, he said:

> *The Watsons have associated themselves with the struggle to change this country for 10 years. Of course they are in danger.*
>
> *I would say that 99 per cent of whites are against them because they rejected white Rugby. Rugby is a religion here. The Watsons could have been national heroes if they'd continued to play it.*[17]

Meanwhile the media in South Africa was depicting the Watsons as criminals. As reported in the *Times on Sunday*, a headline in the *East Cape Evening Post* read that 'Watson was sitting like bat in cupboard'. The article, which described Ronnie Watson hidden in a cupboard when police came to arrest him at 5 a.m., implied the brothers were trying to escape.

> *'In fact, Ronnie was looking for his sandshoes in the wardrobe,' Gavin Watson said. 'When he heard the police he assumed they had come to warn us that our stores had been broken into and he was dressing as quickly as possible.'*[18]

Another local headline reading 'Let Me Stay in Custody – Watson Witness' told how the Watsons' black friend Archie Mkele was in fear of his life from the Watsons because he had decided to testify that they burnt down their own house.[19]

Mkele had managed to smuggle letters out of prison, describing how he was being tortured to force him to make false statements.

The letters were written on toilet paper and passed on by a black prison worker to Archie's wife, Carol. Archie said in the letters that in spite of the torture he refused to inform on the Watsons because they were innocent.

The *Evening Post* published an article headed 'I'd Rather Hang Than Testify'. Although several attorneys believed the notes to be genuine, they were described as being only 'allegedly' written by Archie Mkele.[20]

In another paper Archie's claim that he was being tortured was discounted when the respondents 'submitted affidavits from three magistrates, three doctors, an independent attorney and a number of policemen, all of whom had seen or treated Mr Mkele and found nothing untoward.' The urgent application to seek access to Mkele in prison was dismissed.[21]

At the time the Australian newspaper *Times on Sunday* reported:

> *The letters were apparently disregarded by Judge Eksteen, who refused the Watsons bail. He has also refused permission for Archie Mkele to see his wife, who fears he will die if the torture continues.*
>
> *Leon Schubart, the Watsons' lawyer, said a lot of people in the white community believed, even before the trial, that the Watsons were guilty.*
>
> *Rory Liesching, a Port Elizabeth lawyer who is not associated with the case, said that although many in the legal fraternity were shocked at the judge's decision, more than half were 'not at all unhappy about the Watsons being refused bail'.*
>
> *'South African people are very conservative,' he told the* Times

The Watsons on the farm at Kommadagga. From left to right: Dan, Valence, Cheeky, Gavin, Benny (in hat, Dan's son from his first marriage), Ronnie, 1955.

Cheeky (13), Ronnie (17), Benny, Valence (15) and Sharon (7), at the farm at Alicedale, 1967.

Cheeky (holding ball), captain of Graeme College rugby team, 1972.

Gavin, Archie and a friend conduct 'Township Business', Port Elizabeth, 1992.

Veterans rugby practice, Walmer township, Port Elizabeth, 1993. Valence and Cheeky in the centre.

Political rally, Cheeky and Ronnie in the centre, at Dan Qeqe Stadium, Kwazakele, 1992.

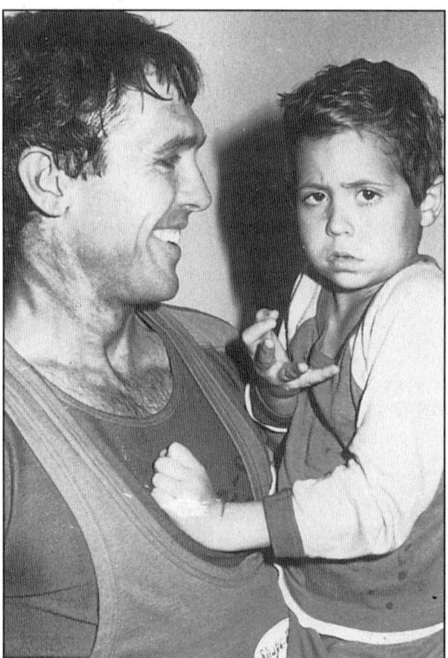

Valence and Eileen's wedding day, 23 June 1979. Left to right: Cheeky Watson, Zolain Sobikwa, Chantal Watson (Cheeky's daughter), Feya Sobikwa. (Photo by D. C. H. Andrews.)

Gavin and Nkosi after the fire destroyed his room in the flat, September 1986. Nkosi is holding up his burnt finger. (Photo by *Eastern Province Herald*.)

The remains of 34 Park Drive, Port Elizabeth, after the fire, October 1985. (Photo by Jeremy D. Acton.)

Carol and Archie Mkele, Port Elizabeth, May 1995.

Crowd outside court on the day the Watsons were released on bail after six months in prison, January 1987. (Photo by Colin Urquhart, *Weekend Post*.)

Three of the Watson brothers, Ronnie, Cheeky and Valence, lifted shoulder high after being released on bail, outside the Port Elizabeth Magistrates' Court, January 1987.

Ronnie Watson and Archie Mkele outside court, after Valence had been convicted of arson and fraud, 31 January 1987. (Photo by Colin Urquhart, *Weekend Post.*)

Cheeky leaving court, 'with mixed feelings', after he and Ronnie were freed and Valence was convicted, 31 January 1987. (Photo by Colin Urquhart, *Weekend Post.*)

The day of release on bail. Left to right: Cheeky, Daniel, Ronnie, Bobbi, and Valence reunited. (Photo by Colin Urquhart, *Weekend Post*.)

The day before sentence was passed on the three brothers, 30 January 1987. Left to right: Leigh Ann, Gavin, Eileen, Valence, Glenda, Ronnie, Tracey, Cheeky. 'Togetherness of the Watson family was an outstanding feature of the trial', noted the local press.

on Sunday. *'They regard the Watsons as extremely left-wing and anti-Government. They are not particularly interested in whether they burnt down their house or not but, at the bail hearing, they were very interested in allegations that Valence and Ronnie had sought political asylum in another country.'*

Gavin Watson said, 'When Valence and Ronnie visited Zimbabwe a few months ago they could have stayed in the country then if they had wanted political asylum.' He is adamant he and his brothers want to stay in South Africa to fight against apartheid.[22]

The letters smuggled out of prison by Archie Mkele were passed on to the *Times on Sunday* in late September 1986 and published in an article headed 'Letters from a tortured prisoner'. Here is an extract:

Written on what appears to be toilet paper, they [the letters] are signed by Archie Mkele, black friend and rugby teammate of the four white anti-apartheid Watson brothers of Port Elizabeth.

Mkele was arrested under a state of emergency on June 10 and has since been in solitary confinement. His letters describe how he has been tortured to force him to testify against the Watson brothers . . . he claims the statements he made incriminating the Watsons and asking to remain in protective custody because he was afraid they would kill him are false. He says he was also forced to say he wanted nothing to do with any lawyer.

In one letter, Mkele says, 'They tortured me from 7.30 a.m. to 2.30 p.m . . . I'm not prepared to testify against the Watsons . . . I went twice to the doctor because I was assaulted . . . I fear for my life. Since they arrested me they keep me alone in a cell. The reason

I don't know. Please help me out . . . I love the Watsons. I am crying tears in jail because of what has happened to them.'

On the toilet paper, a photograph of which was reproduced in the article, Archie described how one torturer tried to get him to change his mind about the Watsons.

'He said to me, "Remember you are alone here today. The Watsons that are protecting you are not here to help today. We know that the Watsons have been using you all these years. Now it is our chance to use you against them as their great friend." He set on something that sounded like an aeroplane. It made a hell of a noise that I thought I was going crazy. I started sweating and shivering my body was full of perspiration. This lasted for about half an hour before it was switched off. Then he said Archie, it's you and us today. He tied both my legs as my hands were already tied behind my back. He kicked me at my back, punched me in my stomach, hit me with the baton on my body and shoulders. He took water and poured it all over my head and face . . .'

The article continued:

A donation of $15,000 from the US towards the Watsons' defence fund has been given to Mkele's wife, Carol, to help pay for Mkele's Supreme Court trial.

'We gave the $15,000 to Archie's wife because the head of police in this region told her not to proceed with his case because she would not have the funds to do it,' said Gavin Watson, the only brother not in jail.

'She will not be intimidated. She wants to expose all the torturing that occurs in the prison which forces people to make false statements.

'We are afraid the system will draw out the trial and drain all our resources.'[23]

The three brothers had now been in prison for a month. They were aware that three of those who shared their cell were Security police posing as prisoners. They had to be extremely careful what they said to each other. Although they had all lost weight the Watsons were not being mistreated.

But at home, things were not so easy. Now that all three wives were working, there were nine children under the age of five to be looked after. The three young black women who minded the children were on their way to work one morning when they were picked up by police and taken to Louis Le Grange Police Station for questioning.

'I got a phone call from them saying, "Please do something. We're scared",' Gavin said. 'I got an attorney to phone the police station and he was told no women had been arrested that day. The police moved the women to Kabega Police Station and continued interrogating them. The women phoned me again. My attorney was told they were not there. Then they were moved to Walmer Police Station. At 6 p.m., after thoroughly disorienting and intimidating them, the police dropped the women back here. That kind of harassment is supposed to break us.'[24]

But more serious harassment was to come. One evening most of the Watson family were in the upstairs flat when a fire broke out in the bedroom where Nkosi, Eileen's eldest son, was asleep. It spread very quickly through the flat. The corridor filled with smoke. Suddenly Eileen sprang up, screamed and tried to get down the corridor towards the bedroom, but was driven back by the heat and flames. Flames were licking the bedroom door where Nkosi lay sleeping. She ran downstairs to get Gavin, who put a wet towel over his head, burst the door open and looked desperately for the child. Nkosi was nowhere to be seen. In the bedroom, the cupboards, the ceiling, even the carpet, were now in flames. Eileen was distraught. Suddenly Nkosi was standing beside her, holding up his mildly burnt hand. He said, 'The fire made me hot so I got up.' Eileen shrieked with relief and then burst into tears.[25]

Later Gavin told the press,

> *'It's a miracle Valence's son is still alive. We were told it [the fire] could have been caused by an electrical fault but we discovered that the lock of the flat had been tampered with. It is very peculiar.'*[26]

Next morning the prison commandant passed a newspaper into the Watsons' cell with front page news of the fire that had almost killed Valence's son. There was a picture of Gavin holding the boy. Valence recalls, 'He sort of laughed, and said, "Do you recognise these people?" He had the paper under his arm and he came across to me, and that's the first I knew of it. I thought my son had been roasted in his bed.'[27]

Valence, who was already depressed, was now really angry.

Eileen decided to try and cheer him up by bringing their youngest child, Jared, to visit him in prison.

'Jared was just over a year old and he'd started to walk. The prison was ugly and scary, so we'd decided not to bring the older children, but Jared was very young so Tracey, Leigh Ann and I thought it wouldn't affect him. I asked the warden for permission to bring him, and Tracey came with me so that if Jared became irritable or started crying she could take him out and I could still talk to Valence. We saw the boys coming and I stood Jared up on a little ledge and told him to hold on to the bars. This was to be the great moment. I said, "There's Daddy!" And Jared looked at Valence and then sort of withdrew. I knew he recognised him but he didn't want Valence to touch him. Valence said, "Look, it doesn't work. Please . . ." And everybody's mouths just dropped and we all felt so deflated. Tracey took Jared out. The visit was a total disaster. I wanted to cry. Valence looked so upset and Cheeky and Ronnie too.'[28]

'I said to Eileen, "Please don't bring him here again,"' Valence said.[29]

Meanwhile, Archie's wife Carol, who was pregnant, had been told by Security that she could see her husband if she agreed to persuade him that he must cooperate with the State. If she did this, they promised, she could give birth to her child in a white hospital and she would be looked after financially until Archie's release from prison. 'They said they would set me up with a house and a car and 30 000 rand', said Carol. She refused the offer. Next they showed Carol an affidavit supposedly from Archie, saying that he didn't want to see her any more because she was part of a plot to kill him. Although she was being followed by Security, Carol managed to secretly meet Gavin and let him know about this.

'Gavin was supportive to me, even though he had three brothers in prison,' she said. 'I told him that the station commander would try and get me to say things against the Watsons. He would say, "I am going to make the Watsons crawl lower than a snake's belly." One time, after I'd been called into his office, I got halfway home and my car started to swerve. I found that all the wheel nuts were loosened in the car.'[30]

Carol sometimes met with Eileen and Tracey, who tried to comfort her. They at least were able to visit their husbands in prison, but Carol had not seen Archie for months. 'It was a very stressful time,' Carol said.

Carol took out a court injunction asking that she be allowed to see her husband, that the torture be stopped and that he be allowed to appear in court to confirm that he was being kept in custody at his own request as a protected witness. Her request was denied. 'I only found out where Archie was being held after seven months. A cook at the prison, Rosie, phoned me and said, "Your husband is here." She met me in a cafe. I would go there as if I was a customer and she would pass me a note.'[31]

Eventually Carol was told by a Security officer named Fourie that she could see Archie if she influenced him to turn against the Watsons. Carol agreed, although she had no intention of trying to influence Archie. 'Before Archie saw me he was allowed to get stronger, not to be starved or beaten, so I would believe he was safe,' Carol said.[32]

'She would put coded messages in my shirt collars to let me know what was really going on,' Archie said.[33]

'On the car journey to the prison Fourie would pretend to me that he was a friend and I would play along with it,' Carol said. She was at that time seven months pregnant and had another child aged five at home. 'Fourie would ask me to work on Archie. He'd say, "Wouldn't you like to be with him?" Later they would telephone me and say they wanted to give me one last chance. I'd say, "You're wasting your time and mine."

Then Fourie said I would have to take the consequences. I said, "Fine". I was working at the Pick and Pay at the time and as a maid for some Dutch people. They couldn't understand how we still associated with the Watsons. But I had strong feelings for them.'[34]

In the meantime the Watson brothers were making such an impression on their fellow prisoners that it was picked up by the local media. The *Eastern Province Herald* ran a front-page story headed, 'Many "converted" in Watsons' behind bars crusade'. It began,

> *The Watson brothers have acquired a nickname in the austere North End Prison where they have been held since their arrest almost two months ago.*
>
> *'The Boys who sing to God' is how fellow awaiting trial prisoners – many of whom claim to have been converted by them – describe the trio who have been holding nightly prayer sessions behind bars . . .*
>
> *The Watson family are all devout Christians and friends said this week that being in jail had served to strengthen the brothers' beliefs . . .*
>
> *The meetings usually last more than an hour with the time being spent reading from the Bible, singing hymns, praying and discussing the meaning of Christianity.*
>
> *Even outside the prison walls, the story of the 'work being done by the Boys Who Sing to God' has spread.*
>
> *Their 'converts' are understood to include two Eastern Cape men who are awaiting trial on several charges of murder and are now fervent participants in the prayer sessions.*
>
> *Mr Tony Fowler, an awaiting trial prisoner who shared a*

communal cell with the brothers until two weeks ago, is one of the people who say they were converted.

'Meeting them really helped me. I was a lost soul before I listened to what the Watsons were saying about God and his love . . .

'At first I didn't get involved in the prayer meetings, but after a while I started listening and what they said really made sense.

'They were always so cheerful – especially Cheeky . . . You can't imagine what it meant to me to meet people like them and have my life changed by finding God.'[35]

Some of the warders were grateful to the Watsons for making the other prisoners easier to handle. But others were resentful of the brothers' power and popularity. The senior prison officers, who were losing credibility amongst the warders who supported the Watsons, became more militant.

All three brothers had lost a lot of weight in prison. The food, in spite of their protests, was still extremely bad.

'I'd lost twenty kilos', said Ronnie. 'In the morning we'd have porridge and some vile-tasting coffee, which was the best meal of the day. At lunchtime we'd have two poor slices of bread with white margarine and a cup of watered-down drink. At night there would be a bit of fish or stewed meat, which was also vile, and what they called 'dehydrates' – vegetables thrown into a big pot of water. The maggots would rise to the top and then be scooped off, according to one prisoner who worked in the kitchen. There was never any fresh fruit or vegetables. So we decided to organise a hunger strike.'[36]

Thirty prisoners began the hunger strike, but only six, including the three Watsons, finished. It lasted nine days.

The prison authorities tried various methods to put a stop to the strike. First they brought in a district surgeon who tried to talk the prisoners out of it. 'As soon as we recognised him as the doctor who had tried to hide the facts of Steve Biko's death we just chased him out of the cell,' said Valence. 'I reminded him of Biko's death and said, "Who are you to talk to us? You're rubbish!" Next they moved us into smaller cells, crammed us up and took all our medication away to make us more uncomfortable. When this didn't stop the strike, they separated us so we didn't have a common bonding. And they left our food in the cells overnight so it stank in the heat.'[37]

When the authorities realised that the remaining strikers were not going to stop fasting they gave in. The strike was successful. The food improved and exercise was permitted.

Prison food was still not exactly plentiful and one visiting day Tracey managed to smuggle two small cans of ravioli to Cheeky, hidden amongst his clean shirts. In the cell that night he held the cans aloft and his cellmates cheered. They set about making a large, tight ball of shredded toilet paper, which they then set fire to. The cans were opened, emptied onto a tin plate and held over the flame. As the delicious aroma of sizzling ravioli wafted to other cells, prisoners began yelling out. The ravioli was shared amongst all in the cell. Next morning a warder appeared and ordered Cheeky to come to him. When he was out of earshot of the other prisoners, the warder grinned and said, 'Smelt good.'

Some weeks later the same warder appeared and commanded Cheeky to go with him. As he was marched down the corridor, Cheeky feared the worst. He was thrust into the warder's office. There on the table was a large plate of steak, chips and eggs. 'Prisoner Watson, sit down,' commanded the warder. Cheeky hesitated, although he was already salivating. 'Don't worry, it's not poisoned,' said the warder kindly, and then, more aggressively, 'It is my duty to warn you that any further attempts to smuggle food into this prison will be severely dealt with. Do you understand?' Cheeky, already devouring the delicious meal, grinned and said that he did.[38]

'The prison warders became very supportive of us,' said Valence. 'Previously they'd been influenced by the media and government propaganda which was very anti-us but in person they found we were different.'[39]

The hunger strike for white prisoners, organised by the Watsons, succeeded. But one that black prisoners tried to organise ended in bitter defeat. Cheeky said:

> *The warders teargassed these guys who had locked themselves in a cell and sent dogs in on them and really beat them up. They then put these guys into single cells, and when they came out they walked with dragging feet. They wouldn't let us speak to the blacks in Xhosa, only English or Afrikaans. There you get hardened criminals in with others, and guys got sodomised and even killed.*[40]

Ronnie said:

> *I saw from the second floor, during this episode, warders holding prisoners down and pushing the guys' legs apart. They were screaming with pain, and on speaking to these prisoners later, they told us that the warders had forced their fingers up their rectums. Grown-up men were screaming. Men's bodies were violated like that.*[41]

The Watsons' trial began on 14 October 1986. They were charged with fraud, arson and the attempted murder of Archie Mkele and Jeffrey Nocanda, by instructing them to set fire to the family home in such a manner that they would be trapped inside the house and killed by the fire.

Leon Schubart, who had not expected the charge of attempted murder to be included, was granted a two week postponement. It was disconcerting for the Watsons to have to return to prison but they remained calm. Schubart said, 'In prison they were very strong and positive throughout. They felt that prison had been an enrichment in retrospect. In court they were model "accused"'.[42]

Jules Browde was the Watsons' defence advocate and senior counsel. He said he felt that theirs was a political trial, not a criminal one. 'The Watsons were not popular amongst whites in the Eastern Cape. Cheeky had been going to play rugby for South Africa, but when he played in the black townships, Danie Craven put an end to his white rugby. The Watsons were making inroads into the gap between black and white and the government resented this.

'When I saw the terrible conditions of the Watsons in jail I said I wasn't prepared to talk to them unless their conditions were improved. I told the police I was going to the newspapers. They were handcuffed to each other! It was unprecedented. They were refused bail, which was an astounding decision. There are two reasons why you don't get bail – you might not be there for the trial and you might intimidate witnesses. The witnesses were in jail. This was just a way of intimidating the Watsons.'[43]

On 22 October, the day the trial began, the court was unusually crowded. Supporters had gathered to give the Watsons a warm welcome. As the public gallery began filling up, the South African Police video crew began filming the arrivals, which was unnerving to some. They also filmed the brothers' reunion with their wives. The case was again postponed, this time until until 1 December. Police were brusque with well-wishers, who crowded around the Watsons afterwards, and threatened one black friend with arrest if he did not 'get moving'.[44]

The wives found the delay of the case particularly disappointing. They had hoped that 'the boys' might be out of prison by Christmas, but now it seemed impossible. 'I would like to say that during that whole Christmas season people stuck by me, but in fact, they didn't,' Eileen said. 'I spent a lot of that period crying at home. I never went out. I stayed home night after night. I wasn't included in activities with friends we'd seen a lot of. I did feel bitter. Valence's mum was my main support; she was fantastic.'[45]

In spite of their unhappiness the Watsons' wives appeared on the first day of the trial looking well groomed, confident and cheerful.

Daniel Watson Senior insisted on being at the trial too, although, because of his recent stroke, his doctor had said he should not go. Defiantly he appeared in his best suit, leaning on a cane.

Ronnie's estranged wife Glenda was also there. And Gavin, of course.

As they approached the courthouse they saw a huge crowd of black people outside. The family was cheered and applauded. They held their heads high and smiled as television cameras rolled and press photographers flashed.

Security photographers with telescopic lenses took photo after photo of individuals in the black crowd.

Inside the courtroom the usher called the three defendants.

When Valence, Cheeky and Ronnie appeared, almost everyone in the court, packed with black onlookers, rose and cheered. The magistrate banged his gavel and called for order. Representing the State was Mr Van der Walt, a small man with a moustache, the same prosecutor who had refused the Watsons bail.

Jules Browde, on behalf of the defence, rose looking impeccable, and denied the allegations of arson and fraud.

At this point the brothers were disturbed to notice that Gideon Niewouldt, a notorious Security officer, had just entered the court. (He would later be found guilty of murdering fellow Security policemen and police informers.) Niewouldt was escorting the first witness, Jeffrey Nocanda, who had been in prison for months. Niewouldt gave the magistrate a cold, implacable stare. The magistrate began fidgeting. He drank a glass of water. It was obvious he found the Security officer's presence unsettling.[46]

'Niewouldt's presence made it clear to us that this trial was being interpreted as an attack against the State,' said Valence. 'Jules Browde questioned his presence. He said, "Who is that gentleman? What is he doing in court?"'[47]

Cheeky said, 'A chair was brought in specifically for Niewouldt. I said to Valence when I saw Jeffrey walk in that something was wrong. Jeffrey's a thin fellow and he had put on weight. He looked directly at me only once, when Jules Browde said, "I want the court to note that you have not looked at the accused once." Jeffrey was looking at Niewouldt and the magistrate. Nobody else.'[48]

Gavin also noticed the affect that Niewouldt had on the magistrate and felt sure he was there to make sure the magistrate exercised his powers appropriately.[49]

A witness, Johan Oliver, described in Afrikaans how he had seen the flames from the Watsons' house at 34 Park Drive on 19 October 1985, and then had seen two figures running away from the house towards the valley behind it.

Another witness, Dr Klatzow, a forensic scientist and a member of the International Association of Arson Investigators, said that he believed the blaze was caused, not by an explosive device, but by some liquid accelerant such as petrol.

Browde said, 'Now it was no secret that that was the view of the police. Do you accept that?'

Klatzow said that he did.[50]

Valence Watson had suspected that an explosive device might have been installed on the first floor of the house, so that it would not leave a crater which would identify it as a bomb. This device could have been used in conjunction with petrol.

On the second day of the trial when Jeffrey Nocanda was led into the courtroom towards the witness box, his head was bowed and his eyes were downcast. He would not look at anyone.

Ronnie looked at Valence and Cheeky, then the three of them looked anxiously back at Gavin and their wives.

Colonel Niewouldt, the Security officer, was watching Jeffrey intensely. 'He seemed to be mesmerising Jeffrey like a snake does to a bird,' Gavin Watson recalls.[51]

The court was shocked when Jeffrey, under cross-examination from Van der Walt, confessed that he and Archie had been instructed to set fire to the Watsons' house.

'Our attorney, Jules Browde, ripped his statement apart and Jeffrey just broke down and said the police had been torturing him for three days so he would say whatever they wanted him to,' Gavin said.[52]

There was a dramatic hush in the court as Nokanda

confessed, 'I admitted that I had burnt the house to the person who was torturing me.'

Jules Browde asked, 'How many days were you tortured?'

'I was tortured for three days; on the first, and then they skipped the second day and the third and the fourth.'

'So you were tortured on three days?'

'Yes.'[53]

Jeffrey then described how a wet sack was placed over his head until he almost suffocated and how he was kicked in the stomach and hit on the back while his hands and feet were tied. He said he was told the police had the power to do with him whatever they wanted.

Jeffrey had written a letter to his girlfriend, Nola, from jail, telling her he loved the Watsons, who were innocent, and he would not testify against them. Nola had given this crucial letter to Leon Schubart, but a few days earlier his briefcase containing the letter had gone missing at the airport. 'When the briefcase was found, the letter was missing,' Schubart said.[54]

'Knowing that the evidence had disappeared, Jeffrey denied ever having written such a letter,' Valence said. 'But Jules Browde said to him, "I'd like you to look at the accused. Now, Nola, stand up. Is that Nola?" He answered yes. "Do you love her?" Again he said yes. "Would you lie to her?" "No." "Did you write a letter to Nola?" "Yes, I did." Van der Walt nearly burst when Jeffrey said that. I didn't know what was coming myself,' Valence said.[55]

It emerged that it was only after Security police had shown Jeffrey 'exhibits', such as a petrol can, gloves and clothing that had his fingerprints on them, and had told him these proved he was guilty, and then continued to torture him, that he had agreed to testify.

Jeffrey said it was Captain Prinsloo who was in charge of the case and he had shown him the exhibits.

Almost ten years later, when questions about the case were put to the prosecutor, Henning Van der Walt, he was asked whether torture was part of the legal system in South Africa at that time. He said, 'Torture was never condoned by the legal system.'

'But despite the fact that Jeffrey Nocanda claimed he was tortured, his evidence was accepted as truthful. Did you feel at all uneasy about the legal system you were in?'

'There were certain laws that were not exemplary. Bad laws have been passed at all times in history. I am not prepared to tell you whether I personally had a problem with these laws, or with my role as prosecutor under these laws. The Watsons trial was not political.'

'But the Watsons' bail was refused on political grounds.'

'I can't remember the reasons why bail was refused. I didn't know anything about the Watsons.'

'But you knew that they had pioneered non-racial rugby? It was big news.'

'What newspapers write about anyone is something I'm not concerned about.'

'Were you happy working under the apartheid system?'

'I'm not prepared to discuss my personal feelings.'[56]

An indemnity was granted for Jeffrey Nocanda and he was free to go.

The court was adjourned for the Christmas recess. It would resume on 14 January. The Watson brothers were taken back to prison.

10

'A DISGUSTING TRIAL'

Christmas was not very festive for the Watson family in 1986. Gavin, the only brother not in prison, tried to play Santa Claus to his brothers' seven children, but it was a lonely time for them all. They had almost no money for food, let alone presents.

On Christmas Day Tracey decided that the wives had to do something to let their husbands know they were thinking of them. 'Why don't we go and wish them a happy Christmas?' she said. Eileen and Tracey jumped into the battered Mercedes, the only remnant of the affluent old days, and drove out to Red Hell Prison. Parking as close as possible to the cell where they knew their husbands were, they tooted the car horn and turned the radio up as loud as it would go, playing cheerful pop songs. Sadly, their husbands did not hear it.

Archie Mkele was still being held as a State witness. He had yet to testify and Security hoped to use him to help get a conviction against the Watsons. Archie had been moved to Kenton-on-Sea, a prison about two hours drive from Port Elizabeth. His wife, Carol, now heavily pregnant, was granted permission to visit him, but she had to agree to be driven there by Security and only to speak to Archie in the presence of a Security policeman. During the long drive Security police would subtly interrogate her, trying to persuade her to get Archie to change his mind and testify. They also tried hard to find out anything they could about the Watsons. Although Carol was seriously short of money and had a young daughter to support, she was never tempted to cooperate with the Security police. 'I had a big hatred for these people who were trying to wreck my life,' Carol said. 'They would offer to buy me anything on the way to that prison.'

Carol said she believed in the work Archie was doing for the ANC and had no intention of betraying him. 'I had always suspected Archie was doing deep underground work for the ANC. Even when we first met he would say he was going to church meetings and he wasn't. Sometimes I'd find ANC literature, but I wasn't worried.'[1]

When Security discovered that neither solitary confinement nor torture could break Archie's resolve to stand by the Watsons, they tried bribery. He was taken out of his isolated cell at the far end of Kenton-on-Sea prison and the prosecutor offered him 50 000 rand. 'That got him as mad as a snake,' Valence recalls, 'He threatened the prosecutor, a very tough Security policeman who had done all the ANC cases for the past ten years, shouting, "Get him out of here. I'll kill him!" The cops had to drag Archie back to the cell.'[2]

In the cell two Security policemen faced Archie and gave him an ultimatum. They told him that the trial was resuming next day and this was his last chance to confess to burning the house. If he wanted to do what Jeffrey had done and say he was tortured, he could do so, but he must confess to burning the house.

Archie remained silent. He was manacled and gaunt after weeks of torture, but he spoke with dignity. 'They said that if I wouldn't cooperate with them, I'd go down with the Watsons and go to prison,' Archie said. 'I said, "You can send me to prison or kill me. I'll never be a state witness." I just said it calmly. Niewouldt then said, "You will go to prison for ten years." Then he left.'

The next day Archie was released.

'Fourie drove me to the court and he worked on me until the last minute. I said "No way!" and jumped out of the car. I ran towards the Watsons,' Archie said.[3]

As Cheeky, Ronnie and Valence were led down the corridor towards the courtroom they saw a wild-eyed, crazy-looking, bushy-bearded black man running towards them. The guards instinctively reached for their pistols. Archie brushed the guards aside and embraced the brothers. 'Why have you got these guys in handcuffs? Take them off!' he told the guards. He had tears in his eyes. He seemed on the edge of hysteria. The brothers tried to calm him.

'They couldn't break me!' he exclaimed. 'How could they think of it? We are brothers. Put me on the stand. I'll tell the truth!'

As Archie entered the courtroom he saw something that intensified his anger. The two Security police who had been torturing him were sitting on the crossbench. There was a murmur of excitement from the predominantly black audience when Archie walked purposefully towards them. The Security police looked up and half stood, preparing to take evasive action, but Archie swept past them, deliberately brushing their knees with great force and dumping one of them, Prinsloo, back in his seat. Then he glared at them.

The black audience muttered its shock and approval.[4]

Leigh Ann, Eileen and Tracey, seated in the gallery, exchanged anxious looks. Had Archie gone mad?[5]

Archie plunged on, straight towards the gallery where he pushed his way towards Gavin and the wives. He embraced them all and then sat down. He told Gavin, 'They must have been crazy to think I'd lie. Tell them to put me on the stand!'[6]

As the court waited for the magistrate, Mr Gert Steyn, to enter, Valence, Cheeky and Ronnie were in conference with Jules Browde.

Ronnie was in favour of putting Archie on the stand as first witness, but Browde shook his head.

He protested that Archie was not rational. He'd been six months in detention, he'd been drugged, he was too emotional, Browde said.

Gavin, who had come down from the gallery, was also inclined to let Archie tell the court the truth.

But Browde warned that if Archie went on the stand Van der Walt would try and make his testimony sound like the ravings of a madman. He said he was delighted that Archie had been released, but that there was nothing to be gained by putting him on the stand.

The brothers agreed that Browde was probably right.[7]

On 15 January 1987, the *Evening Post* in Port Elizabeth reported, 'There was a dramatic turn in the Watson case today when the State told the Port Elizabeth Regional Court that it was closing its case and that Mr Archie Mkele, who had been released from protective custody, would be made available to the defence'.[8]

Other local newspapers showed front page pictures of

Archie being given 'a welcome-back kiss from his five-year-old daughter, Melanie'.

'It was very touching because Archie's son was born within days of his being released,' Valence said.[9]

The trial continued without Archie's testimony for the defence. The State had claimed they had 167 witnesses who were willing to give evidence against the Watsons, but without the evidence of their two prime witnesses, Archie Mkele and Jeffrey Nocanda, not much use was made of the others. The Watsons suspected the other witnesses did not exist.

Also, the State admitted that Archie Mkele had not been in 'protective custody'. In his application to the Supreme Court, through his wife Carol, it had been found that he had been forced into custody.

Two unexpected witnesses appeared to give evidence in support of the Watsons. They were both wealthy women who lived in the Fernkloof flats overlooking their house at Park Drive. Mrs Willis-Dickson, a forthright woman of Scottish descent, said she had reported to the police, twenty minutes after the explosion, that she had seen a white panel van driving away from the burning house. She had seen it from the balcony of her penthouse at midnight and had also heard voices shouting, 'They're going. They're going'. The police had apparently kept her evidence secret. When she came forward with this evidence, the court tried to discredit her, asking if she was a friend of the Watsons. She replied, 'Never met them in my life.' When she was asked, 'How do you feel about the Watsons?' she said stoutly, 'I'm indifferent. All I am here to do is tell the truth and see that justice is done.'[10] This evidence would seem hard for the magistrate to ignore, but he did so.

The second woman, Mrs Jarvis, who was elderly and nervous in court, said that she had seen and heard the same things as Mrs Willis-Dickson. The prosecutor asked if she had been out that evening, to which she replied that she had. 'You had a little something to drink?' he inquired. The woman knew at once that he was trying to undermine her, and said, 'No, I don't drink.'[11]

Both women were adamant about what they had seen and neither of them had ever met the Watsons, but the magistrate put their evidence down to 'a reconstruction of events', meaning that they had imagined it.[12]

Leon Schubart was convinced that these women were telling the truth. 'The Fernkloof ladies' evidence showed that there had to be people on the Watsons' premises just before Archie and Jeffrey left,' he said. 'Steyn tried to cast doubt on their evidence. I had the feeling he was trying to convict the Watsons. There was no reason to refuse them bail. During the court hearing I became convinced that they were innocent. I felt that this trial was being set up to convict them.'[13]

Jules Browde had reserved his judgement on the Watsons. 'I had an open mind about them, although when I saw the treatment they received in prison I felt they had been victimised.' But during the court case Browde too became sure the Watsons were innocent. 'I believe it was a police hit squad that finished the house, because the Watsons were seen as a threat to apartheid. I think the hit squad was surprised by the presence of Archie and Jeff, so they had to improvise and tried to do them in.'[14]

The next witness for the defence was a conservative businessman named Arthur Kotzen, who was managing director of a construction company. He admitted that a few months before the fire he had made an offer of 700 000 rand to Ronnie Watson to buy the family house at 34 Park Drive because he wanted to develop the property and build units.

Browde pointed out that as the house was insured for 440 000 rand the Watsons would have been better off to accept Kotzen's offer than to burn down their house for the insurance.

Van der Walt tried to rule Browde out of order, but the point had already been made.

Almost ten years later Kotzen confirmed what he had said in court. 'Our offer of 700 000 rand was absolutely genuine. The Watsons would have made more money by accepting our offer than from the insurance. I don't believe they would have tried to bomb their house. It was a beautiful property. They would have been crazy to bomb it.

'There is no doubt that the offer I made to the Watsons was a serious one. The guy who was backing us, Stuart McDonald, was very well regarded. We bought the land after the house was bombed, which proves our offer was very serious,' Kotzen said. 'I feel 100 per cent sure the Watsons didn't do it. Only about 20 per cent of the community believed they bombed the house.

'The community was very negative towards the Watsons. They didn't believe that playing rugby with the blacks was a Christian act. Right from the beginning it was not seen that way.'[15]

Valence Watson then took the stand and was questioned about what the loss of the house meant to his family. He said his parents had loved it very much, that the rosewood dining-room suite had been a gift from his father to his mother and was irreplaceable, that all the brothers' rugby trophies and photographs had been destroyed, his wife's clothing and jewellery and, worst of all, the photographs and video tapes of the children. Valence said that he had been devastated by the loss of the house and could not believe it.[16]

There was a hush in the court at the emotion and sincerity of Valence's words.

Van der Walt was not happy that Valence had acquitted himself so well and hastened to state that the Watsons' financial difficulties were so grave that they could have burnt down their house for the insurance and still possess the land, worth some 300 000 rand, on which they could have erected units themselves.

Valence replied that as the total was 700 000 rand in either case, why would the family bother performing such a heinous deed as burning their house rather than accepting a cash offer? He said the family had no experience as developers and that no one would have been prepared to lend them money to build units in any case.[17]

The magistrate then asked Jules Browde whether he wished an adjournment to prepare his final statement.

Browde replied, 'No, Your Worship. On the evidence the State has presented, you wouldn't hang a cat.'[18]

There was applause from the courtroom.

As the magistrate prepared to deliver judgement he looked very pale. He seemed extremely nervous. He took a sip of water and glanced sideways at Niewouldt and Van der Walt. With a frown of defiance he began. He said that the State's case hinged on the accomplice Jeffrey Nocanda. If Nocanda had been assaulted, then he could not express his disapproval of the assault in strong enough terms. He expected the allegation to be investigated without delay.

Niewouldt looked angry. The Watsons looked at each other in surprise. Was justice going to be done?

The magistrate said that whether the assault charges were proved or not Jeffrey's evidence still had to be considered. If he was forced to give the evidence he did, then there was reason for him to lie, but if he was scared of his captors and wanted to please them, then why did he tell the court he had been tortured? The reason surely was that he did light the fire, and he wanted his friends the Watsons to know he would never have admitted it unless he had been brutally assaulted. Therefore, the magistrate said, he found the evidence of Jeffrey Nocanda to be truthful.[19]

There was a murmur of disbelief in the courtroom. Archie, sitting next to Gavin, was incensed. The magistrate called for order.

Jules Browde said later that he found it 'completely inexplicable that Jeffrey's testimony under torture was accepted. It was a disgusting trial.'[20]

The magistrate then dealt with the evidence of the financial situation of the Watson brothers. He said he did not doubt that an offer of 700 000 rand had been made for their house by Mr Kotzen, but there was no evidence that this offer had ever been finalised.

The brothers looked outraged.

Next the magistrate dealt with the witnesses, Mrs Willis-Dickson and Mrs Jarvis. He said Mrs Willis-Dickson was certain she had seen a panel van turn out of the driveway just after the explosion. This aspect was important because it was part of the defence case that Archie and Jeffrey were overpowered by masked men. But with the suddenness of the explosion and the fallibility of human observation, he found that, despite the sincerity of both witnesses, no vehicles left the scene.[21]

At this pronouncement the court erupted and again had to be called to order. The Watsons looked shocked.

The magistrate concluded that Valence Watson's guilt was proved accordingly, but he found insufficient evidence to implicate Ronnie and Cheeky. They were allowed to go free.

The court was adjourned. Sentence would be passed on Valence Watson on the following Tuesday. Until then he was free to leave the court with his brothers. Each of them was on bail of 5000 rand. The brothers' passports were then handed to the clerk of the court and they were required to report to Louis Le Grange Police Station twice daily.[22]

Archie bounded towards the brothers and embraced them.

Outside the courtroom the three Watson brothers and Archie Mkele were carried on the shoulders of a huge, cheering black crowd. As they bore their heroes away they danced the Toyi Toyi and shouted 'Viva!' and 'Amandla!' There were about a thousand people in the crowd, many of them trying to kiss or touch the Watsons. The white police, armed with guns, were pushed into the background. Television cameramen and reporters crowded around the brothers.

A BBC reporter asked Cheeky, 'Is this really an arson trial or is it something more?'

'It's a political trial and everyone knows it.' Cheeky said.[23]

Later, reports in the international press claimed that the trumped-up charges were clearly an attempt to victimise the Watson brothers for their anti-apartheid stance.

But the local newspapers were not so sure. 'In Port Elizabeth one either loves or hates the Watson brothers – there seems to be no middle ground. Some people even appear to love to hate them,' began a report in the *Sunday Star*.[24] After describing the way the brothers were carried by an ecstatic crowd of black supporters, the report continued, 'In Port Elizabeth townships the brothers are hero-worshipped for speaking Xhosa, for supporting black causes and for being the first whites to play in black rugby teams.

'The same reasons make many whites distrust them and the family has endured many years of persecution.'

That evening, for the first time in six months, all the Watsons were able to be at home together. Daniel, their father, who had been admitted to the Provincial Hospital a few days earlier, was allowed out in time to join in the family reunion.

Four days of privacy lay ahead of the Watsons. But the press could not be kept at bay. They followed them everywhere, even to their first meal together. The Watsons, generously, did not appear to mind. 'Less than an hour after they were carried shoulder high from the court building by a crowd of about 1000, the brothers sat down to a seafood luncheon at their brother-in-law's restaurant in Port Elizabeth', wrote Jayne La Mont in the *Eastern Province Herald*.[25]

> *Friends, the defence team and the family gathered around the long table, enjoying their first unrestricted contact with the trio since their arrest early on August 13.*
>
> *Mr Ronald Watson said: 'We didn't expect the issue of bail to come up at all. I couldn't believe it when the magistrate began talking about it.' An equally surprised Mr Valence Watson said: 'We've*

got a lot to catch up on. Right now I'm just listening and getting used to being out.'

Quiet-spoken Mr Cheeky Watson just grinned happily and obligingly posed for the Eastern Province Herald photographer.

'It's been so very long. I can't begin to say what it means to have all my sons back. Now we can face anything. We're together – we're a family again,' said their mother, Mrs Elaine Watson.

Playing hostess to her family at the lunch was Mrs Sharon Taverner, their sister, who said: 'How do I feel about the bail? Wonderful!'[26]

But it was not entirely wonderful.

The whole family knew that Valence would face a long jail term if his appeal failed.

On the morning that judgement was due to be passed on Valence, Eileen described her feelings: 'When we got up this morning Valence and I never said a word about what would be happening today, as though we were both trying to show the other we weren't worried.

'But when he kissed the children goodbye, he hugged them very tightly and I could see he was wondering whether he'd be there when they went to bed that night.'[27]

On the evening before Valence was due to appear in court the four brothers spent some quiet time with their wives and children, held a prayer meeting and then met in a park to talk seriously about the future.

Gavin, Ronnie and Cheeky were afraid that Valence was going to get a long jail sentence, possibly twenty years, and they wanted to assure him that they would fight the sentence and look after his wife, Eileen, and their three children.

'We thought we would have to go to the Supreme Court,' Ronnie recalled. 'We would have to engage ourselves in a three-year fight to prove his innocence. Somehow we had to raise the money for that. We would raise it through the family. We would do something.'[28]

Eileen remembered being quite upset by Valence's insistence that he would have to go to jail. 'I said "Stop talking like that". I said he was lying about having to go to jail and I was a bit weepy.'[29]

Next morning, when Valence went to court, the atmosphere was very different from the jubilance of four days earlier, when the Watsons had been released on bail.

Valence recalled, 'The whole court was surrounded by police. In the streets encircling the building there were yellow buses full of police and dogs. There were police on the roof of the court with guns. My attorney, Leon Schubart, who arrived early, said, "What is happening?" The cop replied, "Haven't you heard? There is a big political trial going on here." Leon says, "No, it is the Watson trial." And another cop says, "That's right. The Watsons."'[30]

'Then we heard from Bishop Bruce Evans, the Anglican Bishop of Port Elizabeth, that he was stopped on his way to the airport because the entrance to the airport had been blocked. They were bringing hundreds of police in from Pretoria as a back-up for those already at the court. The police had declared the court a riot area and cordoned off the whole block. They were allowing none of my supporters into the court while they were sentencing me,' Valence said.[31]

'Every three metres there was a guy with a rifle and every fifty metres, in the streets behind the court, there was a truck with dozens of police in it,' said Ronnie. 'They arrested photographers, took the film out of their cameras. They did not want this trial documented. They did not want the outside world to know.'[32]

'When we came out on bail, SABC television had shown us being carried on the shoulders of the crowd,' said Valence. 'But at the second hearing, where there was a massive show of support – about 3000 people – they showed nothing. But the BBC managed to get some footage and showed it in London.'[33]

Valence had suggested that the wives should dress in ANC colours of green, black and gold when they attended the court. 'I thought, in for a penny, in for a pound. I may as well expose my links,' he said.[34]

At this stage he was feeling so certain that he would receive a heavy sentence that he had prepared a speech to deliver to the magistrate afterwards. 'I was going to get up in the dock and tell the magistrate that I held nothing against him, but I saw him as a weak man, absolutely controlled by the State, who didn't have the courage to speak up and judge according to the law. Then I was going to give a political speech.'[35]

When Leon Schubart heard about this he pleaded with Valence not to attack the magistrate prematurely. He felt confident of winning the case.[36]

The prosecution was trying to prove that the Watsons' business was in such a precarious state that Valence was forced to blow up the house for the insurance but did not want to involve his brothers. Only Jeffrey was aware of this and had assisted him.

Eileen sat in court with Gavin on one side and Cheeky on the other. Both had an arm around her, willing her to be brave. But before the sentence was pronounced, she went outside, unable to bear hearing it.

The magistrate, Gert Steyn, told the court what a good witness Valence had been, how sincere and intelligent. According to a report in the *Eastern Province Herald*, Steyn said Valence was 'a remarkable man from a remarkable family with deep ties in the Eastern Cape' and should not be dealt with as an 'ordinary citizen' but as somebody with strong convictions who had shown in the past with his stand against racism that he had the courage of those convictions.

Steyn explained that Valence was thirty-four, married with three children, aged between five and two years, a devout Christian and an accomplished sportsman. In addition he had been refused bail 'for a good many months' and had already spent a considerable period in custody.

The State contended that the offences were of a serious nature and had been carefully planned. Accomplices had been put in danger while Valence Watson remained 'at a safe distance'.

He had shown reckless disregard for the safety of both his accomplices and the surrounding area, the prosecutor, Mr Henning Van der Walt said.[37]

The magistrate was so full of praise for Valence Watson that it seemed he was almost apologising for the guilty verdict and severe sentence he was about to hand down. So it was a complete surprise when he pronounced that Valence would receive a sentence of five years for each of the counts, of which two and a half years of each sentence would be suspended. Awaiting his appeal he would be released on bail of 15 000 rand and would have to relinquish his passport and report twice a day to the police.

Outside the court a BBC reporter pushed past the police keeping the media at bay and managed to ask Cheeky if he was pleased at the outcome of the trial. 'No, Valence should never have been convicted,' he replied. 'We are going to fight this one to the bitter end.'[38]

Throughout the trial, Eileen and her sisters-in-law had presented a united front. Only once did Eileen's composure slip. Tracey said, 'The only time I saw Eileen cry was when that verdict was passed on Valence.'[39]

That evening at home Valence and Eileen had a serious talk. Valence explained that things were going to get worse, not better. Now that he was awaiting an appeal, he implied, it was not too late to change direction. He was certain that he wished to continue on as before but he wanted to know what Eileen felt. 'Do you want me to pull back?' he asked her.

Eileen said without hesitation, 'No, I wouldn't want it any other way. If the Watsons didn't carry on the struggle now, it would be a great disappointment to a lot of people.'[40]

The next day, as part of the bail regulations, Valence had to go and sign in at the police station at Louis Le Grange Square. This was to happen every day. He decided to take four-year-old Daniel with him for the drive. 'He sees the police and the bars on the windows and I am trying to teach him not to be afraid of police, even though he knows they harass us,' Valence recalls. 'He asks me, "Why do the police hate us?" and I say, "Because we love black people." On the drive home I say to him, "Do you want me not to love black people any more so that I won't have to go to jail?" And he says, "No, you keep loving black people. I will hide you if the police come for you again." And I say, "But where?" He says, "Don't worry. I'll hide you. But don't stop loving black people."

'It was very comforting for me to understand that even my four-year-old child had grown up in surroundings where he was in agreement with what we were doing.'[41]

11

MI6 ATTEMPTS ASSASSINATION

In early 1987 Valence Watson, waiting for his appeal to be held in the Supreme Court in August, decided to enrol at the University of Port Elizabeth to do a degree in Commerce. All the brothers knew that it would not be easy for them to get jobs. They had no money to start a new business and Security was making it as difficult as possible for them to succeed. So Valence, who had always enjoyed studying, went to the university while Eileen worked to support the family. She had two jobs, one as the personal assistant to a marketing manager and one as a computer operator.

At this stage the cupboards were often bare, and Eileen felt indignant that the white community, who didn't know just how financially in need the Watsons were, assumed they were now doing well.

Through the ANC underground network, Archie received a packet from a friend in the Ciskei who had left South Africa to escape political harassment. The friend, Ndzoto, had sent money 'from a Communist to a Christian' to help Valence pay his university fees. 'It was a packet containing 2000 rand. My fees were 1800 rand a year. I desperately needed it, believe me,' Valence said.

'Ndzoto had worked closely with me in ANC underground structures and I had coached the rugby team, the Wallabies, which we both belonged to. But I hadn't had contact with him for a couple of years. He'd been training in Angola and Zambia and had made his way back to Lesotho. He was a comrade in the struggle and one of our closest friends.'[1]

Now that Valence's movements were curtailed by having to report daily to the Security police, they targeted Ronnie Watson as the most political of the brothers. Many men were employed to watch him.

Security knew they could not touch Ronnie inside South Africa, because the Watson brothers had a high international profile, especially since the trial. But outside the country there was a chance of assassinating him.

In March 1987, Ronnie received word that his friend the Reverend Arnold Stofile was on trial for terrorism. Stofile, like so many others, had been a rugby player who had used sport as a means to becoming an activist against apartheid. Now, in the black homeland of Ciskei, he and four others were being charged with terrorism, possession of arms and harbouring terrorists. Ronnie and Archie Mkele decided to go to Bisho, the capital, so that Ronnie could attend the trial. There was another, more sinister, reason for their visit. They had heard a strong rumour that their friend Ndzoto, who had sent the money for Valence's university fees, had been killed by the Ciskei Security. Archie wanted to bring the body back to Port Elizabeth so it could be properly buried, which was an important Xhosa custom.

Ronnie did not think it would be too dangerous to go to the Ciskei, which was just 250 kilometres from Port Elizabeth.

'I thought, Security would be mad to try anything on us

right now. They would be crazy. It is two months since we were found innocent after a trial. We are still hot news.'[2]

Although the Ciskei was a so-called independent country, it was regarded by the ANC as a puppet state of South Africa. The government still took orders from South African Security, as Ronnie and Archie were about to discover.

Judge Pickard, who was conducting the case against the suspected ANC supporters, was a white judge seconded to the Ciskei by the South African Government.

While Ronnie was sitting at the treason trial of his friend Stofile, he noticed that he was surrounded by Ciskei Security.

Ronnie said, 'One of them asked me, "What happened to your house?" I said, "Didn't you ask your father, P. W. Botha?" That is about the worst thing you can say to the Ciskei police. But they are traitors. This one was dressed very poorly. I said, "You look as if you are the orphan son of P. W. Botha." I was joking with him, and he joked back, "I might be the orphan son but you are not even that. P. W. Botha doesn't want you at all."'[3]

Later, when Ronnie spoke to Stofile, the poorly dressed Security policeman was still following him and trying to overhear his conversations. Ronnie told Stofile that Archie was looking for the body of Ndzoto, but Stofile said that Ndzoto was alive, in the cell next to his. Ronnie then realised that he was in danger and had been lured up to the Ciskei by the false story of Ndzoto's death. Surrounded by Security police, he could not escape. He sat and watched the trial continue.

Archie, meanwhile, had heard nothing of the exchange with Stofile, and had gone with another friend to look at the 'body' of Ndzoto. The body he saw was so badly mutilated that Archie could not tell whether it was Ndzoto or not; this particular ANC guerilla had been run over by a kaspir. When Archie came back to Ronnie he said he doubted that the body was Ndzoto's.

Ronnie replied, 'You have reason to doubt. Stofile talked to him this morning.'

Ronnie and Archie realised they were in trouble and thought about trying to escape. 'I told Archie that there were no border posts between the Ciskei and South Africa, just an imaginary line,' Ronnie said.

'A black woman friend called Zoe, who was an ANC underground operative, knew how hot things were getting for us, so when the court dispersed for lunch she invited us to go and have lunch with her.'[4]

As they were driving away from the court, the car was surrounded by armed plainclothes police. Ronnie and Archie were dragged out by separate groups of police, hustled away, and locked up in different police stations.

Zoe phoned Valence Watson in Port Elizabeth, telling him that Ronnie and Archie were being detained. Valence immediately phoned Gavin and urgent messages were sent to the few international journalists who might write about Ronnie's plight in the Ciskei.

'They took away my belt and watch and did not give me a receipt for them,' Ronnie said. 'I thought, "This is it." But they are mad to do this to me. I can't believe they are so stupid.' The youngster who is locking me up says, "I know what you guys stand for. I agree with it. But some people don't understand these things. You must prepare yourself. Be strong."'

When the police did not follow standard arrest procedures Ronnie realised that he was not supposed to emerge from prison alive.

'They locked the steel door and the grille. In fact they wanted no one to see me in there. I thought, "Fine. They haven't killed me yet. They must want information. Once they have got all they want, then they'll kill me. The important thing is for me to stay alert. They'll try to drug me, poison me." The guy brought me food. Lovely food. You wouldn't believe prison could serve such food. And fresh milk. I know their tricks. I played along. I thanked them very much, asked the guard to tell the officer in charge how much I appreciated the meal. When he'd gone I tipped it all down the toilet and flushed it away.'

Ronnie ate and drank nothing but a few sips of water for four days. 'Having no fluid is a killer. But being hungry makes your mind extremely alert,' he said. 'When, on the fourth day, I was taken for questioning, I kept my jacket on so they would not see that I'd lost weight. There were fifteen of them standing around me. One of them said, "Look, Ndzoto has told us that you are part of the ANC, and that you have met him here."

'I said, "That's very nice, that I should be part of something that even I don't know about. Where did I meet him?"

'"You met him in East London; you were commanding operations from there."

'I said, "No, man. Don't make jokes with me."

'They said, "We want to warn you. If we want to kill someone, we can kill them. If we feel you are not responding to us, we will deal with you."

'"You are an independent country. I don't know why you people are trying this with me. Do you have apartheid here? No. That is exactly what we want in South Africa. No apartheid," I said. I thought I would butter them up a bit.'

The Watsons were well known and liked in the Ciskei. Some of the Security police had played rugby with them. Ronnie used this to his advantage: 'I said, "Anyway, there are fifteen of you and only one of me. You never threatened me when we were on the rugby field."

'They laughed. One of them said, "Yes, it was a different kettle of fish when we played rugby together." There was a bit of good-natured banter between us. But then their controllers, the South African Security police, came in.'[5]

Ronnie's interrogation began.

Meanwhile Gavin and Valence were trying without success to find out where Ronnie had been taken, and to get international press coverage to help protect him.

On 29 March, under 'World News' in the Australian newspaper *Times on Sunday*, it was reported that Ronnie and Archie had disappeared in the Ciskei.

> *Ronnie Watson, who was recently acquitted of fraud in a Port Elizabeth case that attracted world-wide interest, and his black friend and former employee Archie Mkele, have been detained under the Internal Security Act and have disappeared.*
>
> *'We can't believe it. No one is prepared to say where they are,' his brother Gavin said from Port Elizabeth this week . . .*
>
> *'The police claim there were altercations in which Ronnie took part,' Gavin said. According to Ronnie's two companions no such thing took place . . . The two companions were questioned for five hours about their relationship with the Watson brothers before being released. Watson and Mkele have not been heard of since.*
>
> *'Our lawyer requested to see them but when he contacted the police station he'd been told they were in, the police said they'd never heard of them.'*[6]

Valence rang another police station in the Ciskei and, speaking Xhosa, asked if they were holding Archie Mkele there. All the Watson brothers spoke Xhosa with such convincing accents that they were often mistaken for blacks on the phone. 'I said, "He plays rugby for the Wallabies." The chap knew that team and he said that Archie was there. I said, "Can you tell me why you are holding him?" and he said. "It is things out there. You know. Politics."

'I said, "Tell me about this guy who was with Mkele, Ronnie Watson. Where is he being held?"

'He said, "What do you want to know that for?"

'I said, "I would just like to know. He was with Mkele at the time."

'He said, "Look here, man, I was kind enough to let you know where Mkele is. Now you want to know about this Watson character. He is a white man. Why are you interested in him?"

'I said, "Actually, he's my brother".

'There was a deathly silence. He said, "Aren't you black?"

'I said, "No, I am white. Ronnie is my brother."

'Once again, silence. He said, "Look, I'm sorry." And he put the phone down.'[7]

It was not until the fourth day of Ronnie's imprisonment that the Watsons discovered, through Zoe's mother, who was also an activist, which police station he was in.

Meanwhile Ronnie was trying with some success to persuade his interrogators, the Ciskei Security police, that he and they shared a common cause against the racism in South Africa. He hoped to appeal to their sense of decency by identifying with them as a victim.

He told them he knew who had been behind the attack on

their President Sebe the month before. They believed it was the Transkei, but Ronnie asked them how the Transkei could have done it without help from South Africa. 'Did South Africa warn you that the Transkei force had crossed their border?' he asked. The police looked uneasily at each other. This question had occurred to them.

Realising that he was winning their confidence, Ronnie decided to reveal to these Ciskei citizens some important information. He told them that, as a member of the ANC, he had discovered that the initial plan of the South African Government was for the whites to retreat to the resource-rich centre of the country and leave the arid extremities to the blacks.

Ronnie then picked up the piece of paper on which the Ciskei Security police had tried to force him to confess that he was part of the ANC and asked if he could draw a map on it. They nodded. He illustrated where the South African Government had planned to draw back the white population into the richest area, Area A. The so-called 'homelands' of the Ciskei and the Transkei were in an all-black area, labelled D. There could be only one leader, either from the Transkei or the Ciskei, and the South African Government had decided that the Ciskei's President Sebe must go, Ronnie said. He explained how power stations, railway lines, dams, every major development of the past fifteen years, had taken place in Area A. Why? Because the whites were planning to retreat there and take it all.

Ronnie continued, 'The Captain of Security, who had been hostile to me when the interrogation started, said, "No more please. I understand exactly what you are saying to me." He then said, "By the way, Ndzoto is alive."'[8]

South African Security were not present at this stage. They did not want to dirty their hands with an interrogation unless the Ciskei police failed to get results.

Ronnie said, 'I asked the Ciskei Security police, "Why have my blood on your hands? Don't you kill me. If the South African Government wants to kill me, let them do their own dirty work."

'They said, "You know we have no argument with you. What you say is true."

'They went away and contacted President Sebe. Now there was tremendous conflict with South African Security. The Ciskei Security had changed its attitude towards me completely. They didn't want me to sign a confession any more. But they had to put on a show for white South African Security, who were listening outside the cell door. The Ciskei Sergeant Major shouted at me and winked. He yelled, "You must sign this thing or I will deal with you!" Then they brought in Ndzoto, in chains. I looked at him and I didn't react. He looked at me and he was wondering if I would betray him. I said I had not seen him since he had fled into exile in 1981. I agreed to sign a statement to that effect in front of my lawyers. Not without them.

'Ndzoto is a brilliant guy, very strong willed, a natural leader. Anyway, they took him back down the stairs. He was cursing and swearing because they were man-handling him.'[9]

The South African Security policeman Engelbrecht then came into the cell and told Ronnie he knew that he was ANC. Ronnie said that was rubbish. He accused Engelbrecht of blowing up the Watsons' house and trying to frame them. 'Engelbrecht said, "Let's leave it. We can always fix that up." I said, "There's nothing you can fix. It's only out of respect for the Ciskei Colonel Nhonhono that I am restrained from attacking you." At this, he gets up out of his chair and comes towards me. I stand up and say, "I would advise you not to take one step closer."

'By this time the Ciskei Security and the South African Security are quite divided. Colonel Nhonhono, who is black, orders Engelbrecht to get out. He goes and the colonel smiles at me, saying,"That is not the way to behave." Then he shouts at me a bit for the benefit of the other white South African Security listening outside. Later he tells me, "We are not going to charge you. Don't sign a thing."

Ronnie denied any involvement with the ANC. The Ciskei colonel looked at him and said, "Watson, you have been with the Xhosa far too long. You can deny having stolen a jacket even while wearing it." Coming from a Xhosa, Ronnie took this as a compliment.

The colonel told him it had been President Sebe who had ordered that he not be charged. In ten minutes he would ring with the final order to release him. While they waited tensely for the phone call, Archie was admitted to the cell. He hugged Ronnie and told him, 'They have nothing on us.' Archie had not been harmed or cross-examined while he was in custody.

'The three of us are sitting there waiting and it is virtually a conspiracy,' Ronnie said. 'Then the colonel asks us if we are hungry, and I haven't eaten for four days. So he orders Kentucky Fried Chicken and Cokes for us. The three of us eat it while we wait anxiously for the phone call. Then, at one o'clock, it comes, and the colonel, with a huge smile on his face, says, "The President says you can go."

'Archie loves telling that story, of how I became such a friend of the Ciskei Security police that instead of offering me a rope after the interrogation, they offered us a feast,' Ronnie said.[10]

Ronnie and Archie drove back to Port Elizabeth in their own car and, being such friends of the Ciskei police, encountered no problems on the border.

Back home they discovered that not only the family but a member of Parliament had been agitating for their release. Mr John Malcolmess, PFP MP for Port Elizabeth, had travelled to Bisho where he talked with the Ciskei Director General of Justice, Mr Nogcantsi, in a bid to free them.

Mr Malcolmess said he was certainly not claiming that he was responsible for the release of the two men, but that if his visit had helped he was pleased he had gone to the trouble.[11]

The following day the *Eastern Province Herald* ran an editorial supporting Mr Malcolmess's claim that the 'Ciskei should not harass South Africans, whether they be visitors, tourists or people in transit . . . we can now add that the South African Security Police should be careful of appearing to assist in such harassment.'[12]

The same newspaper confirmed that the South African Security police officer who had interrogated Ronnie Watson in the Ciskei was Warrant-officer Chris Engelbrecht.

Ronnie could not resist expressing some mock surprise at the presence of South African Security in the Ciskei. The *Eastern Province Herald* reported, 'On his return to Port Elizabeth on Tuesday, Mr Watson said he was "extremely surprised to see a South African security officer in Ciskei, which I thought was meant to be a sovereign state."'[13]

On 30 January 1987, Oliver Tambo had met with US Secretary of State, George Shultz, in Washington for what both sides called 'a serious and substantive exchange of views.'

At the same time, Nelson Mandela, still a prisoner at Pollsmoor, had resumed contact with the Minister for Justice, Kobie Coetsee, and had several meetings with him at his home in Cape Town. Coetsee had proposed that discussions be held between Mandela and a committee of senior government officials.

Mandela consulted his colleagues about these discussions. Walter Sisulu said that although he was not against negotiations in principle, he wished that the government had initiated talks with the ANC, rather than the other way around. Raymond Mhlaba believed that the talks were long overdue but he also felt that 'by initiating talks it would appear that we were capitulating.'[14]

Oliver Tambo, having heard that Mandela was having secret talks with the government, smuggled a note to him, the tenor of which suggested Mandela 'was making an error in judgement.'

Mandela said:

> *I replied to Oliver in a very terse letter saying that I was talking to the government about one thing and one thing only: a meeting between the National Executive of the ANC and the South African government. I would not spell out the details, for I could not trust the confidentiality of the communication. I simply said the time had come for such talks and I would not compromise the organization in any way.*[15]

The Watsons had been briefed about the proposed negotiations between Mandela and the government in early 1987, and like many ANC members who had been committed to an armed struggle, they had reservations about them.

'Like any activists we wanted liberation, a clear break from the past,' said Valence. 'When we heard that insurrection and seizure of power might not be the plan to be followed, but negotiation, we were surprised. I admit that it wasn't our choice. But the ANC had to be sensitive to the frontline states, Mozambique, Angola, Botswana, Zimbabwe, Zambia and Tanzania, because they had been offered refuge in those countries. ANC top leadership had reports that the South African Government was involved in destabilising, militarily and economically, these frontline states. There had been a number of attacks in Gabarone, Maseru, Maputo, Lusaka and Harare. Negotiation wasn't the first choice of most ANC members, including us, but we had no option.'[16]

On 22 March, at talks with ANC leaders in Lusaka, Archbishop Desmond Tutu appealed for a halt in their armed struggle but said that he held out little hope of a cease-fire.

A few weeks later the ten-month-old State of Emergency was once again tightened by the prohibition of any protests on behalf of any political detainees.

Then, on the eve of the white general elections, over half a million workers and students stayed home in a subdued protest. Anti-apartheid leaders called on eligible white voters to boycott the election. The Watsons took part in the boycott. 'We don't vote,' Valence said. 'We expressed our opinions through word of mouth. The first time I ever voted was the last election in 1994.'[17]

President Botha widened his parliamentary majority from 116 to 123 seats and interpreted this as a mandate for more security measures and 'gradual change'.

Archbishop Tutu saw the results as an entry into 'the dark ages in the history of our country.'

Oliver Tambo said they 'blew the whistle for the ANC to intensify the armed struggle'.

'We were aware of this intensification. Absolutely,' Valence said. 'You could not ask Botha and the white community to be "friends" with the ANC. The only way to get them to change was to put the pressure on them.'[18]

In May 1987, Ronnie Watson decided to take a trip to Gabarone in Botswana, ostensibly to sell pharmaceutical products, but in fact to meet with high-level ANC members, including Chris Hani. He knew he was on the South African Security hit list, but Botswana was not a puppet state like the Ciskei so he expected to be safe, even though he knew South African Security had agents in Botswana. Ronnie felt that as the Botha government was sending out the first real signals that they were prepared to talk with the ANC, he had to go to Botswana to meet with ANC leaders to learn what his new instructions would be. Ronnie was excited by the fact that the government was under so much pressure they might actually be contemplating black majority rule.

When he arrived at the Sir Seretse Airport in Botswana that morning, Ronnie was waiting for his luggage when he observed a fit, wiry white man in his late thirties watching him closely.

As Ronnie walked into the hotel foyer a Mercedes pulled up at the hotel entrance, driven by the same wiry man. But this time Ronnie did not notice him. He checked in and went to his room. After he had surveyed the room for bugging devices and bombs, he took off his coat and tie, shirt and trousers and lay down on the bed in his singlet and undershorts. There was a knock on the door. He sprang up, instantly alert, and looked through the peephole. A white man dressed neatly and wearing a tweed jacket stood there.

'Who is it?' called Ronnie, still cautious.

'Service manager, sir. Would you mind if I checked your room?' came the confident reply.

Ronnie hesitated, then decided that the impeccable English voice was to be trusted and he removed the chain and unlocked the door. He turned his back and moved away towards the bed. Behind him the man entered swiftly and drew a Biretta pistol from his belt. Ronnie looked over his shoulder, saw the pistol and recognised the man as the same one who had watched him at the airport.

'Put it away,' Ronnie said calmly. 'You've got the wrong guy.'

The man was temporarily thrown by this reaction but when he spoke his manner was arrogant and assertive. He told Ronnie to lie face down on the bed while he checked his documents.

Ronnie knew that to lie face down on the bed was a prelude to assassination. He would be helpless, and a pillow would be used to muffle the shot at the back of his head.

'My passport's in the pocket of my pants,' he said, pointing to where they hung on a chair. 'Can I put them on?' He indicated that he felt embarrassed in his state of undress. The man nodded. Ronnie handed him the passport and his other documents.

Ronnie explained that he was starting a pharmaceutical business and planning to import medicines. 'That's my contact list of firms.'

The man was not interested in these. He asked him questions about the ANC, which Ronnie pretended to know nothing about.

The man then went into the bathroom, saying he was getting a glass of water. Ronnie moved silently across the room to where he could see the man's reflection in the mirror through the half-open door. The man turned on the tap but did not fill a glass. He then turned it off and reached for a towel, which he wrapped around the muzzle of the Biretta as a silencer.

As the man came out of the bathroom with the pistol pointed at Ronnie's head, Ronnie dived to the floor. 'I heard the pistol shot, and as I landed at his feet another shot over my head. The first shot hit the ceiling and the second hit the concrete. I felt cement hitting my face and I thought I was bleeding, but I couldn't feel where he had hit me.'[19]

Ronnie grabbed the man's legs but he wrenched himself free with surprising strength and fired again, pointing down at Ronnie. The bullet gouged the carpet inches from his head. Ronnie pushed himself up from the floor, grabbed the pistol and forced it high above the man's head as he pushed him back into the corner. The man kicked out at Ronnie with the ferocity and precision of someone trained in unarmed combat, but Ronnie, using the agility and strength that years of competitive rugby had honed, twisted, absorbed the blow, and brought the pistol crashing down on the man's head. Blood flowed and the man staggered, but he would not let go his joint grip on the pistol. Again Ronnie brought it crashing down on his head. This time he used his other hand to throttle the man, who was gasping for breath when Ronnie heaved him down on the carpet. But he was resilient and quickly rose to tackle Ronnie. He was felled with a series of savage kicks and Ronnie then put the pistol to his head. The man's cool arrogance left him and he screamed, 'Don't shoot! Don't shoot!'

'Who are you and who do you work for?' Ronnie demanded.

'I wasn't going to kill you. It was just a scare,' the man protested.

Ronnie kicked him savagely, then repeated the question.

He knew this was an assassin's pistol for killing at close quarters, with low muzzle velocity that penetrated the skull, bounced around and pulped the brain. He threatened to kill the man and began to squeeze the trigger.

The man screamed, 'Please don't kill me!'

Ronnie paused.

The man, looking up at him with a dazed expression, made an astounding admission. He said, 'My name's Steve Burnett. I work for MI6.'

Ronnie was stunned. This was the last thing he expected. Both the physical encounter and the weight of this news made him stagger. He suddenly realised the pervasiveness of the force working against him. It was more than the South African apartheid machine. It was international.

'I said, "Fine. I am not going to kill you. Where are the others?"'

Burnett said there were no others but Ronnie was not convinced. Burnett then admitted that he was an unarmed combat instructor, a British MI6 operative, who had previously served in Northern Ireland killing IRA terrorists and had now been hired by South African Security to kill Ronnie.[20]

Ronnie told Burnett that he was having him arrested. He put his jacket round Burnett's neck and, using him as a shield in case of other attackers, marched him down to the hotel foyer with the pistol behind his head.

'It was quite a funny sight. He was covered in blood, like tomato sauce in a movie. I was in a state of shock, unable to believe I hadn't been shot and this guy was suddenly so calm. I told him to open the door, which he did. Then he saw on the floor a magazine of pistol bullets that had fallen out of the gun. He picked it up and said, "May I put this in my pocket?" I said, "Do as you please with it." I was too agitated to realise the significance.

'I walked down the passage with the pistol at his head. I was shaking, thinking, "This guy could come at me again. He is a trained assassin. He enjoys killing people. There must be others around. Where the heck are they?"'

When Ronnie and Burnett reached the hotel foyer, the manager rang the Botswana Security police. Ronnie relaxed his hold on the pistol for an instant and Burnett suddenly lunged at him, using the magazine to try and knock it out of Ronnie's hands. 'His hands were actually on the pistol so I hit him and he landed in the corner. The receptionist was screaming. I looked like the aggressor. There was not a mark on me, except for a bleeding hand. I said, "For Heaven's sake, Steven, calm yourself. You are finished. You have made a mess. I don't want to hurt you but if you continue in this way, I will have to."

'He said, "Okay. Sorry."

'Then, suddenly, he grabbed a heavy ashtray off the counter. It was huge. He tried to hit me with it. I was standing with my hands on the counter but I saw it coming at the last minute and managed to flick it away. I caught him by his pants, twisted him and brought him down head first. I was annoyed. I gave him a few good kicks in the guts and back, used him a bit like a rugby ball. When he recovered he pointed at me and said to the hotel receptionist, "There is a bloody ANC terrorist."

'All the staff were black except the management. They suddenly realised who the aggressor was and their attitudes changed. They came to stand around me, almost protectively, until the police arrived.

'The police didn't know which of us to arrest,' Ronnie said. 'One of them said to me, "You are ANC?" and I said, "That's got nothing to do with it." They said they would check up on me and I should wait at the hotel. They then handcuffed Burnett and took him away.'[21]

Ronnie went back to his hotel room and rang Valence in Port Elizabeth, told him what had happened and asked him to get in touch with the international press as fast as possible. 'Get the story out or I'm dead,' he said. 'South African Security I can cope with but not MI6. If you don't get the story out immediately, I have got hours left to live.' He told Valence he was going into hiding and not to expect to hear from him for some time.

Valence recalls, 'I have never heard Ronnie so scared. He was also angry. Our father fought for the British and our grandfather. Now suddenly the British were our enemies. When you are of British descent it is like your own brother turning around and fighting you.'[22]

Valence immediately phoned the few international journalists he knew.

That night the London *Observer*, the *Boston Globe*, the *Washington Post* and several other papers ran the story that South African anti-apartheid activist Ronnie Watson had survived an alleged assassination attempt earlier that day, and that

Botswana police had arrested a British citizen, Steven Burnett, an ex-member of 21 SAS, currently working for British MI6, and charged him with attempted murder.

Meanwhile, back in Botswana, the police had returned to the hotel to tell Ronnie he was free to go. He was not to leave the country, however, until after Steven Burnett's trial, which they expected to take place within a month.

Ronnie, still afraid for his life, went into hiding.

While in isolation he thought hard about why British MI6 should want to kill him. He was aware that Britain had six billion pounds worth of investments in South Africa and that if black majority rule came too fast they could lose the lot. Also, he knew there were over a million South Africans eligible for British passports who might all decide to return to the United Kingdom if the majority came to power. They would need jobs, housing, education and social service benefits, which could be economically difficult for Britain. Even Dennis Thatcher had large investments in South Africa. When Prime Minister Thatcher was asked by the press to comment on this, she refused.[23]

Perhaps, Ronnie thought, South African Security had just hired Steven Burnett as a mercenary, and there was no connection with the British Government. But he doubted it.

Botswana Security had put Ronnie into protective custody until after the trial. He described how gentle the people of Botswana were and how very peaceful. During this time he got a call from the ANC, saying that the Executive would like to see him, because they were very concerned about the assassination attempt.

'I went to Botswana Security and asked if I could leave the country and they said, "Just give us your word that you won't go back to South Africa, because if you do they will knock you off or detain you so you can't give evidence at the trial and implicate MI6". So I told them I was flying up to Lusaka to meet with the ANC. In fact I was taken out by car, via a safe route to Lusaka,' Ronnie said.[24]

'We were extremely concerned about Ronnie,' Valence continued. 'He was unarmed and it was dangerous for him to be seen as close to the ANC people at this time, because he had to deny all links with them when he came back to South Africa. That's why I woke Kristin in Sydney at four in the morning and said, "Get the story into the international press." I was sure South Africa would send another hitman after Ronnie.'[25]

When Ronnie met his ANC comrades and the leader, Chris Hani, they congratulated him on 'improvising'. Hani related the story of his own narrow escape, when an ANC house at Maseru, Lesotho, was attacked in 1983. Hani then told Ronnie the startling news that the National Party would be forced to negotiate with the ANC.

Hani and Mzwandile Piliso, head of ANC Security, said that the next ANC task for Ronnie and Valence was to intensify contact with the white community and find out whatever they could about de Klerk's strategy to keep power. Ronnie replied that the white community despised the Watsons. Hani said that once it was announced that the government was going to negotiate with the ANC, they would be surprised at how many whites would suddenly want to know them. Later Hani himself would take an active part in contacting the white community in the Eastern Cape.

'Piliso had been very effective in exposing infiltrators into the ANC ranks and Hani had been a very successful leader of Umkhonto we Sizwe [MK],' Valence said. 'They were both demonised by the South African press and the government. Yet in all our dealings with these leaders, and others like Jacob Zuma of ANC Intelligence, we found them to be gentlemen of integrity with a strong sense of justice and a commitment to peace.'[26]

At his trial in the Botswana High Court, which lasted five days, Steve Burnett pleaded not guilty of attempting to murder Ronnie Watson. The Thatcher Government denied there was any British cooperation with South Africa in hiring Burnett. 'An article in *Time Out* magazine identified Burnett as having worked in the SAS and the Boat Service in Britain as an unarmed combat instructor and claimed he was a very good marksman,' Valence said. '*Time Out* also revealed that he had operated in Ireland.'[27]

Burnett told the court he had never intended to kill Ronnie Watson, just to frighten him. 'He said he was pretending to be James Bond,' Ronnie said. 'People in the court were laughing at him. Judge Barrington Jones, who was British, said his evidence was "a tissue of lies" and his motives were "a lot more sinister than he professed". But he was only sentenced to five years in prison.[28]

Two weeks later the Botswana court sentenced two horse thieves, who had cut off a horse's tail to use as an aphrodisiac, to seven years in prison. A Botswana newspaper printed the news that anti-apartheid activist Ronnie Watson's life 'was not worth a horse's tail.'[29]

After giving evidence at the trial, Ronnie returned to the President Hotel in Gabarone where he had been staying, to check out, and then went to catch a plane home to Port

Elizabeth. Cheeky had flown to Botswana to meet him.

Ronnie discovered that while he had been in court, his hotel room had been completely ransacked and his passport stolen. 'The room had no carpet left, no furniture, no light fittings. Everything was stripped back to the concrete. It was a shock. I had unscrewed a painting on the wall and hidden my documents behind it. They were gone. Botswana is a friendly place. But the hotel manager, I discovered, was a British expatriate. I was nervous that I would be kidnapped at the airport. When Cheeky and I walked into Jan Smuts Airport, there were fifty or sixty Security men lining the walls. I said to Cheeky, "Just walk. Walk on." I think those men were there to make darn sure nothing happened to us.'[30]

Ronnie was interviewed at H.F. Verwoerd Airport, when he arrived back in Port Elizabeth on 25 July 1987.

> *He stressed that he and his family refused to 'bow down to murderers' and said they still stood for non-racial democracy in South Africa, even if this meant losing their lives.*
>
> *He said he 'certainly' felt there could in the future be further assassination attempts on his life, and that he intended to take protective security measures.*
>
> *He further said he expected 'psychological warfare' which had been waged against himself and his family in the past to continue.*
>
> *Following the alleged assassination attempt on his life, Mr Watson said he had moved further north and had stayed with friends in Zambia before returning to Botswana via Harare.*
>
> *His exact whereabouts had remained secret, until his emergence just three days before the trial.*
>
> *Mr Watson said he had also 'chopped and changed' flights from Botswana to Port Elizabeth for safety reasons.'*[31]

Even in adversity the Watson brothers and their wives were able to laugh at each other. Valence recalled, 'When Cheeky and Ronnie got safely home it was a tremendous relief. For two or three months we'd had no idea where Ronnie was. We'd imagined him on the run. We used to rave about how he was vaulting over fences, racing through back yards being chased by Security. It was also a big joke that Ronnie, who is always calm, had sounded so scared on the phone, saying, "Get the story to the press. I've got hours to live."'[32]

But Ronnie and Valence Watson had reason to be scared. In countries as far away as Britain and France underground operatives of the ANC were being targeted.

Two months later, in Wales, Scotland Yard arrested three men who had plans to kidnap Oliver Tambo, Joe Slovo and Thabo Mbeki, senior members of the ANC. 'These people claimed to work with the British Secret Service,' Valence said. 'They said that the issue could not be discussed in the House of Lords or the House of Commons. The three men were allowed to go free. This caused an international outcry.'[33]

'Later in 1987, Dulcie September, a black ANC woman, was assassinated in Paris,' Ronnie said. 'It was a deliberate move by South Africa in conjunction with international agencies against the ANC.'[34]

Ronnie had arrived back in South Africa just in time for Valence's appeal at the Supreme Court in Grahamstown against his thirty-month sentence for arson and fraud.

The Watson family all piled into an eleven-seater Combi van for the two-hour drive to Grahamstown. Jules Browde was to appear on Valence's behalf and one of the judges, van Rensburg, had been a referee in the days the Watsons played schoolboy football. Still, the family was anxious about the outcome of the trial. To allay their fears they made jokes about Ronnie's newly dyed hair, which was bright ginger.

'We thought it looked hilarious. He had done it as a sort of disguise, but we said it would only make the Security police more determined to bump him off, because they would think that with all the pressure they'd put on Ronnie, he ought to be grey by now.'[35] Ronnie and Valence joked all the way to Grahamstown because they knew that Valence was about to be judged under a corrupt system and there was nothing they could do about it.

The case began at 9 a.m.

Eileen was not feeling confident. Daniel, the Watsons' father, was dressed immaculately, with a flower in his buttonhole. Archie had been told by Cheeky to calm down, because he had threatened to scream at Van der Walt, the prosecutor from the first case who was also in court, that he and Jeffrey had not set fire to the house. Jeffrey, having been dismissed as an unreliable witness, was not present. The children, at home with Valence's mother, had not been told about the Supreme Court case.

By 3 p.m. the case was over. At the end of that day, August 28, 1987, Valence Watson had won his appeal against convictions for fraud and arson. Justice van Rensburg concluded that it had not been proved beyond reasonable doubt that the house had been set alight on Valence's instructions.

Afterwards, Valence said he did not feel a great sense of relief. 'I actually felt very deflated. People asked if I was going off to celebrate and I said, "What is there to celebrate? I was innocent at the beginning and I still am." I just wanted to get home. I didn't want to talk to anybody.'[36]

On the front page of the *Eastern Province Herald* next day there was a picture of Valence and Eileen looking serious, rather than overjoyed. Valence commented that 'the success of the appeal was only one of the battles that had been won by the family.

'It won't be the last – the psychological warfare and attempts on our lives will continue. But as we have won this battle, we will win others too.'[37]

12

TREES THAT GROW TALLEST CATCH THE MOST WIND

After the attempt on Ronnie's life, the Watson family entered a stage where they all felt justifiably paranoid. 'It was what kept us alive,' Ronnie explained.[1]

Valence was studying in the university library one evening when he noticed a young man at the next desk with a pistol sticking out of his belt and immediately felt he was the target.

No one in the family would ever park a car under a tree or in shadow. They had to be in the open, under a light, where it would be difficult for anyone to plant a bomb under them. Ronnie would put a small piece of paper in the driver's door, so that he could see if anyone had opened the car when he returned to it. Eileen always said a prayer before she turned the key in the ignition.

One night Eileen heard a loud knocking at the front door at about 11.30, and panicked. No one ever opened the door at night. Ronnie called out, asking who was knocking. When there was no answer he prepared his hunting rifle and waited for the door to be broken down. Eileen, whose children were asleep just beyond the front door, said she almost vomited with fear. 'Then we heard Cheeky laughing outside the door.

He'd been painting his in-laws' house till late and on the way home thought he might just call in on us,' Eileen said. 'Hell, we were mad.'[2]

There were small but infuriating government persecutions of the Watson family. Their electricity and phone bills were always exorbitantly high. 'In the flat the only electrical appliances we had were a fridge, a stove and a kettle. No microwave, heater, fans, nothing else at all,' Eileen said. 'I would query the bill and the municipality would advise me to pay it and then they'd investigate, which they never did. The same happened with the phone. We rarely used it because it was tapped. We'd go to "tickey" boxes, which are public phones. Our phone was locked up all day in a cupboard, only to be used in emergencies, like when the children were sick. Gavin received an account for 3600 rand, which he couldn't pay, so they cut the phone off.'[3]

Tracey said, 'Our electricity and phone bills had always been around the same amount – 125 rand. But suddenly we got bills for 600 rand. We had to pay them.'[4]

The Watsons, having been shunned by the white community for many years, were now under ANC instructions from leaders like Hani, Piliso and Zuma to mingle with whites and find out what they could about their attitudes to a possible change of power in South Africa. They also had to convince the business community that their businesses would not be nationalised. Their task was to shed light on what the ANC was all about so as to counter the negative propaganda against it.

These instructions were received either by way of a courier who brought a message in code or through personal meetings with ANC leaders outside South Africa. The Watsons also had to try and discover how whites felt about the fact that in the event of a change of power, criminals would be brought to justice by an unbiased legal system. There would be trials that could affect not only the Security police but ordinary citizens like themselves.

The Watson children had been told by their parents not to talk about the ANC or their dislike of police at school. Nkosi, Valence and Eileen's oldest boy, who was seven, told them proudly that he had pleased his teacher very much by telling her he thought the orange, white and blue flag was a good flag, but that he and his dad had their own flag, which was green, gold and black. However, Nkosi couldn't resist asking the neighbours and their children how they felt about the ANC and P. W. Botha. 'The neighbours were amused,' Eileen said. 'They were not political people at all, and here was this kid asking bluntly who they supported.'[5]

It was the black community who had kept the Watsons from starving during their most difficult times. Friends would come to visit them with gifts of food and money, making a joke of it to save the family embarrassment. Black street vendors, recognising them, would fill the Watsons' shopping bags with vegetables or cakes, charging them the minimum.

So it was a strain for the Watsons to suddenly have to try and be friendly with the white community who had ignored them when they badly needed support.

'A lot of people apologised,' Valence recalls. 'They said, "We should have helped you, should have phoned or offered some advice. We thought about you during the trial." And we'd just laugh.'[6]

Eileen felt quite bitter. 'There were people we knew, though not well, who'd always seemed nice. They were most critical when the house burned down and when the boys were arrested. Those people, to this day, I will never greet. To me they don't exist.

'I feel that we've actually had to carry the load for peace for the whites; in this region of the Eastern Cape, anyway. It cost us financially as well as emotionally. I haven't seen any other whites suffer what we did. I don't know if Valence agrees with me.'[7]

Valence replied, 'There's an old saying that "Trees that grow tallest catch the most wind". I mean, someone had to do it. We did it because it was a commitment to Christ. But having done it, if He said would I do it again, I'd say, "You're crazy,"' he laughed.[8]

About this time, Gavin Watson became annoyed with the white community. He had been struggling to re-establish the family in business and finding there was a lot of political pressure on him to fail. He had always been a brilliant salesman, and Sharp Electronics had employed him to sell units of office equipment, but he was constantly being told there was no more stock, which he did not believe. Gavin protested, 'We are fighting for a new South Africa, which everyone is going to benefit from, and I am getting kicked in the teeth.'[9]

In October 1987, at a meeting in Vancouver of forty-seven Commonwealth nations, many leaders, including the Australian and New Zealand Prime Ministers, denounced Mrs Thatcher's refusal to cooperate in the imposition of new, tighter economic sanctions on South Africa. Mrs Thatcher continued to maintain that sanctions were more likely to retard than advance the end of apartheid.

Govan Mbeki, senior member of the ANC and colleague of Nelson Mandela, was released from Robben Island Prison after twenty-three years in November. Later the government said it was a trial run for the release of Mandela.

A month later Mbeki, who had been going to address a rally in Port Elizabeth, was prevented from doing so by police. He was to be confined to the Port Elizabeth area, banned from speaking in public and from being published by the media. 'Mbeki was the first of the Treason Trialists to be released, and of course he was under very close surveillance. It was not for us to be seen around him,' Valence said. 'We said hello and that's all.'[10]

In February 1988, the government banned the activities of seventeen leading anti-apartheid organisations, including the UDF. Anti-apartheid leaders vowed to defy the orders.

Archbishop Tutu and two dozen church leaders were arrested as they marched in protest against the banning.

Pretoria Supreme Court granted a stay of execution for the 'Sharpeville Six', six young blacks convicted in 1985 for their role in a mob killing of a black councilman.

A court in Port Elizabeth overturned an old, invalid resolution in May and ruled that the city's beaches must be open to people of all races.

'The blacks would just stand in the water up to their waists and watch the whites catching waves,' said Eileen. 'It was sad. Because they'd never been allowed to use these beaches before, very few of them could swim.'[11]

There were beaches set aside for 'black use' in the Port Elizabeth area but they were the worst available. The currents were dangerous, even for strong swimmers. Swimming pools were almost non-existent in African townships.

In June the government renewed the State of Emergency for another twelve months.

The uncensored version of Richard Attenborough's film *Cry Freedom,* about the anti-apartheid white newspaper editor Donald Woods who fled for safety to Lesotho and then London, opened in more than thirty cinemas in South Africa on 29 July. But seven hours later, after two bombings and some anonymous phone threats, the government over-rode the censor's decision and police began seizing copies of the film.

Valence explained, 'There were two different groups who objected to that film. The outcry from the left was about Steve Biko's Black Consciousness Movement being sidelined. In no way do we blame Donald Woods for this. In his day as editor of the *Daily Dispatch* he was vociferous in his criticism of apartheid. But for American white consumption the film minimised the role of Biko and the BCM and maximised the roles of whites in the struggle. We blamed the producers and director for this.

'The attack from the right-wingers came because they objected to there being any black heroes at all in the film. The bomb threats came from the right.'[12]

Nelson Mandela was moved from hospital to a private clinic outside Cape Town following a diagnosis of tuberculosis. Later he wrote, 'In December I was moved to the Constantiaberge Clinic, a luxurious facility near Pollsmoor that had never had a black patient before.' Because of Mandela's recent illness and his history of high blood pressure, he had been put on a strict low-cholesterol diet, but the kitchen of the luxury clinic had not been advised of this and he was presented with a breakfast of scrambled eggs, three rashers of bacon and several pieces of buttered toast.' He said:

> *I could not remember the last time I had tasted bacon and eggs and I was ravenous. Just as I was about to take a delicious forkful of egg, Major Marais said, 'No, Mandela, that is against the orders of your physician,' and he reached over to take the tray. I held it tightly, and said, 'Major, I am sorry. If this breakfast will kill me, then today I am prepared to die.'*[13]

Meanwhile President P. W. Botha had a stroke. He insisted on remaining President even though his brain had been affected. His Cabinet regarded the situation as unsatisfactory. The National Party elected F. W. de Klerk, a supposed right-winger, as his successor. This did not please Botha. He decided, at last, to meet with Mandela.

Mandela had waited thirty years to meet with a white South African leader. He said, 'He came towards me with his hand outstretched, and smiling'. Mandela explained to Botha why the ANC had taken up the armed struggle and whose example they had been following. He pointed out that the Afrikaners had been the first freedom fighters in South Africa. Mandela believed that the meeting had gone smoothly. But later the National Party tried to exploit it, saying that there had to be a rift in the ANC because Mandela was committed to peaceful development and the rest of the organisation was made up of terrorists.[14]

A general election was imminent. President Botha's conduct was erratic. He went on television and threatened his Cabinet for not supporting him. Then, on 3 February 1989, he said he had no choice but to resign as leader of the National Party, but insisted on staying on as President. F. W. de Klerk became Acting President and soon learned of the three years of secret meetings between Mandela and government committees. He instructed his Intelligence Service to probe deeper into the ANC's position. His message to South African voters was that only the National Party could stop the ANC. He went on television to say, 'The National Party say we don't deal with terrorism and we don't deal with the perpetrators of violence. The ANC is committed to violence at this moment, continually making itself guilty of acts of violence . . .'[15]

Speaking at a National Party rally, de Klerk called for blacks to join whites in a 'great indaba' (Zulu for meeting), in order to negotiate the future of South Africa. Three blacks who turned up at the speech were turned away and told that the hall was reserved for whites.

In spite of de Klerk's apparent insensitivity to the interests of the black population, straight after the election he arranged for two secret agents to meet with Thabo Mbeki and Jacob Zuma, representatives of the banned ANC.

Thabo Mbeki was pleased about the meeting. Later he said, 'When I reported to Tambo he said to me one of his nightmares was that one day there would come a message from the South African government, saying, "We want to negotiate and settle", and because we had not been in contact and prepared we would not understand.'[16]

The secret meeting was held on 12 September 1989. Mbeki and Zuma and the two agents met in room 339 at the Palace Hotel in Lucerne, Switzerland. Switzerland had been chosen because no visas were required. There were no 'tails' or bodyguards. Mike Louw, one of the agents, said, 'We were extremely afraid we were going to make some mistake and botch the thing. What would happen if one of us sprained an ankle? They would say it was a trick of the Boers and so on.'

The agents were anxious as they waited to meet men 'whom their colleagues in the Security Service had attempted to assassinate.' The agents were using assumed names but the ANC representatives used their own. During the meeting Zuma confided to Mbeki in Zulu, 'Sitting here with the enemy I feel my stomach moving.'

The Afrikaners asked questions about the ANC's alliance with the Communist Party and whether an ANC government would abolish the church. 'We wanted to find out what South Africa would feel like if the ANC was in government,' said Louw.[17]

At about this time Jacob Zuma, who would later become Head of Intelligence, instructed Valence and Ronnie Watson to speak to the white business community and tell them that the ANC was not opposed to private enterprise and small family businesses, but wanted a public sector, a private sector and a cooperative sector.[18]

The Watsons realised that Chris Hani had been right about the white community wanting to befriend them. They were suddenly getting invitations at the rate of three a week.

Ronnie was the first to attend a white party. 'I found out that the hit squads were now being exposed. I was just chatting to someone and a woman behind me said, "The Watsons have been warning us for years about these squads but we didn't want to listen. We didn't believe them. Well, what can we say to them now?"'[19]

In spite of her indignation at the white community, Eileen did accept invitations to their homes; she had been told it was ANC orders. After one particularly gruelling cocktail party, she was simmering. 'I was very frustrated because we couldn't feed ourselves. We ate only pizza, tinned soup and bread,' she said.[20]

Tracey Watson also found it difficult to accept the hospitality of whites who had no real interest in what the Watson family had been struggling to achieve for the past decade. 'Cheeky and I went to a dinner party in Walmer with some wealthy business people. One woman asked, "How's Ronnie?" I replied, "He's just had an attempt on his life in the Ciskei and the attacker is being accused of trying to assassinate him." Another woman turned to me and said, "Please, we don't want to hear about the Watsons and their dramas. We want to enjoy the evening." I was so upset I went outside for the rest of the dinner party.'[21]

One evening Andre De Villiers, an old white friend of Valence's from the Crusaders Rugby Club, met him for a walk in the park. He told Valence that when he went back to his office late one night to check the books, he saw something that he was not meant to see. He seemed agitated, saying that what he saw was not right, but could not bring himself to say any more.

Valence said, 'Shortly after this, late in 1989, an ANC operative in one of the government structures reported to us that he'd met with a senior police general. The general had confided to him that de Klerk intended to free Mandela, unban the ANC and the SACP and let the exiles return. Not in five years. Or ten. But very soon.'[22]

Ronnie and Valence reported to ANC leaders that they could hardly believe what they had heard. The Watsons had been told by the operative that the State would not only release Mandela, but all political prisoners in Robben Island jail. However, once the prisoners and others returned from exile there would be an organised backlash. Security and the army would engage in 'donner' (Afrikaans for 'crush' or, more colloquially, 'bugger up'). They would incite black on black violence. While President de Klerk toured the world meeting political leaders and basking in his newfound popularity, death squads of white men in balaclavas, posing as blacks, would exterminate black leaders and help stir up trouble.

Valence recalls, 'The plan was to cause such trouble between blacks that the ANC would poll less than 50 per cent when it came to the vote. I had always said that the day Mandela was released, I'd do flick flacks down Main Street, I'd be so happy. It would be the start of a new South Africa. But now I had extremely mixed feelings.'[23]

Valence wrote a report to the ANC stating that he had been informed that the government planned to 'unban the ANC and SACP, allow the exiles to return, and release political prisoners'. Then he quoted the head of the South African police. He said that after the exiles and prisoners were free the police would take action. *Dan gaan ons hulle in bring en op hulle koppe kap*. (Then we will bring them in and chop them on the head.) He also said that the government would cut the army by 50 per cent and double the police force. He warned of *swart gevaar* (black danger) and *rooi gevaar* (red danger, or communists).[24]

The report also claimed that the confusion and violence that would be generated by the Security forces would be aimed at bringing the ANC's support of the first election to below 50 per cent.

A campaign to defy the laws of apartheid broke out in the

townships and the police reacted brutally. German shepherd dogs were used to attack people, as well as water cannons and real bullets.

Archbishop Tutu was asked to lead a demonstration march through the streets of Cape Town, beginning at St George's Cathedral. "The National Party had always regarded such demonstrations as a threat to law and order," Tutu said. When Tutu was warned that the police would break it up, he said, "Why don't you let your police line the route with their hands in their pockets?" '[25]

The Cabinet was undecided as to whether or not to permit the march. The newly elected President de Klerk said, 'Security indicated that the mood was such that should we suppress the demand to march it would result in very, very strong reaction.'[26]

Crowds of black and white people were already chanting 'Forward to a people's government!' clapping and dancing in the streets.

The march was allowed to go ahead. For the first time the ANC was permitted to raise its banners in public, although it was still an illegal organisation. The National Party was afraid the ANC was controlled by foreign communists. But with the collapse of the Berlin Wall and the whole Soviet bloc at the end of 1989, the threat of communism diminished and it seemed inevitable that change would come to South Africa.

A month later, de Klerk released four leading ANC prisoners, including Walter Sisulu, who had been Mandela's closest friend in jail. But still there was no word on when and if Mandela would be released.

International pressure mounted. In January 1990, a group of American congressmen visited South Africa. It was hoped by the de Klerk government that they would recommend an end to sanctions. But instead one of the congressmen, Howard Wolpe, announced that 'unless the South African government acts decisively to meet the conditions required by the negotiations of the anti-apartheid opposition, the international sanctions will have to be intensified.'[27]

On 2 February 1990, President de Klerk made a momentous speech. Just as the Watsons had been told months before, he announced the official unbanning of the ANC, the SACP and other subsidiary organisations, the release of prisoners, the return of exiles and the unconditional release of Nelson Mandela.

There was wild celebration.

But the Watsons were subdued. 'When we watched Mandela come out of prison on 11 February 1990, we knew what was to follow,' Valence said gravely.[28]

If Mandela was aware of what was to follow, he made no mention of it. His description of de Klerk's announcement of the unbanning of the ANC is full of joy.

> *On 2 February 1990 F. W. de Klerk stood before Parliament to make the traditional opening speech and did something no other South African head of state had ever done: he truly began to dismantle the apartheid system and lay the groundwork for a democratic South Africa . . .*
>
> *It was a breathtaking moment, for in one sweeping action he had virtually normalized the situation in South Africa. Our world had changed overnight. After forty years of persecution and banishment, the ANC was now a legal organization. I and all my comrades could no longer be arrested for being a member of the ANC, for carrying its green, yellow and black banner, for speaking its name.*

For the first time in almost thirty years, my picture and my words, and those of all my banned comrades, could appear in South Africa's newspapers. The international community applauded de Klerk's bold actions. Amid all the good news, however, the ANC objected to the fact that de Klerk had not completely lifted the State of Emergency or ordered troops out of the townships.[29]

This last sentence was perhaps an indication that Mandela knew what was to come. But he did not let this premonition cloud his enthusiasm. He describes his feeling on being released a few weeks later:

When I was among the crowd I raised my right fist, and there was a roar. I had not been able to do that for twenty-seven years and it gave me a surge of strength and joy . . . I felt – even at the age of seventy-one – that my life was beginning anew. My ten thousand days of imprisonment were at last over.'[30]

After the release of the political prisoners Valence became very close to Raymond Mhlaba, one of Mandela's friends from Robben Island, and one of the three who had been transferred to Pollsmoor with him. Mhlaba was now the acting Chair of the Communist Party and part of the internal leadership of the ANC. 'We were asked by his bodyguard to take him out to the beach somewhere, because after twenty-seven years of Robben Island it would be lovely for him to just enjoy a bit of sunshine and a sea breeze. We had a very good relationship with him and found him to be a man who felt no bitterness towards the people who had robbed him of twenty-seven years of his life.'[31]

Suddenly the Watsons found it easier to meet with ANC

leaders because surveillance of the ex-prisoners was not so strict. There were simply too many of them for the Security organs of the South African Government to watch over.

But although the ANC was now legal, the Watson brothers denied that they were members of the organisation for about six months. 'In February, just before Mandela's release, we got a phone call warning us, "Don't raise your heads. Don't come out from underground",' Valence said. 'But by June it was decided we shouldn't remain underground any more. It was nice to be able to say, "Yes, I'm ANC," without going to jail for seven years, to talk openly about our involvement and to work more effectively when called upon.'[32]

Valence and Ronnie were both operatives of the ANC. 'As soon as the operatives were identified there was a danger that they'd all be arrested or eliminated,' Valence said. 'But after 1990 we worked with the ANC Department of Human Resources Development. Piliso asked me to move with him when he changed from head of Security to head of the DHRD.'[33]

Valence's task at this time was to tell the white community what lay ahead, 'to show them that the rubbish you see in the media is not what it's all about, to set up meetings between black and white community leaders and between business leaders.

'We were also investigating the "hit squads",' he said.[34]

Soon after Mandela's release, almost before the celebrations for the beginning of a new era had finished, South Africa erupted into violence. Mandela had urged his supporters to lay down their arms: 'Take your guns, your knives and your pangas and throw them into the sea!'[35] But his plea went unheeded. He then tried to meet with Chief Mangosuthu Buthelezi, leader of the Inkatha Freedom Party, to try and resolve the differences between Inkatha and the ANC, but the ANC leaders in Natal considered it dangerous and vetoed the meeting. It was then that powerful forces were released against the black townships around Johannesburg.

On 26 March 1990, in Sebokeng township, south of Johannesburg, the police, without warning, used live ammunition on ANC demonstrators, killing twelve and wounding hundreds. Mandela said,

> *This sort of action angered me like no other, and I told the press that every white policeman in South Africa regarded every black person as a military target. [He] warned Mr de Klerk that he could not 'talk about negotiations on the one hand and murder our people on the other.'*[36]

For many years single black men had lived in migrant worker hostels on the edge of the city. From these hostels came troops of thousands of men from the Inkatha Freedom Party, heavily armed, to attack innocent people, mainly Xhosa and other blacks, in the township of Sebokeng. ANC supporters retaliated. In three days of fighting, thirty-two people were killed. The government blamed it on 'black on black' violence and did nothing to stop it.

Donner had commenced.

But several Members of Parliament, including Leon Wessels, suspected that the massacre had been planned. 'People from outside were bussed in. They hinted that the State was involved. It was dismissed as black on black violence but I had the suspicion it was institutionalised and not as innocent as it was presented,' he said.[37]

Mandela wrote:

> *On 22 July busloads of armed Inkatha members, escorted by police vehicles, entered Sebokeng in broad daylight . . . I visited the area the next day and witnessed scenes I have never before seen and hope never to see again. At the morgue were bodies of people who had been hacked to death; a woman had both her breasts cut off with a machete. Whoever these killers were, they were animals.*[38]

There were more attacks from Zulus right across central South Africa, all of which were dismissed by de Klerk's government as 'tribal'. Adriaan Vlok, Minister for Law and Order, said, 'It is impossible to have a policeman on every street corner.'

Mandela went to de Klerk several times to ask him to take action and put an end to the violence. 'It became clear he was not moved by the massacre. He still counted black lives like flies,' he said.[39]

There was a further attack from Inkatha members in November, on a squatters' camp called Zonkizizwe, outside the city of Germiston, east of Johannesburg. Twenty-nine people were killed, ANC people were driven out and their property confiscated. Johan Scheepers, an MP who instructed the Deputy Commissioner of Police to investigate the attack and prosecute if necessary, was overruled by the government. Some MPs began to suspect that the police were involved in the killing.

De Klerk defended the police, saying, 'If I look back I have no regrets on how this mission was managed. The majority of police are law abiding.'[40]

Archbishop Tutu said that the government had 'a knee-jerk reaction'.[41]

The violence almost always involved Zulu Inkatha Freedom Fighters. In 1973 Buthelezi had become Chief Minister of Kwazulu. He claimed he was on an ANC hit list. Buthelezi felt that his political future was threatened by Mandela's release. He attempted to stop the ANC from getting organised by staging a series of attacks on pro-ANC townships. He was pleased when the government introduced a regulation allowing Zulus to carry 'traditional' weapons to political meetings. These weapons – spears and knobkerries, wooden sticks with a heavy wooden head like an axe – were used against the ANC.

There was a common belief at the time that a 'Third Force' was masterminding the attacks. Accusations were even levelled at de Klerk. The Watsons, who had prior knowledge of the political strategy to slaughter people and so divide the black community, felt very frustrated but kept on with their work bringing members of the ANC together with the uninformed public and monitoring the hit squads. Their distaste for de Klerk increased as he continued to go on television after attacks by the Security police on innocent people and make excuses for them. In one case he said, 'There were instances where the police did not act as they should but that happens throughout the world.'[42]

In July 1991, a secret memorandum revealed that the Security branch of the South African police had funded Inkatha. Also 200 Inkatha activists were given secret training by the South African Army. De Klerk admitted this was so, but said the activists were necessary to protect VIPs. At the trial of some of these activists the judge found that their training had nothing to do with VIPs. The trainees were involved in hit squad activities.

Also, in July 1991, the ANC held its first annual conference inside South Africa for thirty years. Mandela was elected President and Cyril Ramaphosa Secretary General. Mandela describes Ramaphosa as 'probably the most accomplished negotiator in the ANC'.[43]

By mid-1991 the Watsons' domestic lives were beginning to become a little more comfortable, although they were still under surveillance and their phones were tapped. Eileen now had a good job in the white community. She and Valence and their three boys moved into a rented house and installed a series of spotlights outside that were left on all night.

One night in September 1991, Andre De Villiers, who had been a sporting contact for more than twenty years, approached Valence again. He said that he had some very dangerous information and asked if they could meet to talk. Andre was very nervous. He said that the 'hit squads' Security had said did not exist, did exist. This Valence already knew.

'Andre was extremely afraid that the information he had could lead to him being killed,' Valence said. 'He started by telling me that the business in which he was a partner was involved in a fraud concerning a certain council. He said that if I investigated the fraud, some other very dangerous information would come to light. He did not want to tell me more in case he was identified as the source.'

Valence and Andre met several times during September and October. 'Andre later told me that the hit squad, known as "Hammer", was not purely an SADF operation but that elements within Hammer were involved with "much bigger fish", and were connected with the Security police and the smuggling of drugs. He talked about the killing of trade unionists and politicians in Port Elizabeth and Uitenhage and stressed that there were many more killings than those reported. He told me the names of two white Security police who were involved in kidnapping, torture and killings. He said he had given certain information about this to a senior officer in the police force and two politicians, but that there was a cover-up, which he believed was coming from Cabinet and the highest echelons of the State Security machine. Andre said that the police officer seemed honest but was surrounded by corruption and was scared, especially when the disclosure of the killings was made.

'Andre said he was withholding certain information because he was still investigating. I pleaded with him to tell me everything. He said that he would like to but it was too dangerous. He said, "These people do not play. They are killers."

'He later told me that he had witnessed meetings late at night at his business, between men in blood-stained overalls and gloves, who were burning their balaclavas in a drum at the back of the building and laughing about how many "kaffirs" they'd killed. They had guns and rifles with telescopic sights.

'I went to Andre's business one day, and met a man who told me his job was to change the number plates of certain minibuses that entered the premises after hours,' Valence said.

'One Monday afternoon in late October, Andre phoned me at home at 4 p.m. For the first time, he mentioned the Security police on the phone. At 2 a.m. on Tuesday I was phoned by Francois De Villiers, who told me that Andre had been assassinated at 8.30 p.m. on Monday. I was extremely shocked.

The killing of "ordinary" citizens had started.

'At the beginning of their meetings Andre had dropped one hint to me as to who the members of the hit squads might be. He'd said, "Just look at the guys who have suddenly got rich. Security allows them to run illegal operations such as drug trafficking. Security also pays them to kill."'[44]

When Andre had rung Valence the last time he'd begun to recite a string of names to him. Valence, alarmed, had told him not to say another word. Andre said he had more names and would come over in the morning with them. That night he was shot. He died in his son's arms, saying, "Valence Watson knows everything." The police refused to believe De Villiers' murder was political. They said it was just a robbery by blacks that went wrong.

Valence went on national radio, insisting that De Villiers' murder was political and organised by Security. He demanded a judicial inquiry into the murder and the hit squad allegations. He outlined the Security network and said it all led up to the National Party being murderers.

Mono Badela told Valence he was proud of him, but that he was crazy to call the National Party murderers on the national media.[45]

Eddie Trent, an MP in the Eastern Cape, confirmed that just before Andre De Villiers' death, De Villiers had approached him. 'Andre said he knew things that were dangerous. The Watsons were convinced that the Security police wiped him out. The police were certainly involved in covert things, but they were never arrested.'[46]

Eventually three members of the Security branch were tried for masterminding much of the township violence. One of these was Basie Smit. Another was Engelbrecht, Head of

Criminal Intelligence, who was also found guilty of operating a weapons factory and organising random killings on trains.

It was excruciating for the Watsons to know so much about the operations of 'hit squads', and of drug and weapon smuggling in the Security branch and not be able to do anything to prove it.

In December 1991, de Klerk attacked Mandela in the Parliament, accusing him of letting the ANC keep weapons, which perpetuated the violence. Mandela angrily demanded the right of reply, telling the Parliament that de Klerk had been 'less than frank.'

In September 1992, the ANC launched a campaign of rolling strikes. Hospitals were closed, services stopped, water and sanitation systems demolished. It was an action to destabilise the government. Huge demonstrations showed the government the extent of ANC support in South Africa. The general strike brought the country to a standstill.

Then the ANC organised a march on Bisho, capital of the Ciskei, because the government had prevented the ANC from functioning in its own territory. A hundred thousand people moved across the borders and advanced up the hill towards the heavily armed soldiers. No one expected them to shoot.

Cyril Ramaphosa, chief negotiator for the ANC, said, 'All hell broke loose. The soldiers started to shoot. I was terrified. The massacre was televised worldwide. They took twenty-eight lives. This embarrassed the de Klerk government.'[47]

Mandela refused to negotiate any further with a government that was 'killing our people' until it had agreed to certain conditions.

The conditions were that all ANC prisoners, even criminals,

be released, that Inkatha warriors be banned from carrying weapons, and that razor-wire fences be put around their hostels.

Mandela said, 'My colleagues were doubtful but I was confident. De Klerk wanted us more than we needed him.'[48]

'Our President was as tough as nails,' said Cyril Ramaphosa, 'Incredibly stubborn. I had jelly knees, fearing everything was going to fall apart.'[49]

But de Klerk knew that if he and Mandela did not sign the record of understanding, all would be lost. He agreed to Mandela's conditions.

Security's plan to foster as much black on black violence as possible and blame it on the ANC, so that the National Party would gain 50 per cent of the vote in the election, continued right up until election day in May 1994. But the result was 62.6 per cent of the vote to the ANC.

Mandela was sworn in as South Africa's first black President, with de Klerk and Thabo Mbeki as his deputies. Mandela had lived to achieve his ideal 'of a democratic and free society in which all persons live together in harmony with equal opportunities'. And in a not insignificant way, the Watsons had helped him.

PART TWO

13

'TORTURE AND MURDER? IT'S WATER UNDER THE BRIDGE'

In May 1995, just one year after the election, I went to South Africa to visit the Watsons in their own country for the first time.

As a journalist who was not sympathetic to the apartheid regime I had been refused a visa to enter South Africa under the previous government. Consequently my contact with the Watsons had been confined to phone calls, reading the transcripts of interviews with them as part of the research for a proposed film about their lives, and meetings with Valence, Ronnie and Eileen when they came to Sydney in 1989 for two weeks and again, for a short time, in 1992.

My main source of information about the Watsons until 1995 was what they had told me about themselves. As a journalist my inclination was to be sceptical, in spite of their apparent honesty. Perhaps they had exaggerated. So it was with a sense of excitement and trepidation that I arrived in South Africa to see if the story the Watsons had told about themselves would be validated by their friends, and – indeed – their enemies.

How important had their contribution to the struggle been?

How respected were they by both sides? What was their role now in the new South Africa? Were their powerful enemies still around and would they talk to me?

Port Elizabeth is a port town on the Eastern Cape. Flying in, one sees pale, white beaches that seem to stretch forever, large suburban houses with hedges, gardens and pools and then a mass of tiny shacks like chicken coops with no trees and bare earth – one of the black townships.

On ground level Port Elizabeth is a windy, provincial, industrial town, although the port is almost idle. On the main beach there are coal loaders in the dunes. Black dust mingles with fine white sand and foam from the waves to blow in great stinging gusts across the beach. Large gulls with wide wingspans and strong black bodies gather in a mass on the cold sand before wheeling away to cross the ocean. There are the beginnings of a tourist industry – in the main street a Holiday Inn, oceanarium with trained dolphins, a snake park and the Brooks Hill Pavilion with new apartments, in one of which I stayed. The Pavilion also has a Kaffe Haus overlooking the sea, two restaurants and a tapas bar playing loud rock, which is full of ex-Security men.

The Watsons have been called the Kennedys of Port Elizabeth. To those who know Port Elizabeth this may seem a dubious accolade. But many South Africans who are acquainted with the Watsons told me that they are far more worthy human beings than the Kennedys could ever be. And some of their enemies, still powerful in the new South Africa, felt jealousy, resentment and anger towards them.

These days the Watson brothers do not live all together in a grand house. They are rebuilding their family lives and have rented modest houses in a pleasant suburb of Port Elizabeth, close to good schools, parks, gardens and each other. Only Ronnie lives in a flat in Johannesburg, and he often visits Valence's family for the weekend.

At Valence Watson's family home the steady stream of phone calls is mostly conducted in Xhosa. There are also impromptu meetings round the dining-room table, and comrades from different parts of the country call in at any time for a chat or advice. Coffee, tea and homemade cakes are served at all hours of the day and there is soup with freshly baked bread or a full meal for a comrade who arrives late at night after a long journey. Eileen and Valence's mother, Bobbi, run the household smoothly in spite of the heavy demands on it. The garden is lush and well tended. ('Ronnie planned the garden and whenever he is here for a few days from Jo'burg he adds more plants,' Eileen explains.) There is a swimming pool in the back garden, a small apartment for Bobbi and a study for Valence. Two African women, Grace and Nomvula, relatives of the original staff at the farm, still work for the family, cooking, cleaning and doing the housework.

Cheeky and Tracey, with their two children, live a few blocks away and drop by often. Gavin and Leigh Ann, who have three children, visit regularly too. The children all attend the Grey School, which is part public and part private school. They are well mannered and very affectionate to everyone in the family and to visitors. There is a feeling of great love and pride in this Watson clan.

Since their father, Dan, died, Bobbi has become the matriarch. She is elegant, polite and evidently much respected by everyone who visits the house.

There is certainly an element of the Kennedys in the Watson family. The difference is that the Watsons have survived in spite of their enemies.

When I explained to the Watsons that I intended to interview their enemies as well as those who supported them, there was some consternation, particularly from the women in the family. They had been through years of fear and persecution. They could not bear the thought of ex-Security police and black activists who had turned against them being contacted and asked questions that might bring back painful memories. But eventually they agreed that the story would be unbalanced without the voices of these people; they even became mildly intrigued to see what their adversaries might say.

One of the most distressing experiences for the Watsons was being included in the second boycott of white businesses by the black community in 1986. This seriously affected their business, which was already ailing, and they became bankrupt soon afterwards.

At the time they had been slightly puzzled as to why they had been included in the boycott, but they had accepted the decision of the black boycott committee without question.

Mkhuseli Jack was one member of the boycott committee who did not regard the Watsons as heroes. Described as 'a key UDF leader in the area, twenty-seven-year-old Mkhuseli Jack was in such demand among blacks and whites that he carried a bleeper so he could be paged'.[1]

Jack felt ambivalent towards the Watsons. He strongly resented them for what he saw as their power and paternalism, but could not help admiring them as well. 'I had known the Watsons for a long time, first of all as celebrities,' he told me.

'They were the first white people to have a high profile and enjoy celebrity status in the townships amongst black people. But they couldn't manage that fame of theirs. It became very destructive. They started to venture into politics. They were business people. I have no basis to say they exploited their customers. If you are a celebrity, people will come to your stores. But once they entered into politics the controversy became worse and worse. People were taken in by their paternalistic attitude. The Watsons would fund political activities. It was a bad idea that they controlled people. They turned people into anti-apartheid activists.' Mkhuseli Jack spoke angrily.[2]

I asked him why he thought it was such a bad idea to turn people into anti-apartheid activists. He did not answer the question, but gave further reasons for his objection to the Watsons.

'The Watsons liked having control. They have remote control even now. These guys are bad. They can work with anyone. They're like the Kennedys. They have their own organisation as a family. It's nothing to do with belonging to a political organisation.'

'Is this the majority opinion of people you know in the ANC?'

'I can't speak for everybody. The Watsons tend to deal at leadership level. I'm no hero but I got involved with the struggle. I have fought against apartheid.'

'Are you still an activist?'

'I don't have to be. It's not my priority. Now I'm a businessman. I wish I was more successful.'

'The Watsons were very successful,' I suggested.

'I know. I knew them when they were rich, living like *Dallas*, that film. When I got into their house it was like in a James Bond movie. Imagine me, from a township? For the first time in my life I felt like a human being. I was accepted as a guest in this beautiful, well-run house.'

'So why do you hate the Watsons now?'

'They've been very destructive! They've destroyed some good comrades.'[3]

'Who? Can you give me names?'

Jack became vague. It was clear that he both admired and was very jealous of the family.

The Watsons were surprised when they learned of this conversation, but thought it made sense of something that had puzzled them for a long time. 'At the time of the second boycott we had heard there were a few rabidly anti-white radicals on the committee. Our black friends were too embarrassed to tell us the details. But we abided by their decision that we should be included in the boycott,' Valence said.[4]

It is certainly true that the Watsons were resented in some quarters for their intelligence gathering over the years. The reports they uncovered must have contained negative material about a lot of people. Valence claims that these files were compiled, analysed and evaluated by many people, not just the Watsons. When Valence and Cheeky were told the names of the whites whose careers, according to Mkhuseli Jack, the Watsons had ruined, the brothers looked bewildered. They said they had never reported these people. They thought that some who had failed to do well under the new regime might assume the Watsons were responsible.

Soon after Mandela's release from prison in February 1990, Ronnie Watson had become even closer to Chris Hani, who was then regarded by the ANC as Mandela's likely successor. At the ANC conference in Durban Hani had received the highest number of votes.

In April 1993, Chris Hani was gunned down by a white man in broad daylight in front of his own house. Ronnie was devastated.

It was not so much the fact that Ronnie Watson's car registration number had been found on a piece of paper in the killer's glove box, indicating that Ronnie may have been next on the hit list, that shocked him, but that Hani could be so blatantly murdered. Even today, Ronnie cannot speak about the murder without becoming emotional. He paces, and angrily wipes away tears as he talks.

'I was one of the first there after the shooting. Tokyo Sexuale was there too. He burst out crying. We all to a man walked away and cried. To see people crying . . . The person has been shot in this callous manner, shot in front of his house.

'Chris had more courage than we had. He was a real problem. I'd ask him, "What do they hate most about you?" He'd reply, "They know I will never sell out the African people." (He meant the poor.)

'I am angry about Chris Hani's death,' Ronnie said. 'His murder was planned. We suspected for a long time that Chris was the main target of the National Party government as he was so popular at grass roots. That's why Chris often stayed in my flat and had two bodyguards. The alarming thing is that those psychopaths who planned the murder are still in Security today.

'After the attempt on his life in Maseru, Chris had to leave Lesotho. He was in danger. There were bomb attacks on his house. We'd have to engineer meetings in Gabarone, Lusaka. When I was to meet Chris in Gabarone they tried to kill me. They couldn't discredit us. But I warned our people, "When they fail to discredit, they will kill."[5]

'Chris Hani would not cooperate with any deal,' Ronnie continued. 'Security did not want a man of integrity, a communist and a Christian. His support network was too good. They killed him, but that network is stronger today than it was then.'[6]

'Chris left behind a legacy of activism,' Valence added. 'At his last birthday, his fiftieth, he said, "Look at the back of the crowd and you will see four white youngsters." (He's a few years older than the oldest of us, but in Xhosa it's better to be old.) "These were sports activists. I took them and gave them an ideological basis to their activism." Everyone laughed. In the Xhosa culture it's good to take the credit for everything.'[7]

Ronnie continued, 'I had to organise the party. There were 200 of his best friends. The caterers asked how much alcohol we wanted. When the party was finished, none of the booze had been used. It struck me then, the quality of these people. They drank pure fruit juice, ate food and had fellowship. They were just workers. No one high profile except a few political and trade union leaders were there. The rest were just activists like us.'[8]

Chris Hani's widow, Limpho, is now a member of Parliament. We met in her lunch hour at Parliament House in Cape Town. She is open, friendly, intelligent and has a keen wit.

As we were checked through security before we could enter the dining room at Parliament House, I was asked by the white Security officer if I was carrying a gun. I replied that I was not. The officer then informed me grimly that the metal detector had picked up something the shape of a handgun in my handbag. I was nonplussed and, feeling about in my bag, produced the offending piece of metal, which I held up for inspection. 'She can't do much damage with an oversized front door key, officer,' said Limpho Hani airily as we swept through to the dining room.

Hani spoke with great affection and admiration of the Watson brothers. 'In the process of being activists the Watsons and Chris and I became very close. They were more like brothers to us. I met the whole family, their children, parents, everyone. They are a very warm family. No wonder they got involved in this funny game of politics. They were humanitarians. They hated to see anyone suffering. If I had said, "Give me that shirt you're wearing", they'd have done it. I find it very strange, but those boys think alike. They're very strong. We have lots of African leaders here now who the Watson family built up. One would have thought that the Watsons might want to be in the limelight and in government themselves, but they don't. They work twenty-four hours a day pushing others. When you sit with them in a political meeting, it's not just a serious gathering, they make it fun.'

'Some people are critical of the Watsons; they say they like to be in control. What do you think?' I asked her.

'They don't want control. They're in the background. They do research. If I need information, Valence will get it for me. They prefer working in the background. We, the new politicians, always know they are there for us. Other white people are power hungry. But the Watsons are more than a resource, they're a support group.'

'What do they get out of this?'

'They are not getting any money. They have lost it all. They don't get any financial support from the ANC. They don't like accepting money. It's the way they've been brought up, like missionaries, in my opinion. What they are getting out of being a support group is the love and appreciation of the black community. In the ANC people forget they are whites. They know our culture, can predict our reactions. Ronnie would say to Chris, "Don't do this or he'll do that. Wait and then try this . . . "'

'Did the Watsons ever help you and Chris financially?'

'When our first daughter went to the University of Cape Town, I couldn't afford the things she needed. I couldn't borrow money because I already had a bank overdraft, so Chris phoned Valence and Ronnie. They had very little money themselves but they said, "How much do you want?" The following day that money was in the bank.

'The Watsons are a bit like an African family; the emphasis is on love. I fight with Ronnie a lot. Sometimes I don't speak to him. You always fight with people you love. I'm very stubborn. So is he. He'll make me sit down, like a father, and say, "You have to do this now."

'"No," I will say.

'"You're mad," he will say.

'Ronnie never fought with Chris. Chris used to stay in Ronnie's flat. They were very close. Sometimes they wouldn't talk ANC business; they'd talk about me. Chris would say, "She's not speaking to me. I don't know why." Ronnie was part of us. I'd tease him about his girlfriends. I still call him "brother". Ronnie's son calls me his second mother and when he was little he used to sleep in bed with me. Even now, if I say I've got a problem, Ronnie will leave whatever he's doing in Johannesburg and come here to help me.'

Limpho Hani works mainly in two areas, minerals and energy, and housing. 'Five per cent of the budget now goes on housing. It used to be 1 per cent,' she told me proudly.

I asked whether there was a spirit of camaraderie between the former activists and members of the establishment in Parliament yet. Hani laughed. 'In the beginning it was very interesting, all of us sitting together after being against each other for so long. Individuals would accuse each other, like children, saying, "You did this to us!", but now it's changing and we're all starting to address the real issues. Parliament previously was a boys' club, so at first they treated us like little ladies, as if we were soft and gentle. They now realise we are buddies. We are the seventh country to have a majority of women in Parliament,' she said. 'But there is still no allowance for me to pick up my child at 5 p.m.'

Hani has three daughters, all now at school or university. She feels sad that she is unable to spend much time with them, but believes that her job is more important at this time.

'Our president and ministers are all in government for the first time. Since everybody is new, there are bound to be teething problems. We are constantly told, "According to international standards . . . " but our situation is different. I'm proud of what the ANC has achieved in one year. Apartheid was entrenched. I'm living in Acacia Park; that used to be illegal for blacks. There is free medical treatment for children under six and pregnant women, one free balanced meal a day for children in primary schools. The government is creating jobs. But still there are problems. The other day I went with a comrade, an Indian woman, to address people in the squatters camp outside Cape Town about education. My comrade said to them, "You should watch this educational program on TV", and went on to explain why. I noticed the audience getting angry. Eventually one woman stood up and said, "Let me tell you, comrade, I don't have a house, let alone a TV."'

Even though her job is arduous and requires her to move about the country, Limpho Hani still manages to see the Watsons, particularly Ronnie, quite regularly. She says she is concerned about Ronnie.

'His work is sensitive and dangerous. He'll just say to me, "I have a meeting", and I won't know where or what it is.'

'But now the ANC is in power, aren't the old enemies disappearing?' I asked.

'We are in office, yes, but we don't yet have economic power. The same old faces who don't want to see change are still here. The bureaucracy is still in place. There are thousands of Security police still working in the system, although they are now called something else. The bureaucrats and police try to sabotage the changes proposed by our ministers, which makes us get fed up and impatient. But I am optimistic about the future. Individuals have stopped attacking each other in the Parliament; we are beginning to feel that we are not ANC, IFP or NP but South Africans.'[9]

I arrange to meet one of the Security police still working in the system. His name is Colonel Carl Edwards and he is now Co-ordinator of the Community Policing Program for the Eastern Cape. Although he has never met the Watsons, he knows a great deal about them. He resents the fact that they continued their campaign against apartheid in spite of harassment and great personal danger.

When I phone Carl Edwards to ask if we might meet, he asks light-heartedly why it has taken me so long to call him. He seems well aware of my day to day movements in Port Elizabeth and which people I have already spoken to.

At his suggestion, we meet in the noisy, crowded tapas bar. He points out a friend, also ex-Security, and explains proudly that he is a brave man who has killed over twenty people on the border.

It is only mildly embarrassing for Edwards to be reminded of the role he played in the Security branch, persecuting people like the Watsons who were so recently regarded as 'terrorists'.

'Let's relegate the past to the past,' he told me firmly. 'It's water under the bridge. Everybody was culpable. We regarded it as a revolutionary war. Anybody who got involved was a terrorist. Our job was to go in search of them.'

Edwards, who is about the same age as the Watsons, grew up in the Eastern Cape. He says that Ronnie, as a schoolboy, once defended him in a fight. What is chilling about Edwards is that he seems so ordinary. He could well have been the Watsons' next-door neighbour. He is smart, agile and feels no remorse for the part he played in the 'revolutionary war'. He is resentful of the way the international media portrayed the South African Security Service in the 1980s and early 90s and seemed, at the beginning of our interview, to be directing some of his anger towards me. 'They portrayed us as narrow-minded, ignorant and stupid,' he said threateningly. 'We were never stupid! We were following the laws.'

'But surely that's the Nuremberg defence?'

'I've never made excuses for what I did. I'm very proud of

it. It's easy to say, "So and so was involved with these murders, this torture." It's water under the bridge. We did a lot of naughty things in the past. But so did the ANC.'

'You see yourself as professionally proud of what you did. But do you believe that the ANC was right to insist on one man, one vote?'

'The problem is that the people vote with their feet, not their heads,' Colonel Edwards said.

'What do you think of the Watson brothers?'

'They are totally acceptable to the black population, 100 per cent, which accounts for their powerful position. They are brilliant propagandists.'

'But they were regarded as outcasts by the whites after playing rugby with the blacks. They were severely ostracised. They went bankrupt. Then they were criminalised. They had no power at all.'

'The Watsons went against the run of play. South Africa wasn't ready for it. Why didn't they go to the other side? You believe according to the way you've been brought up. You make choices. Everyone has to decide which way to jump. I believed change would come to South Africa eventually. I continued as I was. In the struggle to change too quickly a lot of people fell by the wayside. It's a dirty game. Nobody comes out clean. The Watsons were always businessmen. They've got their agenda.'

'Do you ever feel a grudging respect for them?'

'They're all men's men. They're good at handling the media.'

'Is that why they weren't killed, because they appealed to the international media?'

'We had no interest in killing the Watsons. There was no proof in my opinion that they were involved in what people said they were. Anyway, our resources were small. We were not infallible. We didn't have the manpower or time for fancy footwork.'

'Three of the four brothers claim there have been attempts on their lives. Do you know why MI6 tried to kill Ronnie?'

'Somebody inside South Africa thought Ronnie was worth wiping out. I certainly didn't and nor did my colleagues in Port Elizabeth. If the Watsons had been involved in MK, transporting terrorists or weapons, they'd have been under intense surveillance. We got everyone we were after. Shot them. Anyway, it's not prudent to dig up the past. We've got to bury the hatchet. It was war.'

'When I read descriptions of the torture that Security police inflicted on people like Archie Mkele, it sounded too detailed to be invented. Was torture just accepted as part of the game of war?'

Colonel Edwards bristled defensively. 'I was mentioned as one of those guys torturing, but I was on leave. They were bullshit allegations.'

'Even if you never tortured, you must have known it was being done.'

'Our function was to keep the wolf from the door, to stop innocent people being blown up,' he said grimly. 'It was war.'

'Do you feel happier now it's over?'

'Shit, what a relief! In those days we worked like demons, keeping the wolf from the door. Late nights. Early mornings. You should talk to my wife.'

'What do you think the Watsons will do in the future?'

'Well, they certainly know all the role players. They've got their agenda.'

'And what is that?'

'A decent lifestyle?'

Colonel Edwards seemed to feel that the Watsons were on moral high ground that he could not touch, and this frustrated him. He regarded them with a mixture of controlled anger, envy and fear.

'Have you met any of the Watsons recently?' I asked him.

'I've never had anything to do with them. At some point in time we should meet. Some Members of Parliament have recently thought of getting old pals together – Security police, UDF, ANC, etc. – for a good old chin wag. The Watsons would be invited to one of those meetings, certainly.'[10]

He says this without a trace of irony.

The Watsons were surprised that Colonel Edwards had said they might be invited to a reunion of ex-Security police and ex-terrorists. Valence was mildly amused by the idea but he did not think that he or his brothers would go.

I asked if he thought Archie Mkele might go to such a meeting.

There was a pause and then Valence said gravely, 'Every morning Archie gets up before it is light and prays for an hour, then he goes for a run for an hour to help get rid of the anger he still feels towards those Security guys who tortured him. Only then does he feel ready to go to work.'[11]

Ntsikelelo Bungane is now personal assistant to Premier Raymond Mhlaba of the Eastern Cape. He too was tortured when he was an activist. He is young, intelligent and sincere and talks positively about the future of the new South Africa. Often, in his job, he comes face to face with ex-Security policemen. 'I'm working with them but I do not trust them.

We are encouraged to let bygones be bygones. The Premier is always giving such orders. But the three guys who tortured me, I don't see myself forgiving them.'

One of the reasons for Bungane's torture was to get information about Ronnie Watson's whereabouts in Lesotho. I asked if the Security police got the information they were after.

'No! Not at all,' Bungane said proudly. 'I trusted the Watsons, regarded them more like my brothers in blood. They were exceptional. We risked operations together. They would never disappoint you.'[12]

Mike Nzotoyi is General Secretary of the ANC in Port Elizabeth. He joined the ANC while he was a prisoner on Robben Island for seven years. When he was released in 1985 he met the Watsons. 'I recruited people to MK with the Watsons. I trusted them. Their house in Park Drive was the only place that was safe.'

'Why didn't the police raid the Watsons as they did to other ANC members?' I asked.

'They were scared of the Watsons,' he said.[13]

Moki Cekisani is Chairman of the Ubuntu Environmental Trust in Port Elizabeth. He was a strong supporter of Steve Biko and the Black Consciousness Movement. After Biko's death he joined the Pan African Congress. He is volatile, passionate and speaks loudly, because he is deaf as a result of being beaten about the head while in prison. He also has scars from being electrocuted. 'I was attracted to the Watsons in the early seventies because of their tolerance for black politics. It could not have been easy for them as whites to accept black consciousness. When I was released from detention in 1978 I was under house arrest for eight years, confined to a house in the black township of Walmer, and not allowed to talk to people. The system was vicious. If you broke the rules it could kill. The police could arrive at any time. But the Watsons were never scared to visit me. At one stage they smuggled me out and hid me in their house for two weeks. I was very close to their late father. The family supported me financially and I was able to start a small upholstery business. My banning order was one of the last to be lifted – not until 1986.'

While Cekisani was under house arrest for eight years he got to know the Security police who visited to check on him. 'Some of the guys were very close to me. One guy was conscripted to go to Angola. I said, "Why go there? You're being used to kill unnecessarily." A few days later he shot himself. I cried. It was the first time I'd cried for a dead white man, a Security policeman. For the new South Africa to work we've got to have a spirit of reconciliation.' Cekisani said.[14]

Some former political assassins have been given amnesty as part of the process of reconciliation in the new South Africa. Mandela's government pledged to create a 'Truth Commission', where those who were guilty of crimes could confess and apply for amnesty. But bitterness runs deep, and the relatives of black activists who have been murdered find it difficult to forgive the former policemen responsible, just because they say in their defence, "We were brainwashed, taught that blacks were not human beings, but like animals."[15]

Relatives say they do not want revenge, but justice, and cannot understand how a white policeman like Dirk Coetsee, who was exposed as a former hit squad commander, is not behind bars. Coetsee is now a member of the ANC. Recently he agreed to meet the family of Griffith Mxenge, the black hero and ANC-supporting lawyer he had murdered in November 1981 in Natal. Coetsee said on television that he was dreading the meeting. He told the dead man's family that he was sorry for what he had done. They replied that they would like to see him arrested and charged.

Coetsee said that he had not been charged because this would have been embarrassing to the new regime, as he had been one of the few ex-Security police to have a change of heart and stand up against the old system.

After meeting with Coetsee, the dead man's brother said with dignity that his worst suspicions had been confirmed. Coetsee had become a folk hero, who was cheered when he went on television talk shows to confess that he'd had a change of heart about killing black activists. In fact he was still dangerous and untrustworthy.[16]

The Watsons are inclined to take a similar view of ex-Security police who claim to have seen the error of their ways. Neither are they particularly tolerant of certain white members of the ANC.

Eddie Trent is the white Eastern Cape Democratic Party leader. 'There is huge friction between the Watsons and other white members of the ANC,' he said. 'I have heard that they exercise influence over our Parliament in Bisho, which has a strong communist representation. I am told the Watsons are on the SACP side.

'I think that what drives them more than anything is an abhorrence of the apartheid system. I don't accept that they are just clever businessmen. They would have capitalised on that and sought money and power.

'The Watsons were hounded by the Security police for years and years but they were never arrested on political grounds. Why? Maybe it was because nothing could ever be proved. Molly Blackburn was very positive about them. [Molly Blackburn was a political activist who died in a road accident after her brakes failed. It has recently been proved in a Truth Commission hearing that she was murdered by Security, who tampered with the brakes.]

'What I find strange is the intrigue about these guys. If anyone suggested to them that Valence took the rap in their court case, they would of course deny it. When Valence came out of jail he got an Honours degree in Commerce and worked for the Development Corporation.

'If you look at Valence in public he doesn't sound like a socialist, but then many South African communists don't really seem to be. It's an historical thing. The Watsons' Communist Party connections arouse some discontent in the black community as well as the white.

'When we were trying to amalgamate the police forces after the ANC won the election, Valence was initially heavily involved. He produced a paper and was prominent at meetings but then he just seemed to fade away. None of the Watsons were on our lists [of parliamentary candidates] so perhaps they were not very ambitious. I wouldn't know. But I would have thought that Valence could have got on a list.'[17]

It is baffling to many people in the Eastern Cape why the Watsons did not try to enter Parliament after the ANC won the election.

Valence explained with a smile that he had acted as

Strategic Manager of Police for two months. 'It was an ironic situation. At my first meeting with the police I said, "Gentlemen, I think you all know who I am." These were the guys who'd been trying for years to get hold of us.'[18]

But since then he has accepted no official position in the new government.

'But why, when the people trust you and you have been with the struggle for so long?' I asked.

'I'd never take a position in the ANC. I'm an activist, not motivated to take political office. I don't want to gain anything financially from the new South Africa. It's better people don't know what I do. In the past I brought businessmen, political parties and the Trade Union movement together and helped to form the Regional Economic Forum. I was on the Directorate of the ANC's Department of Human Resources Development until the government of National Unity came into being.'[19]

Valence is not being coy when he says 'It's better people don't know what I do'. He really believes he can be more effective as a resource to the black community and the new government if he does not have a high profile. He is simply called a consultant, which means that his phone rings day and night.

'No one in our family seeks publicity,' Valence insisted. 'There was a time during the years of anti-apartheid struggle when publicity kept us alive. But now we would rather fade into the background.'[20]

Some people, however, refuse to believe that Valence Watson does not have political ambitions.

Rory Riordan is a white ANC member of the Transitional Local Council in Port Elizabeth. 'I would say the Watsons are ambitious to be in politics,' Riordan said. 'Valence was on the list initially but he was re-shuffled. He will get something. Ronnie is the most intensely paranoid. He's deeply involved in the business of finding plots. Gavin and Cheeky seem to me to be less so. Cheeky is almost out of politics. He's intent on making a living.

'There was an unbelievable focus of anger on the Watsons from white Afrikaners. To them they were white thuggies who'd broken rank, the ultimate traitors. They certainly went for them,' he told me. 'When the Watsons were being tried for arson and fraud in court I went along as an observer. There were more police than I'd ever seen in my life.

'The Watsons got involved in politics through rugby. They were quite unschooled in politics, but their contribution to the struggle against apartheid in the late seventies was stunning. Magnificent. They did a tremendous job. They were hounded and victimised but they stuck to it. They are a close-knit force. An injury to one is an injury to all. They were pioneering. They are still doing very good work. But a change in their approach to politics came at about the time of the second consumer boycott. They ran very successful businesses, starting with one and ending up with four. When they were included in the second boycott they went broke. At this stage they became incredibly supicious of the motives of a lot of people. They became involved in the ANC underground, which is a very hard world. They were brave, but a certain amount of paranoia set in.'

'Would you say there was some reason for that paranoia?'

'The State was unquestionably out to get them. When their house was burnt down, I was uncertain. But after Steve Burnett attempted to assassinate Ronnie, I felt the State was unquestionably behind it, although it has never been proven. There was amongst certain people an absolute hatred for the Watsons. It was difficult. They lost balance and began vilifying people. They've done it to me. They believe that white people in the ANC are either subservient to the Watsons or they're some sort of Security police.

'The Watsons have very close associations with influential people in government. They obtain enormous loyalty. A number of white people in the ANC have been subjected to strong attacks by them, the same way as the Watsons were attacked. The Watsons operate easily within the ANC.'[21]

'Is it true that you, the Watsons, have attacked white people within the ANC with whom you disagree?' I asked Valence.

'I wouldn't say it's true at all,' he replied. 'We are outspoken on issues. I don't apologise for that. The Watsons are known as being critical of people with an agenda, who try to use the ANC for their own political ends. If you join the ANC you don't join for personal gain or aggrandisement.

'Some people who have previously been in the PFP [Progressive Federal Party] have decided to join the ANC. There's nothing wrong with having a Damascus road experience. But ANC members have a right to ask why the PFP and its members supported the slaughter of people in Mozambique and Lesotho. We have been vocal about that. We say, "Tell us your deeds and we'll forgive you." Having been in the underground struggle we've learned to question everything. Otherwise we'd be dead today. Many of our comrades were killed because they cooperated with the wrong people.

'Any loyal ANC person couldn't possibly deny the Watsons. We were in the ANC when it wasn't popular in the white community. Throughout the years of struggle we've always cooperated with people who were beyond reproach. But we've never allowed people with a hidden agenda close to us. That's why we're still alive today. Of course there will be certain people who are not pro the Watsons. They have their own agendas and they have a democratic right to oppose our views.'[22]

14

'WHEN WE DIE I WOULD LIKE TO THINK WE MADE A DIFFERENCE'

What are the agendas of each Watson brother in the 1990s? Valence is re-establishing his family life in Port Elizabeth and works as a consultant. He is completing an MBA at the University of South Africa and has been a research fellow at the entrepreneurial centre at Wharton, a prestigious business school in Pennsylvania in the United States. He uses his business skills to advise in many different areas in the new South Africa.

Ronnie lives in Johannesburg and is a trader of imported goods. On a voluntary basis, he uses his skills to assist the new ANC politicians. He has just bought a 'farm', which his brothers describe as 'absolutely wild and untamed'. (Recently the brothers and their children went camping there, got lost, and had to be lifted out by helicopter.)

Cheeky is beginning to get back into business in the Eastern Cape. His business is going 'reasonably well', although he finds the new government is slow in making decisions due to the fact that bureaucrats from the old order are still in place and often manage to sabotage government ministers. He is trying to get the new government to 'rediscover tourism as a big industry'. Cheeky is also involved in preaching.

Gavin advises and helps to facilitate business and education within the black community in Port Elizabeth. He is currently using his business expertise to assist the Entembeni Enrichment Centre and the Umzamo Trust Community Development.

The Entembeni Enrichment Centre is for black pupils who want to repeat their matriculation exam because of failure or a poor pass. In 1994, 726 students sat for the examination. They achieved a 91 per cent pass rate, which is 40 per cent above the national average.

As we approach the gracious, white building on a hill overlooking the sea, Gavin explains that he is only one of a team who helped establish the school. Reverend Brian Bird, his longtime friend and a member of Concerned Citizens, was one of the founders and so was Sicelo Duze, who now directs the centre.

How could students who had practically given up any hope of passing their matriculation well enough to enter university now be doing so well?

Duze said he thought the good results hinged on 'discipline, hard work and a "tough-love" approach towards pupils.' There are five 'non-negotiables' at the centre – attendance, time, homework, respect and monthly tests. If the pupils fail in any of these they are given no second chance. 'We are preparing them for the real world,' said Duze. 'Arrive late to class, fail a test or show disrespect to teachers or fellow pupils and you're out. The onus is on the pupils and the family to achieve. We do not believe in spoon feeding and are determined to go past simple head-learning.'[1]

Gavin Watson has helped to provide the centre with eighty

computers and a computer laboratory to teach the students, most of whom had never seen a computer before.

'We go to various schools in the townships and bring children in for further education. Any kid who wants to can come. We send buses to collect them between 2 p.m. and 5. We go to New Brighton, Zwide, Kwazakele, Kwambele and Walmer,' he told me.[2]

I watch the students walking down the corridors of this well-kept building and chatting in small groups in the grounds. They seem relaxed, mature and well motivated. Entembeni is a great contrast to most of the schools in the black townships.

'We've linked this computer system up to the one at the University of Port Elizabeth, which is checking the kids' progress,' Gavin explains enthusiastically. 'The system cost about two million rand. We got the money from various trusts and organisations, both in South Africa and overseas.'[3]

There are plans to extend the Entembeni program to Cape Town and possibly other cities.

Next morning we are off to a meeting of the Umzamo Trust, the other organisation that Gavin is passionate about. He drives fast, explaining with enthusiastic gestures, just what the Trust aims to do. His brothers make jokes about Gavin's bad driving, which gets worse as he gets more involved in his subject.

The aim of the Umzamo Trust, Gavin explains, is 'to get blacks into the mainstream economy, to teach them how to be entrepreneurs, to get black builders to contract for their own shopping centres, to teach them how to run their own food, clothing and entertainment outlets.'[4]

The philosophy of the Umzamo Trust is that there should be empowerment, not by handouts but through successful business partnerships between private enterprises and the communities in which business operates.

'The need for community and entrepreneurial development is obvious, with an unemployment rate in this region of 65 per cent. Black people have been deliberately kept out of the mainstream economy for the last forty years,' states the Umzamo Trust Community brochure.[5]

At the meeting of the Umzamo Trust, about sixty black people, mostly men, are packed into a small council room. Gavin Watson and a group of six others sit at a long table out the front. The chairman, Peace Malinda, opens the meeting. The atmosphere is one of intense interest. Gavin, dressed immaculately as usual, gives a short rousing speech, partly in English and partly in Xhosa. He incites the assembled electricians, builders and plumbers not to become sub-contractors but joint developers in certain buildings about to be contracted in the Central Business District. He tells them that government and corporate programs must be complemented by micro-entrepreneurs. This is a challenge for them. Umzamo Trust will help them to create jobs and stop poverty in the black community. But they must take the initiative. Gavin gets up to demonstrate on a whiteboard the way the Umzamo Trust can coordinate the development. 'We're not just developing this for whites. It's so that we can work and live there.' He looks around at the assembled black people. Nobody mutters that Gavin Watson is not black. 'Let's get involved!' he finishes.[6]

Gavin's speech is greeted with loud murmurs of agreement and a few cheers. There are many questions, mostly in Xhosa.

Some builders seem uncertain of their ability to take responsibility for a whole development in the CBD. It is daunting to contemplate such a thing, they say, after generations of taking orders. Others disagree. There are jokes, at each other's expense. One giant of a man with a surprisingly soft, gentle voice admits that sticking to a particular date to finish a building would be a problem for him.

The room fills with sympathetic laughter.

Next the chairman produces a letter with a fake Umzamo Trust letterhead. A small black building company has been illegally calling itself Umzamo Trust. It is decided that rather than penalise this company they will invite them to the next meeting of Umzamo Trust and encourage them to join.

At the end of the meeting, the feeling is one of optimism. There have been few people who haven't participated in the decision making.

Afterwards I comment on this and Gavin explains. 'In the new South Africa they *have* to participate. Some of them are a bit shocked at having to take responsibility. But it's necessary. They have political freedom but they're not economically free yet. We have the ideas which help give people self-confidence. The Umzamo Trust is helping to empower them. There is good camaraderie. We have a collective. The major directors of companies now want to be our friends. The Trust is busy with a 300 million rand project. We were the only ones to unlock that deal. People like working with us.'

'Do you personally make any money from this deal?'

'No, I make money from being a consultant. It's enough to live on.'[7]

None of the Watsons is affluent, but compared with the

way they were living in the 1980s, they are now quite comfortable.

Cheeky Watson lives in a small suburban house with a pleasantly overgrown garden, which he shares with Tracey and their two children, Candy and Luke.

These days he loves to cook rather than play rugby, and his brothers tease him about having put on weight. Cheeky is unfazed by this. He sits with his feet up in a comfortable chair in his lounge room, while delicious smells waft in from the kitchen. He speaks slowly, has a deep voice, a commanding presence and a droll sense of humour. Cheeky has been described as the least politically involved of the brothers, and one senses that he is a little battle weary. He has found it immensely difficult to get re-established in business, in spite of his considerable skills.

'In 1991 I tried to establish a financial services business. The bureaucrats were still in power and I found that I could not get contracts. I approached the five biggest insurance companies in the country to try and sell their products. They stonewalled me. I asked why and they told me: my political background was too controversial.

'I had been searching for a job for about a year when I eventually got one with Federal Life, a British-based firm, but they wouldn't give me a contract. The branch manager showed great confidence in me. He flew me up to Durban to meet the new chairman, who had just changed the name of the firm to Norwich Life. I had no idea why the new chairman wanted to meet me. When we met I said, "Your company has been racist. Because of my political background they wouldn't give me a contract." He investigated and found this was true.

He then said, "I'm here to right the wrongs of the past", and gave me a 30 000 rand cheque to help establish my broking business. That was my first breakthrough.'

The years before the Norwich Life job, things had been grim. 'We were living with Tracey's parents to save money and driving an unroadworthy, unregistered vehicle,' Cheeky recalls. 'It was a little yellow Mazda that ran on a teaspoon of petrol. God bless the Japanese. The problem was that the top had rusted and whenever it rained I had to drive with a raincoat over my knees.'[8]

Tracey adds that she was afraid of being caught by traffic police in this unroadworthy car. 'I stayed at home to mind the children, who were little, and did Cheeky's books. I waitressed for a time, but when Cheeky started making money I stopped. I was doing gospel singing twice a week and was involved with my church group.'[9]

'Tracey helped me tremendously in my insurance business. It was a battle. Although Norwich Life assisted me greatly I was restricted to selling their products, and only earning 50 per cent of the profits. I tried to break into other areas of business, at first selling watches and later on overalls.'

Tracey laughs. Apparently this had not been successful.

'The guy who owned the overall company was a rabid right-winger, but he took a shine to us,' Cheeky explains with a puzzled expression. 'We told him we were Watsons, but he didn't seem to mind. We thought, "We've made it!" Then we discovered he thought we were the "shoe" Watsons, not the political activist Watsons. By that time we had developed a good relationship with us and he let us sell his overalls.'

In 1993 Cheeky Watson began a transport business. 'I transported oil and gas in big trucks. Fortunately you didn't need any capital. If you had the contract you could negotiate with finance companies to get the trucks. At the end of 1994 I expanded the business. But one of the enormous new vehicles I bought gave trouble. I found out it was secondhand. Eventually it exploded. Unless you're mechanically minded you've got a problem. I was always covered in grease and oil. I managed to sell the other truck without losing anything. I sold the business at the end of the year and just kept my brokerage business going.'

Cheeky and Tracey are both very involved in church activities.

'I'm not preaching at the moment but I always do a little sharing at house groups,' Cheeky says.[10]

'The other brothers are very politically motivated,' Tracey explains. 'Valence and Ronnie are called to work in politics, Gavin in business. For Cheeky and I, our hearts' desire is to be in the ministry.'[11]

Cheeky says he would like to spend 80 to 90 per cent of his time in the ministry, but admits he has had differences of opinion with the Pentecostal Church. 'We were some of the few Christians who spoke out against apartheid. The churches should be thanking the Watson brothers for the prophetic role they played in this country. The sad thing is they ostracised us for years. They made us feel unwanted. We had no place to worship. I was glad to minister when I was asked to at the Assemblies of God. I was given a title on which to preach: "Adam, where art thou?" They sent me out to practise on a coloured church, where they learned to perfect their ministering before they preached to whites. I said to the congregation, "I've come to practise on you so-called coloureds. But there's so much you can tell me that

I'm going to allow Tracey to sing and then will you please minister to me." I was never asked to minister again. So I said, "That's it." Since then I have ministered only to small groups at home. I'm just waiting on God for the next task I've got to do.

'My philosophy is, "Wait upon the Lord. Let Him direct you. Once He's placed the ball in your hands then it's up to you to run with it." We believe that He has divinely provided for us. He caused an unknown man to write out a 30 000 rand cheque to right the wrongs of the past. That was incredible. We are just waiting for the next stage of God's plan for us.'[12]

Does Tracey feel the same?

'Definitely. We've both grown up in the Church. My mother's a preacher. Cheeky's father was a preacher. We've had a similar background spiritually. My heart's desire is to sing for God, so people's lives are touched, their hearts are changed.'[13]

Tracey has a very fine singing voice. She has performed on television and made an album, but she refuses to record pop music. She sings only gospel.

When Cheeky is called away to the phone she races to the piano, sits down and accompanies herself in a song called 'I'm Gonna Be Free'. She sings with such spirituality and power that I, a non-believer, am moved to tears. When Cheeky returns and notices this he does not seem surprised. Apparently Tracey's singing often affects people this way.

Tracey and Cheeky tell me the story of how their daughter, Candy, at the age of three, was found, apparently drowned, in their swimming pool. They gave her mouth to mouth resuscitation, but she did not respond. She was blue and swollen with water. After a few minutes she vomited, but was still unconscious. They raced her to hospital. Medical staff tried to convince them that Candy was dead, but Tracey would not believe it. 'I prayed and cried out to the Lord to help us.' Cheeky tried to convince Tracey to give up, but she wouldn't. She stayed by Candy's bedside all night, praying. In the morning the child opened her eyes and said she was hungry. Her brain had not been damaged in any way. 'The medical staff told us it was a miracle,' Tracey says.[14]

It was his Christian faith that made Cheeky speak out against apartheid in 1976. But these days he sometimes wonders whether it might have been better to have become a Springbok after all. 'I ask myself, "Was it the wise thing to have done, to have given up the Springbok blazer I'd been promised in 1976?" Maybe it would have been more effective if I had just hung in there and got the blazer and played mixed rugby afterwards. But it did seem as though God's hand was guiding the whole thing. We weren't that aware of the political situation in 1976, when the school riots were at a peak. But once we'd played rugby with the blacks we became completely involved.'

These days Cheeky also admits that he worries about his brothers' safety, particularly Ronnie's. 'Ronnie is pushing it. He's too aggressive,' he says gravely.[15]

Although the brothers may still be resented by many in the white community, the blacks show no lack of affection for them. Everywhere I go in Port Elizabeth, with any one of the Watson brothers, they are recognised by black people and greeted warmly.

Valence drives me through Walmer township, where there was once a large sign saying 'No Whites Allowed'. He is instantly hailed by a crowd of youngsters, who wave and shout at us to stop. We get out and while he is chatting to them in Xhosa the crowd grows larger. As more young people come running the others shout, 'It's Valence Watson, who used to play for Wallabies!' After many hugs and jokes we climb back in the car. Valence tells me that it is ten years since he played for the Wallabies. Many of these kids are too young to have ever seen him play, but obviously the legend lives on.

At a restaurant the same evening, I am having dinner with three of the Watson brothers when one waiter greets them warmly. Suddenly every black waiter in the restaurant is at our table, leaving the other diners stranded. There is laughter, talk, jokes and questions. More staff emerge from the kitchen. The white manager looks pained. Eventually Valence breaks up the party and with much handshaking and exchanging of affection the staff return to their duties.

There is some criticism of the Watsons in the black community, I am assured, but it seems extremely rare. Even PAC members like Arabeleng Mosia, Chairman of the PAC in New Brighton, who does not agree with all that the ANC stands for, has no quarrel with the Watsons. 'When a white man becomes loyal to Africa he becomes an African. These Watsons are Africans. Like Joe Slovo. He was also an African. In the seventies I saw their place as a refugee camp.'

'These men are our examples. They were hated by the whites. The police were after us and them too. We had to pray in their shop. I used to pray for Ronnie when he went to Lesotho to see Chris Hani. God saved him because we prayed for him. Rugby was a big recruiting ground for the Church and a fertile ground for liberation. The Security branch couldn't get us at prayer meetings.'[16]

I talk to Mosia outside the Ascension Church in the black township of New Brighton just before attending the funeral of Sipho Nozewu, a top rugby coach, businessman and former Eastern Province 'King of Swerve'. Cheeky Watson is the only white speaker at this vast gathering. He speaks in Xhosa so I do not understand why ripples of laughter spread throughout the church. Later he tells me he made a joke about the 'King of Swerve's' ability to trip him up, even after his death, by tricking him into giving an impromptu speech at his funeral.

The funeral is not at all a gloomy affair. Sipho lived a full and interesting life and the congregation is here to celebrate that fact. His open coffin is displayed for all to see. The church is packed with friends and relatives dressed extremely well – the men in suits, the women in fashionable dresses, hats and gloves. The choir sings splendidly and everyone joins in. I am engulfed in the sound and feel I am being carried inside a wave of exultation.

When the various speakers make jokes about Sipho's small failings, there are gusts of laughter. When they speak of his great virtues there is applause and loud murmurs of agreement. Gavin Watson explains to me quietly that whatever an African's shortcomings in life, he is praised to the skies at his funeral. Gavin adds with a smile that Sipho died owing him a considerable amount of money. There are tributes from visiting preachers, local councillors, presidents of rugby clubs, coaches and former players. (In the local newspaper report next day, headed 'Glowing Tribute to the "King of Swerve"', even I am mentioned as a 'visiting Australian dignitary'.)[17]

Reverend Mxolisi Mfazwe is a fiery preacher, who describes Sipho as a man who was 'able to withstand the demons of apartheid in this country. He had vowed in his lifetime not to accept defeat.'[18]

The preacher then becomes very passionate, shouting at the congregation. He seems to be exhorting them to political action. They shout back, giving ANC salutes. I ask Gavin to translate. 'He is telling them that although they've won the election they won't be liberated until 1999, when the present bureaucracy is dismantled. He says that at this stage of our liberation we must carry things forward by having our local government elections at the end of this year [1995].'[19]

There are many old friends of the Watsons at the funeral. After the service they greet each other with hugs, followed by the comrade's handshake, then talk rapidly in Xhosa, laugh and give each other more spontaneous hugs. It is easy to see how the South African whites, whose body language towards the blacks is utterly restrained, if not disdainful, would find the Watsons' uninhibited affection for their black friends alienating.

People have travelled from Bisho, Durban and Cape Town for this funeral. Mono Badela has come from Johannesburg. Max Mamase, Minister for Housing and Local Government in the Eastern Cape, explains why people have travelled so far to bid farewell to Sipho Nozewu, an old rugby hero.

'Our eyes were opened through non-racial rugby. In 1976 when Mono Badela led Kwazakele rugby union and when Cheeky Watson actually forsook a Springbok blazer to play non-racial rugby, from that moment on the movement was unbreakable, right up to the stage where the ANC won the fight. That's why when one of our rugby heroes falls, you see people coming from many, many areas.'[20]

It is evident from talking to a number of people at the

funeral that the Watsons are an important part of the legend of rugby heroes who transformed themselves into fighters for the ANC.

Mamase tells me about the part played by the Watsons in the struggle against apartheid and the ANC's triumph in the election. He also talks about how the Watsons fell from favour with a few black activists, and how this ruined their business.

'I first heard about the Watsons when I was at school. Ronnie would come to the township to coach us. He was a hard player and a bloody fast runner. He was not good on the backline but excellent on the frontline.

'Later we played rugby with the whites. We wanted non-racial sport and were opposed to multi-racial sport (whites playing against blacks). At that time there were group areas acts; players could not go to the bar after a game. ANC policy was that we were all South Africans, black and white.

'Although you could not openly be ANC, rugby was a convergence of non-racialists. When the ANC introduced military combat most of us went outside the country for training. It was easy for us to go to Lesotho; we'd say we were going on holiday.

'We became a threat to the country. With the assistance of outside comrades we got the Springboks barred from international competition and that had a tremendous impact here in South Africa. As a result of that we were perceived as mobilising for the ANC. Rugby was a disguise.

'We began to meet with the Watsons. I went on a trip to Lesotho that was financed by them. We took clothes from their shop in East London to comrades in Lesotho and used their Mercedes to get there. The Watsons spent their money financing the revolution. Thus we felt that their consumer boycott exemption was just. But that caused a division, because some activists wanted a blanket boycott. There were individuals in the community who said the Watsons were making money out of the black community, but only a very few.

'In the second boycott the Watsons were included. At the time there was a strong anti-white feeling across the spectrum, although we, who were non-racial rugby players, were opposed to it. To us the Watsons were not whites. They were part of us. But a few key people felt the Watsons were making money out of the boycott.

'In the mid-1980s we activists were between life and death. We are fortunate to be still alive. The police were a law unto themselves. There were mass funerals every weekend. One could refer to this as a mini genocide. People running away from the police were hiding in houses and shops owned by the Watsons. At that time the Watsons had international recognition, so if the police touched them, they would get bad publicity, but the police knew that people being hidden by the Watsons couldn't stay long, and then they would pursue them again.

'We were working in closed networks. I don't think Colonel Carl Edwards' informers were as capable as he thinks. At no stage was I caught. I had a network I could trust. We knew some of the informers and were careful never to say anything in their presence. It was an extremely difficult period.

'Carl Edwards was wrong to believe he and his police were in control of the townships. The Security police had Combis with tinted windows. They would cordon off areas and get informers in cars to identify the activists. If they had to go to that extent, then they were not in control. I lost some good friends, but I was never arrested.

'The Watsons' commitment was crucial. They are not holding any high positions in government now. They never had vested interests. When they got exposed to township life they contrasted this with their own lives. As a result of their strong Christian values they felt they must assist in the total transformation of their society. The Watsons still enjoy a lot of respect in the community.'

'What did the Watsons mean to black Africans during the struggle against apartheid?' I ask.

Mamase gravely repeats what he has told me already. 'To us they were not whites. They were part of us.'[21]

Knox Tsotsobe owns a tavern, which was once a shebeen, in the township of East Brighton. The township is a mass of small houses crammed close. There are no trees, only bare earth, over which plastic and papers blow and children amuse themselves by rolling and chasing after abandoned car tyres.

Knox Tsotsobe's tavern stands out like a beacon in East Brighton. It is painted bright orange on the outside. Inside the lighting is dim, the radio plays African pop music and people sit about drinking and chatting in booths. It is neat and clean. A neighbour's three-year-old boy and a puppy mingle with the patrons. Tsobe is proud of the tavern, explaining that it has recently been upgraded and now attracts a better clientele. At the back he has added a comfortable bedroom for his wife. His teenage daughter, just home from school, follows him about and listens with admiration to him speaking fluent English to the only white woman in the township.

We walk outside and more children follow. A stream of cars and trucks are entering the township, as the day's work has finished. Drivers wave and hoot their horns at us. A white man who entered the township a few days ago to deliver some merchandise was shot. I am feeling apprehensive about walking near the main road, but Knox is pleased to be seen with me. The crowd of children and dogs behind us grows larger.

Knox Tsotsobe is fifty-four and Regional President of the Pan Africanist Congress in the Eastern Cape. 'I stepped down as Chairman after the election. I had played my innings. I said to myself, "Let the young blood take over".' He smiles. 'I have taken the people to where they wanted to be. They have elected their own government.'

The PAC, which believes in 'one settler, one bullet', has often been opposed to the ANC. But Tsotsobe is philosophical about the differences. As a result of being a prisoner on Robben Island from 1963–68 and mixing with ANC prisoners, he became more tolerant of ANC politics. 'When Mandela arrived we had already been at Robben Island for some time. In fact we built his residence. There was no difference of opinion between the presidents of the PAC and the ANC, or between the prisoners at all. We were a network of activists.'

When Tsotsobe came out of prison he met the Watsons. 'I went into one of their shops to buy a shirt and I'd never heard whites speaking my language so well. I was highly impressed with them. They offered me a job as a salesman. My wife had known them as boys because she grew up at Alicedale, where they had a farm. The Watsons were not seen as liberal whites. They were like black Africans.'

Knox Tsotsobe played rugby with Cheeky and Valence and discovered that although there was 'a lot of racism within the coloured camp, the ANC and PAC in this region were able to resolve their differences. That is why the Eastern Cape is so stable.

'No other whites were as strong as the Watsons. Their mother and father were both strong. They'd taught them since childhood to be involved with the blacks. They had played with black children. Christianity played a big role too. Even before you opened the shop, or closed it, you must pray.

'I had doubts about the Watsons after their house was burnt down. I thought, "Now these people will give in." When they didn't, I had great respect for them.'

'Did you ever try to win them over to join the PAC?' I asked.

'Yes! I argued with them but they always came up with facts to defend their position. Unfortunately they are ANC.'[22] He laughed.

Early one morning Cheeky, Valence and I leave the flat coastal town of Port Elizabeth to drive the two hours to Alicedale, where the Watsons spent their early years.

Along the shore black coal loaders loom up out of the mist like ghosts. An eerie fog horn sounds. Ships like silent cities lie at anchor until the blanket of white has lifted. We stream past the deserted Brooks Pavilion, and the Kaffe Bar with a splendid view for tourists, the oceanarium and the Holiday Inn, and soon we are out on flat, deserted roads on the way to Karoo country.

The road begins to wind and climb. There are blue hills and deep, wide valleys. 'One of our first farms was here,' Cheeky says. 'There were wild goats. Dad said to me, "If you catch those goats you can have them." I thought I'd get

Valence to help. I was eight. He was ten. I said, "Let's catch these goats." He said, "No, Cheeky, we'll get in trouble." After hours and hours we caught a goat. Valence said, "How do we tie it?" I said, "With my coat." The goat tore the coat to shreds. We caught two goats, slaughtered them and sold the meat,' he says proudly.[23]

The country is a mass of rocky outcrops, with only cactus and a few scrubby thorn trees growing. 'Thorn trees are the staple diet of goats,' Cheeky explains.

We follow a dirt road towards Kommadagga. Now there are plains, with sheep and cattle grazing. Monkeys race across the road. The earth is red, the scrubby grass a dull green. The sky is wide, blue and cloudless. There are no houses, just the occasional broken windmill where one might have been. Craggy red bluffs rise up out of the dry earth. 'This is where I was born, pal,' says Valence proudly.' This is where I grew up.'[24]

'I prefer rivers and lush mountains,' says Cheeky, unimpressed.

'Here it is. Kommadagga.' Valence leaps out of the car. We have stopped in an almost abandoned village. We all get out, breathing the clean, crisp air, taking in the bright sunlight and the silence. 'Very good sheep farming country. This was a construction village. They were building the railway line. Mother ran the store.' Valence strides around enthusiastically. Cheeky smiles and shrugs. Buildings have collapsed and weeds grow on what was once the main street. All that remains of the store is three chimneys. In the distance two small black children stare at us curiously.

We drive on, towards the farm the Watsons bought after leaving Kommadagga. The roads are just as rough, red and earthy as they were when the Watsons were children. Angora goats stand on their hind legs eating the thorn trees. The aloe cactus, which blooms with a brilliant red flower in June, is still green. We pass a cluster of farms, the houses built in the 1820s. One of these was a Watson farm. 'The houses were built close together for safety,' Valence explains.

The country is much more rugged than I had imagined. Grey rocky outcrops completely cover the earth in many places. The Watson boys would clamber over the boulders as they chased rock rabbits with their dogs. 'When we caught one we'd skin it and roast it on a spit, down by that pool there,' says Cheeky. The pool looks to me like a tiny pond. 'Look! There on top of that rock. There's a rock rabbit.'

The rock rabbit looks like a weasel; it is big and dark with short ears and sharp teeth.

On the road to Alicedale there is no traffic. No person walking. Not a living thing, except for rock rabbits.

'There used to be blue cranes here. They were beautiful,' Valence says nostalgically. 'But they were killed by powerlines and insecticides. Now they're almost extinct.'

Cheeky is driving and looks straight ahead. 'This is called "the hard country",' he says with a droll smile.

A family of baboons lopes across the road, in no hurry. 'Baboons can kill a dog very easily,' says Cheeky.

'See that prickly pear?' Valence asks. 'It has lovely fruit. In severe drought you can burn off the thorns and feed it to cattle.' We pass a purple rocky gorge. Now there are high ridges on either side of the road. 'Father and I used to minister to blacks out here,' says Cheeky. 'I was about ten.'

Valence grins. 'Cheeky stuck to our father like glue.'

'For protection?' I ask. They laugh.

We pass an ostrich farm. The tall, long-necked birds running fast with beaks open are covered in red dust, the same colour as the mountains.

The town of Alicedale has not changed much since the Watsons lived there in the late 1950s. It has a wide main street, bordered by trees, which when we visited were covered in autumn leaves. A river flows through the town. It seems a pleasant place. The school, where Ronnie organised fights, is still exactly the same.

'There were three main avenues in town: for whites, coloureds and blacks,' says Valence. 'We were closest to the blacks. There was an unwritten rule that no blacks could stay in the white or coloured part of town. Only later was it legislated. We were here when apartheid was being entrenched. As a kid I remember feeling absolutely confused. We had black friends, but we found ourselves drifting apart for no reason. Then, one day, we found out what it was. The master plan. It affected the media, the passing of laws and it was called apartheid.'

We drive on out of Alicedale to the last farm that the Watsons lived on before moving to Port Elizabeth. The farmhouse is a long way off the road and has a new owner, so we don't go in, although we can see it clearly. The sign on the gate says 'Happy Valley'.

'When we owned it we called it "Wilton". People used to stop driving on their way to town to admire the garden my mother had planted. It was huge,' Valence says.

'We used to race our horses along this driveway,' Cheeky remembers. 'My brothers would give me a start but Gavin always used to win.'

Driving back towards Port Elizabeth I suggest that growing up in this harsh environment amongst pro-National Party farmers should have made the Watsons' politics rather conservative.

'It's an absolute miracle that the opposite happened,' Valence says.

Cheeky thinks that the brothers' political beliefs had a lot to do with their parents. 'They led by example, not by being authoritarian. Our mother thought correctness in manners was important. But she was very soft and gentle.'

Cheeky tells a story to illustrate their mother's gentle firmness. When Cheeky was thirteen he and Gavin drove to the local store to buy supplies. On the way home Gavin, who was nineteen, wanted to read the newspaper so he let Cheeky drive. Cheeky was wearing flip flops (thongs) and when one got stuck under the accelerator he leaned down to retrieve it. 'When I looked up again I was flattening thorn trees,' Cheeky recalls. 'I rolled the van. Apart from a few thorns in the skin neither of us was hurt, but the van was a mess. Gavin said, "Don't tell anyone you were driving." But our mother was not convinced. She took me aside and said quietly, "Cheeky, let's hear the truth." So I told her. Our father then said, "It's your fault, Gavin. You should never have let him drive."'

'Our father taught us to have a strong sense of justice and equality,' Valence explains. 'His ancestors were Scots, warlike, not scared of a fight, a physical confrontation. He taught us that if a thing's got to be done, it's got to be done. He taught us to be stubborn, to fight for equality in this country.

'Our mother taught us to care about people's feelings. We were brought up to be chivalrous. She would make sure we did the right thing. She wouldn't lecture. She would show us.

She was half Italian. She believed cleanliness was next to Godliness, that you should always serve guests "a good table" no matter how little you had for yourselves, and that familiarity breeds contempt. She taught us to be gentle and consequently we were popular with the opposite sex.'

We laugh. Valence, in particular, has a fine reputation in this area.

He protests, genuinely embarrassed. 'I didn't work at that; it just happened. In the rugby environment most of the guys would make jokes about women and tell each other about their conquests. I wouldn't. I treated women sensitively.'

'Our mother would try to hide our bad deeds from our father to stop us getting a hiding,' Cheeky says. 'I never got a hiding because I was such a lovely child.'

'I had two hidings in my life, both because of Cheeky,' Valence says ruefully.

'We grew up in a very protected atmosphere. Our father was an easygoing fellow. I can't ever remember wanting to sleep out at a friend's house. I was so happy at home,' Cheeky says.[25]

'We were strong kids who grew up in a tough, wild country,' Valence says thoughtfully. 'I'd hate to be seen as the heroes of the struggle, as we were just a few amongst tens of thousands of activists. But when we die I would like to think we made a difference. I would like to believe that.'[26]

NOTES

PART ONE

'NAUGHTY BUT CHIVALROUS'

1 Valence Watson to Kristin Williamson (KW), 1 May 1995.
2 ibid.
3 Bobbi Watson to KW, 8 May 1995.
4 Gavin Watson to KW, 2 May 1995.
5 Cheeky Watson to KW, 1 May 1995.
6 Allister Sparks, *The Mind of South Africa: the story of the rise and fall of apartheid*, William Heinemann, Great Britain, 1990, p. 51.
7 ibid., p. 57.
8 ibid., p. 62.
9 Valence Watson to KW, 1 May 1995.
10 Bobbi Watson to KW, 8 May 1995.
11 Valence Watson to KW 1 May, 1995.
12 In Sparks, p. 185.
13 ibid.
14 ibid., p. 182.
15 Valence Watson to KW, 10 October 1992.
16 Valence Watson to George Miller (GM) and David Williamson (DW), October 1992. (Tape 6, p. 3.)
17 ibid., p. 19.
18 Bobbi Watson to KW, 8 May 1995.

19 Gavin Watson to DW, July 1986. (Tape 4, p. 21.)
20 ibid.
21 Cheeky Watson to KW, 11 April 1996.
22 Ronnie Watson to KW, 15 April 1996.
23 Cheeky Watson to DW, July 1986. (Tape 4, p. 21.)
24 Steven Geldenhuys to KW, 4 May 1995.
25 Margaret Geldenhuys to KW, 4 May 1995.
26 Cheeky Watson to KW, 1 May 1995.

2 FEELING THEIR HEARTBEAT

1 In James North, *Freedom Rising*, New American Library, New York, 1985, p. 41.
2 Allister Sparks, *The Mind of South Africa: the story of the rise and fall of apartheid*, William Heinemann, Great Britain, 1990, p. 196.
3 In North, p. 42.
4 Rian Malan, *My Traitor's Heart*, The Bodley Head, London, 1990, p. 59.
5 Ronnie Watson to DW and GM, December 1989. (Tape 1, p. 9.)
6 Valence Watson to DW and GM, December 1992. (Tape 11, p. 4.)
7 Archie Mkele to DW, 7 May 1995.
8 Valence Watson to DW and GM, December 1992. (Tape 11, p. 4.)
9 Cheeky Watson to KW, 11 April 1996.
10 ibid.
11 Ronnie Watson to DW and GM, December 1989. (Tape 1, p. 9.)
12 Mono Badela to KW, 7 May 1995.
13 Cheeky Watson to DW, July 1986. (Tape 4, p. 18.)
14 Valence Watson to DW and GM, December 1989. (Tape 6, p. 11.)
15 Mono Badela to KW, 7 May 1995.
16 ibid.
17 Gavin Watson to DW, July 1986. (Tape 6, p. 17.)
18 Ronnie Watson to DW and GM, December 1989. (Tape 7, p. 15.)
19 Cheeky Watson to DW, July 1986. (Tape 2, p. 6.)
20 Valence Watson to KW, 1 May 1995.

21 Cheeky Watson to DW, July 1986. (Tape 2, p. 26.)
22 ibid.
23 ibid.
24 ibid.
25 Ronnie Watson to DW and GM, October 1989. (Tape 7, p. 26.)
26 Cheeky Watson to DW, July 1986. (Tape 2, p. 29.)
27 Staff reporter, *Evening Post*, Port Elizabeth, 11 October 1976.
28 Cheeky Watson to DW, July 1986. (Tape 2, p. 9.)

3 FROM RAND MILLIONAIRES TO WHITE KAFFIRS

1 Geoff Bird, 'Craven Lashes Mixed Game', *Weekend Post*, Port Elizabeth, 12 October 1976.
2 ibid.
3 Mono Badela to KW, 7 May 1995.
4 Donald Woods, 'A Warning to Craven', *Rand Daily Mail*, Johannesburg, 15 October 1976.
5 Staff Reporter, 'Editor warns Craven: don't interfere', *Eastern Province Herald*, Port Elizabeth, 15 October 1976.
6 Nic van Oudtshoorn and Mel Channer, 'Rebel Rugby Trio Hounded', *Sunday Times*, Port Elizabeth, 13 February 1977.
7 ibid.
8 Cheeky Watson to KW, 11 April 1996.
9 ibid.
10 Valence Watson to DW and GM, December 1989. (Tape 8, p. 21.)
11 ibid., p. 24.
12 Ronnie Watson to DW and GM, December 1989. (Tape 8, p. 23.)
13 ibid. (Tape 5, p. 12.)
14 Valence Watson to DW and GM, December 1989 (Tape 5, p. 13.)
15 Ronnie Watson to DW and GM, December 1989. (Tape 8, p. 23.)
16 Cheeky Watson to DW, July 1986. (Tape 4, p. 24.)
17 Ronnie Watson to DW and GM, December 1989. (Tape 2, p. 15.)
18 ibid., p. 23.

19 ibid., p. 27.
20 Valence Watson to KW, 4 May 1995.
21 Valence Watson to DW and GM, December 1989. (Tape 4, p. 2.)
22 ibid., p. 7.
23 Cheeky Watson to DW, July 1986. (Tape 7, p. 22.)

4 SECURITY STRIKES

1 Archie Mkele to DW, 8 May 1995.
2 Valence Watson to DW and GM, December 1989. (Tape 10, p. 11.)
3 Cheeky Watson to KW, 2 May 1995.
4 Valence Watson to KW, 4 May 1995.
5 Cheeky Watson to KW, 2 May 1995.
6 Gavin Watson to DW, July 1986. (Tape 6, p. 11.)
7 Valence Watson to DW and GM, December 1989. (Tape 12, p. 24.)
8 Gavin Watson to DW, 1986. (Tape 6, p. 13.)
9 Eileen Watson to DW and GM, October 1992. (Tape 6, p. 3.)
10 Valence Watson to DW and GM, October 1992. (Tape 6, p. 3.)
11 Eileen Watson to DW and GM, October 1992. (Tape 6, P. 3.)
12 Cheeky Watson to KW, 2 May 1995.
13 Valence Watson in interview with Rory Riordan, *Monitor*, the Journal of the Human Rights Trust, Port Elizabeth, October 1988, p. 9.
14 Eileen Watson to DW and GM, October 1992. (Tape 6, p. 3.)
15 Valence Watson to DW and GM, October 1992. (Tape 14, p. 16.)
16 Eileen Watson to DW and GM, October 1992. (Tape 14, p. 16.)
17 Valence Watson to DW and GM, October 1992. (Tape 14, p. 16.)
18 Ronnie Watson to DW and GM, December 1989. (Tape 14, p. 24.)
19 Cheeky Watson to KW, 11 May 1995.
20 ibid.
21 Valence Watson to DW and GM, October 1992. (Tape 14, p. 16.)
22 Valence Watson, in *Monitor*, p. 6.

23 Archie Mkele to DW, 6 May 1995.
24 Ronnie Watson to DW and GM, December 1989. (Tape 14, p. 28.)
25 ibid.
26 Valence Watson to DW and GM, October 1992. (Tape 15, p. 36.)
27 ibid., p. 32.
28 ibid.
29 Cheeky Watson to KW, 11 April 1996.
30 Valence Watson to KW, 30 September 1996.
31 Nelson Mandela, *Long Walk to Freedom: the autobiography of Nelson Mandela*, Little, Brown and Company, London, 1994. p. 493.

5 DON'T GIVE THEM THE PLEASURE OF SEEING YOU CRY

1 Valence Watson to KW, 15 April 1996.
2 Cheeky Watson to DW, July 1986. (Tape 4, p. 10.)
3 Gavin Watson, ibid.
4 Eileen Watson to DW and GM, December 1992. (Tape 12, p. 16.)
5 Nelson Mandela, *Long Walk to Freedom: the autobiography of Nelson Mandela*, Little, Brown and Company, London, 1994, pp. 350–351.
6 ibid., p. 351.
7 Ronnie Watson to KW, 3 May 1995.
8 Linda Mti (alias 'Richman') to KW, 8 May 1995.
9 Ronnie Watson to KW, 3 May 1995.
10 Valence Watson to DW and GM, October 1989. (Tape 14, p. 18.)
11 Leigh Ann Watson to KW, 8 May 1995.
12 Gavin Watson to DW and GM, July 1986. (Tape 7, p. 1.)
13 Leigh Ann Watson to KW, 8 May 1995.
14 ibid.
15 Cheeky Watson to KW, 2 May 1995.
16 Tracey Watson to KW, 2 May 1995.
17 ibid.
18 Cheeky Watson to KW, 2 May 1995.
19 Tracey Watson to KW, 2 May 1995.

20 Cheeky Watson to KW, 2 May 1995.
21 Valence Watson to KW, 4 May 1995.
22 Ronnie Watson to KW, 2 May 1995.
23 Valence Watson to KW, 4 May 1995.
24 Eileen Watson to KW, 6 May 1995.
25 ibid.
26 Mandela, pp. 497, 501–3.
27 Valence Watson to KW, 15 April 1996.
28 Valence Watson to KW, 4 May 1995.

6 DEEP UNDERGROUND

1 Gavin Watson to DW, July 1986. (Tape 7, p. 18.)
2 ibid.
3 Cheeky Watson to KW, 7 May 1995.
4 Valence Watson to DW and GM, October 1992. (Tape 14, p. 26.)
5 Cheeky Watson to KW, 7 May 1995.
6 Valence Watson to KW, 15 April 1996.
7 Nelson Mandela, *Long Walk to Freedom: the autobiography of Nelson Mandela*, Little, Brown and Company, London, 1994, p. 506.
8 Valence Watson to DW and GM, October 1992. (Tape 15, p. 26.)
9 Valence Watson to KW, 7 May 1995.
10 Valence Watson to KW, 15 April 1996.
11 Valence Watson to KW, 7 May 1995.
12 ibid.
13 ibid.
14 Mandela, p. 509.
15 ibid.
16 ibid.
17 ibid.
18 ibid., p. 514.
19 Valence Watson to DW and GM, October 1992. (Tape 15, p. 12.)
20 Valence Watson to KW, 15 April 1996.
21 ibid.

22 Cheeky Watson to KW, 3 May 1995.
23 Gavin Watson to KW, 4 May 1995.
24 Mono Badela to KW, 6 May 1995.
25 ibid.
26 In April 1996, after the first week of hearings of South Africa's Truth and Reconciliation Commission into human rights abuses during the apartheid era, Joe Mamasela, a former Security officer, confessed on SABC television that he and other police had been involved in the murder of between thirty and thirty-five anti-apartheid activists. These included the PEBCO Three.
27 Mono Badela to KW, 6 May 1995.
28 Cheeky Watson to DW, July 1986. (Tape 7, p. 20.)
29 Gavin Watson to KW, 4 May 1995.
30 Mono Badela to KW, 6 May 1995.
31 ibid.
32 ibid.

7 THE BURNING OF THE HOUSE

1 Valence Watson to KW, 5 May 1995.
2 Cheeky Watson to KW, 6 May 1995.
3 Gavin Watson to KW 18 August 1986 (reprinted in *Times on Sunday*, 24 August 1986).
4 Cheeky Watson to KW, 6 May 1995.
5 Eileen Watson to KW, 6 May 1995.
6 ibid.
7 Tracey Watson to KW, 2 May 1995.
8 Cheeky Watson to KW, 2 May 1995.
9 Eileen Watson to KW, 6 May 1995.
10 ibid.
11 Cheeky Watson to KW, 2 May 1995.
12 *Death of Apartheid*, Part 1, BBC TV 1995.
13 Eileen Watson to KW, 4 May 1995.
14 Tracey Watson to KW, 2 May 1995.

15 Eileen Watson to KW, 4 May 1995.

16 ibid.

17 Tracey Watson to KW, 2 May 1995.

18 Leigh Ann Watson to KW, 8 May 1995.

19 *Death of Apartheid*, BBC TV, 1995.

20 Allister Sparkes, *The Mind of South Africa: the story of the rise and fall of apartheid*, William Heinemann, Great Britain, 1990, p. 367.

21 Nelson Mandela, *Long Walk to Freedom: the autobiography of Nelson Mandela*, Little, Brown and Company, London, 1994, p. 516.

22 ibid.

23 ibid.

24 Cheeky Watson to KW, 2 May 1995.

25 ibid.

26 Valence Watson to DW and GM, October 1992. (Tape 11, p. 10.)

27 Gavin Watson in Michael Parks, '4 White Brothers Spark Anti-Apartheid Struggle', *Los Angeles Times*, Los Angeles, 6 October 1985, pp. 22–23.

28 Valence Watson in Parks, '4 White Brothers Spark Anti-Apartheid Struggle'.

29 Ronnie Watson in Parks, '4 White Brothers Spark Anti-Apartheid Struggle'.

30 Eileen Watson to KW, 4 May 1995.

31 Tracey Watson to KW, 2 May 1995.

32 Cheeky Watson to DW, July 1986. (Tape 7, p. 5.)

33 ibid., p. 7.

34 Gavin Watson to DW, July 1986. (Tape 7, p. 7.)

35 Cheeky Watson to DW, July 1986. (Tape 7, p. 5.)

36 Brett Adkins, 'Watson Home Gutted in Fire Blast', *Evening Post*, Port Elizabeth, 21 October 1985.

37 Eileen Watson to DW and GM, October 1992. (Tape 12, p. 22.)

38 Adkins, 'Watson Home Gutted in Fire Blast'.

39 Michael Parks, '4 White Brothers Spark Anti-Apartheid Struggle'.

40 Cheeky Watson to DW, July 1986. (Tape 7, p. 8.)

41 Gavin Watson to DW, July 1986. (Tape 7, p. 9.)

42 Cheeky Watson to DW, July 1987. (Tape 7, p. 8.)

43 Cheeky Watson to DW, July 1987. (Tape 7, p. 10.)
44 Cheeky Watson to DW, July 1987. (Tape 7, p. 11.)

8 CRIMINALISING THE WATSONS

1 Cheeky Watson to DW, July 1986. (Tape 7, p. 16.)
2 ibid.
3 ibid.
4 Eileen Watson to DW and GM, December 1989. (Tape 17, p. 3.)
5 Gavin Watson to KW, 5 May 1995.
6 ibid.
7 ibid.
8 ibid.
9 Valence Watson to KW, 7 May 1995.
10 Cheeky Watson to KW, 2 May 1995.
11 Valence Watson to KW, 7 May 1995.
12 Gavin Watson to KW, 2 May 1995.
13 Gavin Watson to KW, 5 May 1995.
14 Max Mamase to KW, 6 May 1995.
15 Cheeky Watson to KW, 2 May 1995.
16 ibid.
17 Gavin Watson to KW, 5 May 1995.
18 Valence Watson to KW, 8 May 1995.
19 ibid.
20 ibid.
21 Nelson Mandela, *Long Walk to Freedom: the autobiography of Nelson Mandela*, Little, Brown and Company, London, 1994, p. 518.
22 Gavin Watson to DW, July 1986. (Tape 4, p. 16.)
23 Valence Watson to DW and GM, December 1989. (Tape 17, p. 11.)
24 Leon Schubart to KW, 7 May 1995.
25 Eileen Watson to KW, 5 May 1995.
26 Bobbi Watson to KW, 6 May 1995.
27 Eileen Watson to KW, 6 May 1995.

28 ibid.

29 Tracey Watson to KW, 6 May 1995.

30 Eileen Watson to KW, 6 May 1995.

31 Court Reporter, 'Watson Case: The charges', *Evening Post*, Port Elizabeth, 13 August 1986.

32 Bobbie Watson to KW, 6 May 1995.

33 Tracey Watson to KW, 6 May 1995.

34 Eileen Watson to KW, 6 May 1995.

35 Valence Watson to KW, 4 May 1995.

36 Leon Schubart to KW, 7 May 1995.

37 Valence Watson to KW, 10 May 1995.

38 Debbie Booysen, 'Watson denies seeking asylum', *Evening Post*, Port Elizabeth, 10 August 1986.

39 Valence Watson to KW, 10 May 1995.

40 Debbie Booysen, 'Wide Public Interest in Watson Case', *Weekend Post*, 16 August 1986.

41 Debbie Booysen, 'Watson: I did not stop police', *Evening Post*, Port Elizabeth, 14 August 1986.

42 Valence Watson to DW and GM, December 1989. (Tape 18, p. 2.)

43 Ronnie Watson, p. 4.

44 Valence Watson to DW and GM, December 1989. (Tape 18, p. 2.)

45 Debbie Booysen, op. cit., 14 August 1986.

46 ibid.

9 INSIDE RED HELL

1 Valence Watson to KW, 7 May 1995.

2 ibid.

3 Ronnie Watson to DW and GM, December 1989. (Tape 18, p. 8.)

4 Valence Watson to KW, 7 May 1995.

5 Valence Watson to DW and GM, December 1989. (Tape 18, p. 9.)

6 Eileen Watson, p. 11.

7 Eileen Watson to KW, 6 May 1995.

8 ibid.

9 Bobbi Watson to KW, 6 May 1995.
10 Tracey Watson to KW, 6 May 1995.
11 Bobbi Watson to KW, 6 May 1995.
12 Eileen Watson to DW and GM, October 1992. (Tape 17, p. 23.)
13 Eileen Watson to KW, 7 May 1995.
14 Tracey Watson to KW, 6 May 1995.
15 Leon Schubart to KW, 7 May 1995.
16 Gavin Watson to KW, 4 May 1995.
17 Kristin Williamson, 'Anti Apartheid Watson brothers refused bail while trial is stalled', *Times on Sunday*, Sydney, 14 September 1986.
18 ibid.
19 ibid.
20 Chris Rennie, 'I'd rather hang than testify', *Evening Post*, Port Elizabeth, 26 August 1986.
21 Mncedisi Saliso, 'Let me stay in custody – Watson witness', *Eastern Province Herald*, Port Elizabeth, 20 August 1986.
22 Kristin Williamson, 14 September 1986, op. cit.
23 Kristin Williamson, 'Letters from a tortured prisoner', *Times on Sunday*, 28 September 1986.
24 Kristin Williamson, 14 September 1986, op. cit.
25 Eileen Watson to KW, 7 May 1995.
26 Kristin Williamson, 14 September 1986, op. cit.
27 Valence Watson to DW and GM, December 1989. (Tape 19, p. 6.)
28 Eileen Watson to KW, 7 May 1995.
29 Valence Watson to KW, 7 May 1995.
30 Carol Mkele to DW, 6 May 1995.
31 ibid.
32 ibid.
33 Archie Mkele to DW, 6 May 1995.
34 Carole Mkele to DW, 6 May 1995.
35 Jayne La Mont, 'Many "converted" in Watsons' behind bars crusade', *Eastern Province Herald*, Port Elizabeth, 11 October 1986.
36 Ronnie Watson to DW and GM, October 1989. (Tape 19, p. 1.)
37 Valence Watson to KW, 15 April 1996.
38 Cheeky Watson to KW, 2 May 1995.

39 Valence Watson to KW, 5 May 1995.

40 Cheeky Watson to Rory Riordan, in an interview for *Monitor*, the Journal of the Human Rights Trust, Port Elizabeth, October, 1988, p. 8.

41 Ronnie Watson in *Monitor*, op. cit.

42 Leon Schubart to KW, 7 May 1995.

43 Jules Browde to DW, 7 May 1995.

44 Jayne La Mont, 'Police film Watsons, spectators in court', *Eastern Province Herald*, Port Elizabeth, 3 October 1986.

45 Eileen Watson to DW and GM, October 1992. (Tape 18, p. 19.)

46 Valence Watson to KW, 4 May 1995.

47 ibid.

48 Cheeky Watson to KW, 2 May 1995.

49 Gavin Watson to KW, 5 May 1995.

50 D. J. Klatzow, Transcript of proceedings of the regional court for the regional division of the Eastern Cape held at Port Elizabeth, 1 December 1986, p. 89.

51 Gavin Watson to KW, 7 May 1995.

52 ibid.

53 P. C. Nocanda, Court transcript, op. cit., p. 142.

54 Leon Schubart to KW, 7 May 1995.

55 Valence Watson to KW, 7 May 1995.

56 Henning Van der Walt to DW, 4 May 1995.

10 'A DISGUSTING TRIAL'

1 Carol Mkele to KW, 6 May 1995.

2 Valence Watson to DW and GM, October 1989. (Tape 18, p. 19.)

3 Archie Mkele to DW, 6 May 1995.

4 Valence Watson to KW, May 1995.

5 Eileen Watson to KW, 4 May 1995.

6 Gavin Watson to KW, 5 May 1995.

7 ibid.

8 Chris Rennie, 'Watson drama as witness freed', *Evening Post*, 15 January 1987, p. 1.

9 Valence Watson to DW, October 1989. (Tape 18, p. 18.)

10 ibid., p. 19.

11 ibid.

12 ibid., p. 20.

13 Leon Schubart to KW, 7 May 1995.

14 Jules Browde to DW, 8 May 1995.

15 Arthur Koetzen to DW, 8 May 1995.

16 Valence Watson to KW, 5 May 1995.

17 ibid.

18 Jules Browde to DW, 8 May 1995.

19 Valence Watson to KW, 7 May 1995.

20 Jules Browde to DW, 8 May 1995.

21 Valence Watson to KW, 7 May 1995.

22 ibid.

23 Cheeky Watson to KW, 2 May 1995.

24 Ken Vernon, 'Joy as Watsons get bail', *The Sunday Star*, Port Elizabeth, 18 January 1987, p. 2.

25 Jayne La Mont, 'Watsons celebrate after court grants bail', *Eastern Province Herald*, Port Elizabeth, 17 January 1987, p. 1.

26 ibid.

27 Eileen Watson to KW, 6 May 1995.

28 Ronnie Watson to DW and GM, October 1989. (Tape 22, p. 9.)

29 Eileen Watson to KW, 6 May 1995.

30 Valence Watson to DW and GM, October 1989, (Tape 22, p. 10.)

31 ibid.

32 Ronnie Watson to KW, 3 May 1995.

33 Valence Watson to KW, 3 May 1995.

34 Valence Watson to DW and GM, October 1989, (Tape 22, p. 11.)

35 ibid, p. 12.

36 Leon Schubart to KW, 7 May 1995.

37 Jayne La Mont, '"Unrest" move as Watson gets two and a half years', *Eastern Province Herald*, Port Elizabeth, 31 January 1987, p. 1.

38 ibid.

39 Tracey Watson to KW, 2 May 1995.
40 Eileen Watson to KW, 5 May 1995.
41 Valence Watson to DW and GM, October 1989. (Tape 22, p. 22.)

11 MI6 ATTEMPTS ASSASSINATION

1 Valence Watson to KW, 4 May 1995.
2 Ronnie Watson to DW and GM, October, 1989. (Tape 22, p. 27.)
3 Ronnie Watson to KW, 3 May 1995.
4 ibid.
5 ibid.
6 Kristin Williamson, 'Watson brother disappears after arrest', *Times on Sunday*, Sydney, 29 March 1987.
7 Valence Watson to KW, 7 May 1995.
8 Ronnie Watson to DW and GM, October 1989. (Tape 23, p. 3.)
9 ibid, p. 11.
10 ibid., p. 23.
11 Michel Desmidt, 'Watson, Mkele are released by Ciskei', *Eastern Post*, Port Elizabeth, 24 March 1987, p. 2.
12 Editorial, 'The Watson puzzles', *Eastern Province Herald*, Port Elizabeth, 26 March 1987, p. 16.
13 Herald Reporters, 'Watson: SA Security Police led questioning', *Eastern Province Herald*, Port Elizabeth, 26 March 1987, p. 2.
14 Nelson Mandela, *Long Walk to Freedom: the autobiography of Nelson Mandela*, Little, Brown and Company, London, 1994, p. 523.
15 ibid., p. 524.
16 Valence Watson to KW, 5 May 1995.
17 ibid.
18 ibid.
19 Ronnie Watson to DW and GM, October 1989, (Tape 23, p. 39.)
20 Ronnie Watson to DW and GM, October 1989. (Tape 24, p. 1.)
21 ibid., p. 5.
22 Valence Watson to DW and GM, October 1989. (Tape 24, p. 2.)
23 ibid.

24 Ronnie Watson to KW, 4 May 1995.

25 Valence Watson to DW and GM, October 1989. (Tape 24, p. 14.)

26 Valence Watson to KW, 4 May 1995.

27 ibid.

28 Ronnie Watson to KW, 4 May 1995.

29 Ronnie Watson to DW and GM, October 1989. (Tape 28, p. 29.)

30 Ronnie Watson to DW and GM, October 1989. (Tape 24, p. 33.)

31 Juliette Saunders, 'I am back to stay says Watson on return', *Eastern Province Herald*, Port Elizabeth, 25 July 1987.

32 Valence Watson to DW and GM, October 1989, (Tape 24, p. 35.)

33 Valence Watson to DW and GM, October 1989. (Tape 25, p. 4.)

34 Ronnie Watson to KW, 4 May 1995.

35 Valence Watson to DW and GM, October 1989. (Tape 25, p. 11.)

36 ibid.

37 Barbara Orpen, 'Watson Wins Arson Appeal', *Eastern Province Herald*, Port Elizabeth, 29 August 1987, p. 1.

12 TREES THAT GROW TALLEST CATCH THE MOST WIND

1 Ronnie Watson to KW, 4 May 1995.

2 Eileen Watson to DW and GM, October 1989. (Tape 25, p. 18.)

3 Eileen Watson to KW, 5 May 1995.

4 Tracey Watson to KW, 5 May 1995.

5 Eileen Watson to KW, 5 May 1995.

6 Valence Watson to KW, 5 May 1995.

7 Eileen Watson to KW, 5 May 1995.

8 Valence Watson to KW, 5 May 1995.

9 Gavin Watson to KW, 7 May 1995.

10 Valence Watson to KW, 5 May 1995.

11 Eileen Watson to KW, 5 May 1995.

12 Valence Watson to KW, 5 May 1995.

13 Nelson Mandela, *Long Walk to Freedom: the autobiography of Nelson Mandela*, Little, Brown and Company, London, 1994, p. 530.

14 *Death of Apartheid*, Part One, BBC TV, directed by Mick Gould, 1995.
15 ibid.
16 ibid.
17 ibid.
18 Valence Watson to KW, 8 May 1995.
19 Ronnie Watson to KW, 4 May 1995.
20 Eileen Watson to KW, 5 May 1995.
21 Tracey Watson to KW, 2 May 1995.
22 Valence Watson to KW, 8 May 1995.
23 ibid.
24 ibid.
25 *Death of Apartheid*, Part One, op. cit.
26 ibid.
27 ibid.
28 Valence Watson to KW, 8 May 1995.
29 Mandela, p. 546.
30 ibid.
31 Valence Watson to KW, 8 May 1995.
32 ibid.
33 ibid.
34 ibid.
35 Mandela, p. 566.
36 ibid., p. 568.
37 *Death of Apartheid*, Part Two, 1995.
38 Mandela, p. 566.
39 *Death of Apartheid*, Part Two, 1995.
40 ibid.
41 ibid.
42 ibid.
43 Mandela, p. 583.
44 Valence Watson to KW, 8 May 1995.
45 Mono Badela to KW, 6 May 1995.
46 Eddie Trent, MP, to DW, 7 May 1995.
47 *Death of Apartheid*, Part Two, 1995.

48 ibid.

49 ibid.

PART TWO

13 'TORTURE AND MURDER? IT'S WATER UNDER THE BRIDGE'

1 Allister Sparks, *The Mind of South Africa: the story of the rise and fall of apartheid*, William Heinemann, Great Britain, 1990, p. 338.

2 Mukeseli Jack to KW, 7 May 1995.

3 ibid.

4 Valence Watson to KW, 8 May 1995.

5 Ronnie Watson to KW, 4 May 1995.

6 Ronnie Watson to KW, 4 May 1995.

7 Valence Watson to KW, 4 May 1995.

8 Ronnie Watson to KW, 4 May 1995.

9 Limpho Hani to KW, 9 May 1995.

10 Carl Edwards to KW, 5 May 1995.

11 Valence Watson to KW, 6 May 1995.

12 Ntsikelelo Bungane to KW, 4 May 1995.

13 Mike Nzotoyi to DW, 4 May 1995.

14 Moki Cekisani to KW, 4 May 1995.

15 Dirk Coetsee, in *Confronting the Hit Man*, Yorkshire Television documentary, 11 July 1995.

16 Dr Mxenge, in *Confronting the Hit Man*, op. cit.

17 Eddie Trent MP to DW, 7 May 1995.

18 Valence Watson to KW, 8 May 1995.

19 ibid.

20 ibid.

21 Rory Riordan to KW, 8 May 1995.

22 Valence Watson to KW, 8 May 1995.

14 'WHEN WE DIE I WOULD LIKE TO THINK WE MADE A DIFFERENCE'

1 Sicelo Duze, in 'Ethembeni finds the key to success' by Peter Du Toit, *Evening Post*, Port Elizabeth, 11 January 1995.
2 Gavin Watson to KW, 4 May 1995.
3 ibid.
4 ibid.
5 Umzamo Trust Community Development brochure.
6 Gavin Watson at Umzamo Trust meeting, Port Elizabeth, 3 May 1995.
7 Gavin Watson to KW, 3 May 1995.
8 Cheeky Watson to KW, 2 May 1995.
9 Tracey Watson to KW, 2 May 1995.
10 Cheeky Watson to KW, 2 May 1995.
11 Tracey Watson to KW, 2 May 1995.
12 Cheeky Watson to KW, 2 May 1995.
13 Tracey Watson to KW, 2 May 1995.
14 ibid.
15 Cheeky Watson to KW, 2 May 1995
16 Arabeleng Mosia to KW, 6 May 1995.
17 Jimmy Matyu, 'Glowing Tribute to the "King of Swerve"', *Evening Post*, Port Elizabeth, 9 May 1995.
18 ibid.
19 Gavin Watson to KW, 6 May 1995.
20 Maxwell Mamase to KW, 6 May 1995.
21 ibid.
22 Knox Tsotsobe to KW, 2 May 1995.
23 Cheeky Watson to KW, 7 May 1995.
24 Valence Watson to KW, 7 May 1995.
25 Cheeky Watson to KW, 7 May 1995.
26 Valence Watson to KW, 7 May 1995.

BIBLIOGRAPHY

BOOKS

Adam, Herbert, *Modernizing Racial Domination: the dynamics of South African politics*, University of California Press, Berkeley, 1971.

Amnesty International, *South Africa State of Fear: security force complicity in torture and political killings, 1990–1992*, Amnesty International Publications, London, 1992.

Benson, Mary, *South Africa: the struggle for a birthright*, International Defence and Aid Fund for Southern Africa, London, 1985.

Biko, Steve, *I Write What I Like*, Edited by Aelred Stubbs, Harper and Row, San Francisco, 1978.

Breytenbach, Breyten, *Return to Paradise*, Faber and Faber, London, 1993.
The True Confessions of an Albino Terrorist, Taurus, Johannesburg, 1984.

Butler, Guy, *The 1820 Settlers: an illustrated commentary*, Human and Rousseau, Cape Town, 1974.

The Commonwealth Group of Eminent Persons, *Mission to South Africa*, Viking Penguin, New York, 1986.

Davidson, Basil, *The African Genius: an introduction to African social and cultural history*, Little, Brown and Company, Boston, 1969.

Davis, Richard Harding, *With Both Armies in South Africa*, New York, 1900.

De Klerk, W. A., *The Puritans in Africa: a story of afrikanerdom*, Penguin, Harmondsworth, 1976.

Du Toit, Andre, and Hermann Giliomee, *Afrikaner Political Thought: analysis and documents*, vol. 1, 1780–1850, David Philip, Cape Town, 1983.

Edwards, Isobel Eirlys, *The 1820 Settlers in South Africa: a study in British colonial policy*, Longmans, Green, London, 1934.

Elphick, Richard, *Khoikhoi and the Founding of White South Africa*, Ravan Press, Johannesburg, 1985.

Gandhi, M. K., *The Selected Works of Mahatma Gandhi*, Vol. 3 Navajivan Publishing, Ahmedabad, 1968.

Kane-Berman, John, *Soweto: black revolt, white reaction*, Johannesburg, 1978.

Katzew, Henry, *Apartheid and Survival: a Jewish view*, Simondium Publishers, Cape Town, 1965.

Lelyveld, Joseph, *Move Your Shadow: South Africa, black and white*, Times Books, New York, 1985.

Lodge, Tom, *Black Politics in South Africa Since 1945*, Ravan Press, Johannesburg, 1983.

Luthuli, Albert, *Let My People Go*, Collins, London, 1962.

Malan, Rian, *My Traitor's Heart*, The Bodley Head, London, 1990.

Mandela, Nelson, *Long Walk to Freedom: the autobiography of Nelson Mandela*, Little, Brown & Company, London, 1994.

Mandela, Nelson, *The Struggle Is My Life*, International Defence and Aid Fund for Southern Africa, London, 1978.

Martin, C. A., *The Concentration Camps, 1900–1902*, Howard Timmins, Cape Town, 1957.

McGregor, Robert, *Who Owns Whom?* Juta, Cape Town, 1989.

Moodie, Duncan Campbell Francis, *The History of the Battles and Adventures of the British, the Boers and the Zulus, etc. in Southern Africa*, Murray and St Leger, Cape Town, 1888.

North, James, *Freedom Rising*, New York: Macmillan, 1985.

Reader, D. H., *The Black Man's Portion*, Oxford University Press, Cape Town, 1961.

Slovo, Shawn, *A World Apart*, Faber and Faber, London, 1988.

Sparks, Allister, *The Mind of South Africa: the story of the rise and fall of apartheid*, William Heinemann, Great Britain, 1990.

Swan, Maureen, *Gandhi: the South African experience*, Ravan Press, Johannesburg, 1985.

Thompson, Leonard, *The Political Mythology of Apartheid*, Yale University Press, New Haven, 1985.

Welsh, David, *The Roots of Segregation: native policy in colonial Natal, 1845–1910*, Oxford University Press, Cape Town, 1971.

Wilson, Monica, and Leonard Thompson (eds), *The Oxford History of South Africa*, Volumes One and Two, Oxford University Press, Oxford, 1969.

JOURNAL AND NEWSPAPER ARTICLES

Bird, Geoff, 'Craven Lashes Mixed Game', *Weekend Post*, Port Elizabeth, 12 October 1976.

Booysen, Debbie, 'Watson denies seeking asylum', *Evening Post*, Port Elizabeth, 10 August 1986.

– 'Watson: I did not stop police', *Evening Post*, Port Elizabeth, 14 August 1986.

– 'Wide Public Interest in Watson Case', *Weekend Post*, 16 August 1986.

Channer, Mel, and Nic van Oudtshoorn, 'Rebel Rugby Trio Hounded', *Sunday Times*, Port Elizabeth, 13 February 1977.

Court Reporter, 'Watson Case: The charges', *Evening Post*, Port Elizabeth, 13 August 1986.

Desmidt, Michel, 'Watson, Mkele are released by Ciskei', *Evening Post*, Port Elizabeth, 24 March 1987.

Du Toit, Peter, 'Enthembeni finds the key to success', *Evening Post*, Port Elizabeth, 11 January 1995.

Editorial, 'The Watson puzzles', *Eastern Province Herald*, Port Elizabeth, 26 March 1987.

Herald Reporters, 'Watson: SA Security Police led questioning', *Eastern Province Herald*, Port Elizabeth, 26 March 1987.

La Mont, Jayne, 'Police film Watsons, spectators in court', *Eastern Province Herald*, Port Elizabeth, 3 October 1986.

– 'Many "converted" in Watsons' behind bars crusade', *Eastern Province Herald*, Port Elizabeth, 11 October 1986.

– 'Watsons celebrate after court grants bail', *Eastern Province Herald*, Port Elizabeth, 17 January 1987.

– '"Unrest" move as Watson gets two and a half years', *Eastern Province Herald*, Port Elizabeth, 31 January 1987.

Matyu, Jimmy, 'Glowing Tribute to the "King of Swerve"', *Evening Post*, Port Elizabeth, 9 May 1995.

Orpen, Barbara, 'Watson Wins Arson Appeal', *Eastern Province Herald*, Port Elizabeth, 29 August 1987.

Parkes, Michael, '4 White Brothers Spark Anti-Apartheid Struggle', *Los Angeles Times*, Los Angeles, 6 October 1985.

Rennie, Chris, 'I'd rather hang than testify', *Evening Post*, Port Elizabeth, 26 August 1986.

– 'Watson drama as witness freed', *Evening Post*, 15 January 1987.

Riordan, Rory, in *Monitor*, the Journal of the Human Rights Trust, Port Elizabeth, October 1988.

Saliso, Mncedisi, 'Let me stay in custody – Watson witness', *Eastern Province Herald*, Port Elizabeth, 20 August 1986.

Saunders, Juliette, 'I am back to stay says Watson on return', *Eastern Province Herald*, Port Elizabeth, 25 July 1987.

Staff Reporter, 'Editor warns Craven: don't interfere', *Eastern Province Herald*, Port Elizabeth, 15 October 1976.

van Oudtshoorn, Nic, and Mel Channer, 'Rebel Rugby Trio Hounded', *Sunday Times*, Port Elizabeth, 13 February 1977.

Vernon, Ken, 'Joy as Watsons get bail', *Sunday Star*, Port Elizabeth, 18 January 1987.

Williamson, Kristin, 'Anti Apartheid Watson brothers refused bail while trial is stalled', *Times on Sunday*, Sydney, 14 September 1986.

– 'Letters from a tortured prisoner', *Times on Sunday*, 28 September 1986.

– 'Watson brother disappears after arrest', *Times on Sunday*, Sydney, 29 March 1987.

Woods, Donald, 'A Warning to Craven', *Rand Daily Mail*, Johannesburg, 15 October 1976.

FILM AND TELEVISION CREDITS

Death of Apartheid, Parts One and Two, Directed by Mick Gould, BBC, London, 1994.

White Tribe of Africa: drowning in blood, Part One, BBC 1, London, Panorama, 1990.

White Tribe of Africa: no way back, Part Two, BBC 1, London, Panorama, 1990.

Rian Malan, *Tales of Ordinary Murder*, BBC 1, London, Panorama, 1990.

Sport and the Boycott, David Dimbleby, BBC, London, 1987.

The Comrades, BBC 1, London, Panorama, 1986.

Confronting the Hit Man, Yorkshire Television, 1995.

Burning Down the House, Yorkshire Television, 1995.

INDEX